The Laban Sourcebook

Rudolf Laban (1879–1958) was a pioneer in dance and movement, who found an extraordinary range of application for his ideas; from industry to drama, education and therapy. Laban believed that you can understand human beings by observing how they move, and devised two complementary methods of notating the shape and quality of movements.

The Laban Sourcebook offers a comprehensive account of Laban's writings and includes extracts from his five books in English and from his four works in German written in the 1920s, translated here for the first time.

This book draws on archival research in England and Germany to chart the development of his groundbreaking ideas through a variety of documents, including letters, articles, transcripts of interviews, and his unpublished *Effort and Recovery*. It covers:

- the beginning of his career in Germany and Switzerland in the 1910s
- his astonishing rise to fame in Germany in the 1920s as a dance teacher, choreographer and creator of public dance events
- following his move to England in 1938, the application of his ideas to drama, education, industry and therapy.

Each extract has a short preface providing contextual background, and highlighting and explaining key terms. Passages have been selected and are introduced by many of the world's leading Laban scholars.

Dick McCaw is Senior Lecturer at Royal Holloway, University of London, UK. He co-founded the Medieval Players theatre company in 1981 and he was Artistic Director of the International Workshop Festival from 1993–2001. He trained with Geraldine Stephenson, a former pupil and colleague of Rudolf Laban. He is the co-editor of eight DVD ROMs with Peter Hulton on theatre movement and practice, and is the author of a book on Warren Lamb.

The Laban Sourcebook

- Edited by Dick McCaw

Routledge
Taylor & Francis Group
LONDON AND NEW YORK

First published 2011
by Routledge
2 Park Square, Milton Park, Abingdon, Oxon OX14 4RN

Simultaneously published in the USA and Canada
by Routledge
711 Third Avenue, New York, NY 10017

Routledge is an imprint of the Taylor & Francis Group, an informa business

Collection and editorial matter © 2011 Dick McCaw; individual chapters, the contributors

The right of Dick McCaw to be identified as the author of the editorial material, and of the authors for their individual chapters, has been asserted in accordance with sections 77 and 78 of the Copyright, Designs and Patents Act 1988.

All rights reserved. No part of this book may be reprinted or reproduced or utilised in any form or by any electronic, mechanical, or other means, now known or hereafter invented, including photocopying and recording, or in any information storage or retrieval system, without permission in writing from the publishers.

Trademark notice: Product or corporate names may be trademarks or registered trademarks, and are used only for identification and explanation without intent to infringe.

British Library Cataloguing in Publication Data
A catalogue record for this book is available from the British Library

Library of Congress Cataloging-in-Publication Data
Laban, Rudolf von, 1879–1958.
The Laban sourcebook / edited by Dick McCaw.
  p. cm.
Includes bibliographical references.
1. Dance. I. McCaw, Dick.
II. Title.
GV1594.L33 2011
792.8′2—dc22   2010024030

ISBN: 978-0-415-54333-0 (hbk)
ISBN: 978-0-415-54332-3 (pbk)
ISBN: 978-0-203-85284-2 (ebk)

Typeset in Sabon
by Keystroke, Station Road, Codsall, Wolverhampton

Printed and bound in Great Britain by
TJ International Ltd, Padstow, Cornwall

I dedicate this book to Geraldine Stephenson, who introduced me to Laban's ideas about movement.

Contents

List of illustrations   xi
Notes on contributors   xiii
Preface   xvii
Acknowledgements   xxi
List of abbreviations   xxiii

Editor's introduction   1
Dick McCaw

1 **Dance activities and schools, 1912–1917, Ascona and Zurich**   21
   Introduction, Dick McCaw

2 ***The World of the Dancer* (1920)**   41
   Introduction, Stefanie Sachsenmaier

3 ***Gymnastics and Dance for Children* (1926)**   69
   Introduction, Dick McCaw

4 ***Gymnastics and Dance* (1926)**   83
   Introduction, Dick McCaw

CONTENTS

5 *Choreography* (1926)   97
Introduction, Dick McCaw

6 Texts on Laban's choreographies: *Gaukelei* (1923) and *Titan* (1927)   113
Introduction, Dick McCaw

7 The Choreographic Institute Laban (1926–1929) and Laban's presentation at the first Dancers' Congress, Magdeburg (1927)   121
Introduction, Vera Maletic

8 The Pageant of the Trades and Crafts, Vienna, June 1929   139
Introduction, Dick McCaw

9 Laban and Movement Notation   155
Introduction, Roderyk Lange

10 Rudolf Laban's dance films   167
Introduction, Evelyn Dörr

11 *Choreutics*, written in 1938, published 1966   175
Introduction, Valerie Preston-Dunlop

12 Laban's concept of Effort and his work in the 1940s and 1950s   197
Introduction, Dick McCaw

13 The Art of Movement in Education, Work and Recreation (mid-1940s)   207
Introduction, Dick McCaw

14 *Effort* (1947)   217
Introduction, Warren Lamb

CONTENTS

15 Answers to Ten Questions on Industrial Rhythm (early 1950s) — **231**

16 *Modern Educational Dance* (1948) — **237**
Introduction, Anna Carlisle

17 Shadow Moves — **257**
Introduction, Marion North

18 *The Mastery of Movement on the Stage* (1950) — **265**
Introduction, Dick McCaw

19 *Effort and Recovery* (early 1950s) — **283**
Introduction, Dick McCaw

20 Excerpts from *Effort and Recovery* and notes taken from Withymead (early 1950s) — **299**
Introduction, Janet Kaylo

21 The Harmony of Movement (early 1950s) — **317**
Introduction, Carol-Lynne Moore

22 Themes and contradictions in Laban's work and thinking — **333**
Dick McCaw

Glossary of terms as used in Movement Psychology — 351

Glossary of German terms — 359
Stefanie Sachsenmaier and Dick McCaw

Bibliography — 363
Index — 369

List of illustrations

Figures

Prelim.1	Laban drawing from the John Hodgson Archive, Brotherton Library, University of Leeds	xx
Prelim.2	Laban drawing from the John Hodgson Archive, Brotherton Library, University of Leeds	xx
0.1	Illustration of the octahedron from *Choreography* (1926)	11
0.2	Illustration of the three planes of movement from *Choreography* (1926)	12
1.1	Laban School in Ascona (1913)	22
1.2	Laban School in Ascona (1913)	22
1.3	Laban School in Ascona (1914)	23
6.1–6.4	Images from Laban's stage-plan of *Titan* (1927)	114
6.5	Hamburg Movement Choir	116
7.1	Directory of Laban Schools in 1927	121
7.2	List of Laban vocational training schools	122
7.3	What is necessary?	130
7.4	Rehearsal for *Agamemnon* (1927)	134
7.5	Gleisner Movement Choir (1927)	135
7.6	Herta Feist School, Berlin	135

LIST OF ILLUSTRATIONS

7.7	Rehearsal for *Titan* (1927), photo given to John Hodgson by Albrecht Knust	136
7.8	Rehearsal for *Titan* (1927), photo given to John Hodgson by Albrecht Knust	136
7.9	Rehearsal for *Titan* (1927), photo given to John Hodgson by Albrecht Knust	137
9.1	Dance instruction in the work by M. Toulouze, *L'Art et Instruction de bien Danser*, Paris, 1488	156
9.2	The minuet recorded in the Feuillet system	157
9.3	'Pas de Zéphire', recorded by A. Zorn, 1887	159
9.4	Example of movement notation	159
9.5	Example of Kinetography	165
10.1	Photograph of the icosahedron (1928)	169
11.1	Notation of symbols	187
11.2a	The cluster	188
11.2b	The girdle	188
11.3	[Illustration of transversal movements]	189
11.4a	[Peripheral standard scale]	191
11.4b	[Peripheral standard scale]	191
11.5	[Knot-form around an axis]	194
12.1	The Effort Cross	202
12.2	The eight Effort actions	202
14.1	The Efforts	223
18.1	[Human expressiveness in the art of movement]	273
22.1	Dietrich Eckhart Stadium, venue for the 1936 Berlin Olympics	345
22.2, 22.3	Dress rehearsal of *Vom Tauwind und der neuen Freude* at Dietrich Eckhart Stadium from the brochure commemorating the opening of the Dietrich Eckhart Stadium, venue for the 1936 Berlin Olympics	346

Tables

12.1	Effort	200
12.2	Drives and attitudes	204

Notes on contributors

Walter Bodmer undertakes research on human genetics and cancer. He has been Professor of Genetics at Stanford and Oxford Universities, and Director of the Imperial Cancer Research Fund. He was elected FRS in 1974, was knighted in 1986, and has more than 30 honorary degrees, memberships and fellowships of scientific and medical societies.

Anna Carlisle trained with Lisa Ullmann at the Art of Movement Studio. She was Head of Dance at Lewes College, Lecturer in Choreological Studies at LABAN, London and is currently President of the Laban Guild and Chair of the Lisa Ullmann Travelling Scholarship Fund. She was awarded the MBE for Services to Dance in 2003.

Evelyn Dörr wrote her doctoral dissertation on the life and work of Rudolf Laban, after first studying theatre. Research for her thesis uncovered a great deal of archival material on Laban which resulted in the publication of two books: *The Dancer of the Crystal* (2008) and *Rudolf Laban: The Complete Choreographic Works* (2004). She works as a teacher of theatre, dance and German literature and is also an author for German radio and theatre.

NOTES ON CONTRIBUTORS

Janet Kaylo has an extensive background as a professional dancer, teacher and director. As Founder/Director of Laban/Bartenieff and Somatic Studies International, she presents Certificate Programmes in Movement Analysis and BodyMind Practice™, and has trained dancers, teachers and dance therapists in the USA, Canada, England, Europe and India over the course of three decades.

Warren Lamb crystallised the Effort/Shape Framework, based on his training and apprenticeship with Rudolf Laban from 1946 until Laban's death in 1958. He used it in teaching Irmgard Bartenieff and Judith Kestenberg, with whom he worked in the development of their respective systems. His main work has been the development of Action Profiling, now renamed Movement Pattern Analysis (MPA), and its application to decision-making. His consultancy practice, Warren Lamb Associates, has used MPA in advising senior executives of large and small organisations in more than 30 countries.

Roderyk Lange is a choreologist and anthropologist. He taught at the Laban Art of Movement Studio from 1967 to 1972, and at the Laban Centre from 1976 to 1993, as well as in several universities in Poland. He was a Professor at the Mickiewicz University, Poznan, where he has also been the Director of the Institute of Choreology from 1993 to the present. He has published numerous books including *The Nature of Dance* (1975) and *Handbook of Kinetography* (1975). In Paris in 2005 he was made a *Chevalier de L'Ordre des Arts et des Lettres*.

Vera Maletic, Professor Emerita, received her initial training from her mother Ana Maletic, one of Laban's disciples in Europe, and subsequently studied at the Laban Centre in England. Her book, *Body-Space-Expression: The Development of Rudolf Laban's Movement and Dance Concepts* was published by Mouton de Gruyter in 1987.

Dick McCaw is Senior Lecturer at Royal Holloway, University of London, UK. He co-founded the Medieval Players theatre

NOTES ON CONTRIBUTORS

company in 1981 and he was Artistic Director of the International Workshop Festival from 1993–2001. He trained with Geraldine Stephenson, a former pupil and colleague of Rudolf Laban. He is the co-editor of eight DVD ROMs with Peter Hulton on theatre movement and practice, and is the author of a book on Warren Lamb.

Carol-Lynne Moore, PhD, has been involved in the field of movement analysis as a writer, lecturer and consultant for over 30 years. Her publications include *Beyond Words* (Routledge, 1988), *Movement and Making Decisions* (Rosen, 2005), and *The Harmonic Structure of Movement, Music, and Dance According to Rudolf Laban* (Mellen, 2009).

Marion North has worked as an educationalist, therapist, researcher and creator of buildings for dance, to help young people achieve their aims in dance. She was Principal of the Laban Centre from 1973–2003, now in its award-winning building at Creekside. Her ground-breaking research into early movement patterns of children is now being developed by colleagues in the United States. She worked as Laban's assistant for the last ten years of his life.

Valerie Preston-Dunlop is a consultant and Honorary Research Fellow at Trinity Laban. She received her initial training from Rudolf Laban, Lisa Ullmann and Albrecht Knust. An internationally renowned author, practitioner and lecturer, her current publications include *Rudolf Laban: An Extraordinary Life* (winner of the Dance Perspectives book of the year, 1999, 2nd edn), *Looking at Dances: A Choreological Perspective on Choreography* (Dutch commission), and *Dance and The Performative*, DVD *Living Architecture* with Anna Carlisle.

Stefanie Sachsenmaier is a lecturer in Theatre Arts at Middlesex University. She completed a Masters degree in Performance at Goldsmiths College, a DEA (Diplôme d'Etudes Approfondies) in Théâtre et Arts du Spectacle at the Sorbonne Nouvelle, and a PhD in Performing Arts at Middlesex University. She has

XV

been teaching at several universities in London and works as researcher with choreographer Rosemary Butcher. She has been performing for the past decade, more recently her own solo work. She is also a qualified teacher of Wu-style Tai Chi Chuan.

Preface

This book is a carefully selected anthology of Rudolf Laban's writings with comments by many who either knew him or have studied and performed his work. It succeeds in giving an overview of the extraordinarily wide range of Laban's interests and reflects very well the combination of his artistry, his mysticism and spiritualism, and his analytical, quasi-scientific thought. He was indeed a visionary, in the best sense of that word.

The reason why I, a scientist with virtually no experience in Modern Dance, am writing this preface is because my mother, Sylvia Bodmer, was one of Laban's pupils in the early 1920s and was a key figure in the development of his work in the UK.

Laban wrote: 'dance . . . has something in its essence that fulfils the whole of the physical, emotional and spiritual being' and this was really the basis of his own life's work. In her description of how Laban worked with the dancers on the project *Gaukelei*, Rita Zabekow emphasises how he encouraged them to improvise without imposing any choreographically rigid plan, and this is exactly how my mother described her experience, some ten years earlier, with *Tanzbuhne Laban*.

What is Modern Dance? According to Laban, 'One of the most obvious differences between the traditional European dances and modern dance is that the former are almost exclusively step dances, while the latter uses the flow of movements pervading all articulations of the body.' No doubt this is why he called the school he founded with Lisa Ullman and Sylvia Bodmer, in Manchester, England after the Second World War, 'The Art of Movement Studio'. In an article on 'The Harmony of Movement' (see Chapter 21), Laban wrote: 'One question may occur to the attentive observer: why is it that musical harmony and disharmony are more conspicuous than the harmony or disharmony of movement?' I went to a summer dance holiday course at Dartington in 1952 where Laban did give some special extra lessons for the few men attending the course. My diary entry at the time said, 'In these we were taught harmonic movements and movement sequences designed to exercise all parts of the body to their fullest extent. This we certainly succeeded in doing in a most exhilarating way.'

Laban was very concerned with the theatre and drama. Thus, he said, 'It is movement which is the basis of poetry, drama, music, dance and the other arts.' Later, however, after he came to England, he commented, 'It is not so long ago that the fashion in acting suddenly changed from pompous gesticulation to a naturalism devoid of any movement-expression at all.' The Art of Movement Studio provided movement training for Joan Littlewood's Theatre Workshop, no doubt with the practical aim of redressing this tendency.

Laban, in general, became more practically oriented after he came to Manchester, largely through the influence of the management consultant Fredrick Lawrence with whom he wrote *Effort* (1947). It was Lawrence who also influenced his English writing, which became much clearer and more direct than his earlier German writings. Lawrence was the major influence in the development of Laban's interest in industrial workplace applications. As Laban wrote,

> The growing realism of the theatre of those days led me to a thorough investigation of working movement in

agriculture and industry. . . . My interest in the theatre has never entirely faded, but my movement observation became more acute during all these years and also gained a broader significance.

This was the stimulus for his notion of 'Effort'. As Laban pithily put it: 'Any inappropriate use of movement is just a waste of effort!' In the introduction to a previously unpublished manuscript, *Effort and Recovery*, he writes, 'One has to search, to hunt, to notate, to compile and to compare movement impressions in order to get more clarity.' There can be no doubt that he had extraordinary powers of observation of movement and an ability to describe them clearly.

Another important practical application of his dance ideas was in education in schools. As Anna Carlisle puts it in her introduction to Chapter 16, Rudolf Laban was the 'founding father of dance in the English state education system', but his role in this is now largely forgotten. Laban also promoted the therapeutic applications of dance on the basis that

> The knowledge that movement has power to influence mood, and even ways of thinking and behaviour, has been used consciously and unconsciously at all times, and still today people can go to a recreational dance class weary and dispirited, and feel refreshed and invigorated afterwards.

Rudolf Laban's uniqueness was his ability to combine extraordinary artistic talent with a real analytical ability, almost scientific in nature, and to work out ways of systematising the study, and of course the notation, of human movement. That entirely distinguishes him from other key figures in Modern Dance in the twentieth century.

I hope that in these brief comments I have made it clear that this is not just a book for the specialist, but is a book that can be appreciated by anyone with even the slightest interest in human movement, and in that extraordinary mind of Rudolf Laban.

Sir Walter Bodmer

PREFACE

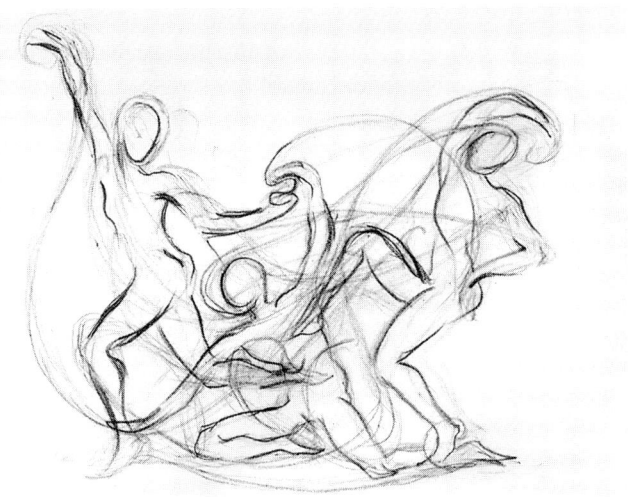

Figure Prelim.1 Laban drawing from the John Hodgson Archive, Brotherton Library, University of Leeds

Figure Prelim.2 Laban drawing from the John Hodgson Archive, Brotherton Library, University of Leeds

Acknowledgements

First of all, to Steffi Sachsenmaier who has done far more than work on the translations from German, and her work on *The World of the Dancer*. I also acknowledge my huge debt to Franc Chamberlain who took on the role of copy editor and who has made this a much more readable and useful book. The mistakes are still mine, but there are an awful lot less thanks to Franc and Steffi.

To all the contributors who did far more than simply select and introduce their passages from Laban's writings – each of them provided me with encouragement and advice.

For help in mining the archives: Helen Roberts and Sharon Maxwell at the National Resource Centre for Dance; Sam Gibbard, Oliver Pickering and Chris Sheppard from the Special Collections at the Brotherton Library; and Jane Fowler from the library at Trinity Laban.

For giving me books from their collection: Tonja and Gerard Bagley. For giving me unlimited access to his personal collection of Laban materials and for his unstinting support: Gordon Curl.

To David Pearce for his work on the photographs and to David Wiles and David Wolfe for their always enjoyable and illuminating conversations.

ACKNOWLEDGEMENTS

To Elaine Turner for proof-reading the typescript.

To Eden Davies who suggested I edit the book, and to the Routledge team: Talia Rodgers and Catherine Foley who saw it on its first steps, to Ben Piggot and Niall Slater who saw the book into production.

Thanks to William Elmhirst and the Dorothy Whitney Elmhirst Trust, and Donald Howarth of the John Hodgson Theatre Research Trust for their financial support – without them this book would not have been possible.

List of abbreviations

Ch *Choreography*
Cho *Choreutics*
E *Effort* All extracts are from the second edition of 1974
ER *Effort and Recovery* Although *Effort and Recovery* was never published, it was prepared for publication by MacDonald and Evans. The National Resource Centre for Dance holds the manuscript and has housed each chapter into one or two folders. For long extracts, the full file reference is given in notes. There is a typescript numbered from 1–280 and shorter references are made to this paginated typescript.
GD *Gymnastics and Dance*
GDC *Gymnastics and Dance for Children*
JH John Hodgson (in connection with interviews he conducted)
JHA References to the John Hodgson Archive at the Brotherton Library, University of Leeds. Although the material has not yet been catalogued, it has all been put in numbered boxes and folders.
LD *A Life for Dance*
MED *Modern Educational Dance*

LIST OF ABBREVIATIONS

MM	*Mastery of Movement on the Stage* All extracts are from the first edition of 1950, but references are made both to the first and second edition of 1960 (which includes quite considerable changes by Lisa Ullmann).
NRCD	National Resource Centre for Dance, University of Surrey
PDN	*Principles of Dance and Movement Notation*
VDS	*A Vision of Dynamic Space*
WD	*The World of the Dancer*

Editor's introduction

Dick McCaw

The aim of this sourcebook

Rudolf Laban (1879–1958) was one of the pioneers of modern dance in Germany in the 1910s and 1920s and of movement education in England in the 1940s and 1950s. Although his career focused on dance and movement, he succeeded in applying this seemingly specialised knowledge to a bewildering breadth of fields – architecture, aesthetics, theatre, education, ethics, mental and physical health, industry, and management. As a pioneer of dance, he created institutes of dance to promote research, helped organise congresses, and wrote ten books and countless articles to raise awareness of dance as an art and of dancers as artists. As a social visionary, he created ideal communities and retreats. This list of his achievements is far from complete and will be filled out over the course of this book whose primary aim is to give readers an idea of the astonishing breadth of his writing about, and activities in, the field of dance and movement.

Of Laban's five books in German, the first four books in German (written between 1920 and 1926) still remain untranslated into English, and though his autobiography of

1935 was translated,[1] it is now out of print, as are his four books written in English. Thus there is a need for a publication which gives students access to a representative selection from his writings. This sourcebook consists of published and unpublished writings of Rudolf Laban between 1912 and 1958, as well as documents and images illustrating his various activities. The aim is to give the clearest examples of Laban's thinking in specific areas of activity and with passages of sufficient length to allow a reader to engage with his ideas. A secondary aim is to present previously unpublished material – notes, letters, manuscripts – from two archives: the John Hodgson Archive at the Brotherton Library, University of Leeds, and the National Resource Centre for Dance, University of Surrey.

Laban's writing and practice crossed so many different disciplines that it would be foolhardy for one editor to claim a similar breadth of knowledge or competence. It is for this reason that acknowledged Laban scholars have been invited to contribute to this book – each one being asked to select writings that cover their particular field of expertise and to explain their choice in a short introduction. Many were taught by him and have gone on to develop his ideas in their own ways; thus each of the contributors brings their own perspective of Laban. This Sourcebook thus offers many ways of understanding this multiform thinker and the bibliography will assist readers who want to take their research further.

What this book does not aim to be is a practical manual – either of how to move, or how to notate movement. If there are examples of his exercises or his forms of notation, these are to illustrate a broader point being made about movement in general and how Laban understood it. Although Laban constantly noted the inherent contradiction of writing about movement – it is an activity better understood through physical doing rather than intellectual reflection – he did write ten books on the subject, many of them including passages of philosophical reflection upon the meaning of movement. This Sourcebook aims to identify key principles, terms, themes and images through which he articulated his meditations upon movement. The contents of the Sourcebook are ordered chronologically so that the reader can see the development in Laban's thinking. In short, this book aims to make available this exciting and tumultuous pioneer of dance and movement to the widest possible readership.

One thing this book cannot offer is any comprehensive impression of Laban's work as a visual artist. He was a wickedly evocative caricaturist, as well as being a talented draftsman, capable of representing three-dimensional geometry with incredible accuracy and imagination. It would require a large, full-colour book[2] to do justice to the way that he imagined and conceived of movement shapes in three-dimensional space through their representation on a two-dimensional page.

Brief biography of Rudolf Laban

Rudolf Laban was born on 15 December 1879 in Bratislava (called *Poszony* in Hungarian and *Pressburg* in German), then in the Austro-Hungarian Empire which ceased to exist as a political entity after World War I. His father was a highly respected military governor in the Austro-Hungarian Army and was posted to Bosnia-Herzegovina where Laban encountered the Muslim culture and more particularly the Dervish dance of its Turkish inhabitants. Although Laban writes about these experiences in both *The World of the Dancer* (WD) and *A Life for Dance* (LD), Mary Wigman offers a succinct account of how Dervish dance profoundly influenced him:

> The earliest, strongest and most long-lasting impression of dancing came to Laban in the Orient. The exercises of dancing Dervishes which he saw there as a boy excited him, urged him to dance himself. Only years later did this strong childhood experience become clear to him, he understood the meaning of these dances and their living, animated symbolism. The founders of the order of dancing dervishes called universal occurrence, 'The dance of the spheres around god'. To experience this dance and

to reproduce it in his own dancing became not only a task for Laban but also for dancers in general, the ethical basis of the theory of dancing, cosmic experience, religion.[3]

Wigman here touches on several themes that will be developed over the course of this book: the connection between dance, religion, ethics and the symbolism of the circle.

Laban's country of origin caused him problems in later life. Lisa Ullmann, Laban's partner from 1938 to 1958, reflects on which languages he spoke as a child: 'French was probably the first language he came across consciously because of his governess. He also spoke Hungarian because he went to proper school, not private tuition.' He only 'learned German properly in his later teens when he came to Germany', and his first attempts at speaking and writing the language 'were very much laughed at'.[4] There was also the problem of citizenship – Laban's first 20 years in Germany were plagued by his status of being an alien which required him to make repeated requests for residency. He finally obtained German nationality on 5 November 1935.[5]

Another important fact about this pioneer of dance and movement is that he began his career as a painter and not as a dancer or choreographer. Far from being an initial wrong-turning, collaborators noted the profound connection between the two. Suzanne Perrottet recalled:

> He always saw movement in his paintings, whatever he did. Everything became a group dance with a soloist. There was always movement in what he drew... When he went out he was never still, he would sketch the landscape or the houses or anything which he wished, very quickly. A tree, falling leaves, anything which was interesting in its structure.[6]

Lisa Ullmann adds: 'He was fascinated by people moving around and seeing ordinary people moving in the streets and he was in a way disgusted with the dance he saw because it was all so rigid and unnatural.'[7]

If Laban began his life in a culturally remote part of Europe, by 1900 he had found his way to the cultural centre of Paris after having left the prestigious Military Academy in Vienna where his father had wanted him to pursue a career as a soldier. In Paris, he continued his studies of painting and architecture as well as exploring Rosicrucian thinking. Following the tragic death of his first wife, Martha Fricke (mother of his first two children, Arpad and Azra) in 1907, he then moved to Munich which was another crucible of European cultural experiment, with composer Arnold Schönberg, artists Franz Marc and Wassily Kandinsky (together they formed the *Blaue Reiter* group in 1911), Hans Obrist (a close friend of Laban), and theatre pioneer Georg Fuchs, all resident there in the early 1910s.

Switzerland and Germany, 1910–1937

From 1910, Laban started to become known for his ideas and experiments in modern dance and it is quite extraordinary how he managed to create this reputation in such a short space of time. These activities included organising *Faschings* (Easter carnivals) in Munich, setting up a 'festival community' in Ascona, a school in Zurich, giving brilliant illustrated lectures, as well as creating and performing his first dance pieces. On 15 May 1918, he wrote to his friend and collaborator Hans Brandenburg:

> The idea of a performing society has become a reality, to the extent that I have given over two hundred performances in the past few years, which were received initially with mistrust by a small circle as well as by the press, but which have now gained full recognition.[8]

The 1920s saw his activities focused solely in Germany, with an important stay in Hamburg between 1922 and 1926. In this decade, he created over 30 major pieces of dance, pieces for what he called movement choirs, countless smaller pieces, as well as two major processional pieces. On top of this, he helped organise two Dance Congresses, published four books – *The World of the Dancer* (1920), *Gymnastics and Dance for Children* (1926), *Gymnastics and Dance* (1926), and *Choreography* (1926) – as well as formulating his dance notation in 1928. In addition, he became more involved in the emerging new art form of cinema. During this period movement choirs and Laban Schools sprang up throughout Germany (and beyond in Paris, Zagreb and Zurich). Irmgard Bartenieff recalls this period:

> We had at least twenty schools by the mid-twenties. And the interesting thing was that he worked with people personally, and also developed a staff of people that he could use as teachers. A group leader founded the *Folkwang* School in Essen. He kept those schools together, and every head of a school came together every year. So, the new ideas of Laban were immediately transferred. It was only ten or twelve years really. . . I still can't believe it was such a short time. We had very high standards.
>
> He also had this whole Hungarian vitality . . . He just lived! It was interesting that he should have started these schools in Germany with all these problem-ridden people. But, he always used to say, 'I feel my work is still best understood in Germany because of their intuitive and sensitive nature.' That was also part of it. . . . He also created something that is still a marvel to me. He created the proletarian movement choir. It was full of political background, with a speaking choir possible, and very modern music – unthinkable![9]

To have achieved all this in ten short years constitutes a truly staggering output of work.

The 1930s were a period of official recognition, political catastrophe, and ultimate disgrace and exile to England. In 1930, Laban was appointed Ballet Master at the Berlin State Opera, a position which acknowledged his reputation within Germany, remaining there until August 1934, by which time Adolf Hitler's National Socialist Party had been in power for

18 months. He then accepted the post of Director of the *Deutsche Tanzbühne* (German Dance Organisation): his brief was, 'to organise performances of artistic dance works, choreographing them where necessary, and to promote young German dancers, especially those who were out of work because of the recession'.[10] In 1936, he was asked to produce a massive pageant *Vom Tauwind und der neuen Freude* (Of the Spring Wind and the New Joy) to celebrate the opening of the stadium – the Dietrich Eckhart Theatre – for the 1936 Berlin Olympics. Both Hitler and his head of propaganda Dr Josef Goebbels attended a dress rehearsal after which the performance was cancelled. In his diary, Goebbels noted: 'I do not like it. That is because it [Laban's dance] is dressed up in our clothes and has nothing whatever to do with us.'[11] Very soon Laban was a *persona non grata* and eventually found his way to Paris where he became seriously ill (his life was dogged by bouts of chronic illness). His last two works written in Germany were his autobiography, *A Life for Dance*, published in 1935, and an unpublished manuscript written in 1937, 'A Statement on the Setting Up of the German Dance Theatre'.[12]

England and Wales, 1938–1958

Lisa Ullmann, who was later to become his partner, brought him to England in 1938 where he wrote the text of *Choreutics* (published in 1966) during his recuperation. They stayed in Dartington Hall, an important centre for cultural and scientific innovation created by Dorothy and Leonard Elmhirst and where Kurt Jooss and Sigurd Leeder (both former pupils of Laban) ran their ballet school and company, and Michael Chekhov had his theatre school (where Ullmann taught movement). They were still at Dartington near the Devon coast when World War II broke out in 1939 but, following the Dunkirk retreat in the summer of 1940, all 'aliens' were evacuated from vulnerable coastal areas. Thus, Laban and Ullmann were obliged to move to Newtown in mid-Wales, and later to Manchester where Laban's career had a final, extraordinary flourishing. In Dartington, he had met a management consultant called Frederick Lawrence, and together they started to adapt Laban's ideas about movement to help people working in factories – particularly women who had replaced the male workforce – achieve greater productivity. Their work together resulted in the book *Effort* (1947).

In October 1946, Ullmann opened the Art of Movement Studio in Manchester and, as a result of her tireless activity, it soon became recognised by the Department of Education for training movement teachers in primary and secondary schools. This resulted in Laban's second English publication *Modern Educational Dance* (1948). Following his teaching at Esmé Church's Northern Theatre School in Bradford, a third book, *The Mastery of Movement on the Stage*, appeared in 1950. The Studio moved to new premises in Addlestone, Surrey, in 1953, thanks to funds from the Elmhirst family. Here he continued his researches into applied movement, dance history, movement in theatre, expanding later into Movement Therapy. At the same time his dance notation was continuing to develop, and, in order to assure his copyright, he published *Dance and Movement Notation* in 1956. His later researches focused ever more upon what he called Movement Psychology, a subject he explored with William Carpenter until his death in 1954, after which Laban abandoned this field of research. Laban left an unpublished book on the subject called *Effort and Recovery*.

An overview of Laban's thinking

Although each selection of excerpts has its own explanatory introduction, the following brief review of Laban's concepts aims to give an idea of the field of thought that will be covered in this book. Since Laban published little in the 1910s, the first section consists of accounts of his educational work. According to correspondence with Hans Brandenburg, Laban established his first school in Munich in 1910. Apart from his correspondence with Suzanne Perrottet, I have found no documents about his activities in the early 1910s so we pick up his educational activities in 1917 in Zurich when his teaching was interdisciplinary and was entitled Dance Music Word (*Tanz Ton Wort*).

Themes in *The World of the Dancer*

His first book, *The World of the Dancer*, is one of his most challenging works, as much because of the form as the content. In Laban's explanation of the book in a letter of 29 April 1920 to Brandenburg, we find many of the themes he will pursue throughout his career in dance and movement.

> Two essential themes run through my work in general. First, to give to dance as an art form and the dancer as an artist their proper value, and second to stress the influence of dance education on the rigid psyche of our time.
>
> Spatially experienced movement, tension between forms and the transformation of forms is the basis of all perception, all feeling, all knowledge and all awareness. Employed from time immemorial as ceremony, ritual, sign (gestural and graphic) and symbol, human movement is the archetype and image of all tensions that both are and produce thoughts, feelings, acts of volition, etc.[13]

Certainly, Laban devoted the first 25 years of his career to ensuring that 'dance as an art and the dancer as an artist' were given their proper value. In this sense he can be compared to Stanislavsky (five years his senior) who demanded that theatre be taken seriously as an art form, and the actor as an artist. Both men spent their lives engaged in the transformation of their art form through their teaching, writing and artistic productions.

The second paragraph quoted from the letter deals with his theory of spatial movement. When proposing that 'spatially experienced movement . . . is the basis of all feeling, all knowledge and all awareness', he names three forms of perception, which recur in various forms throughout his early writing and which correspond to body/mind/spirit. He insists that none of these forms should outweigh the other, but that our perception should involve a balance of all three. This insistence upon totality, of feeling with the whole self, which in turn is related to the unity of body and mind, is another major theme in Laban's writings. From his first to his last writings, he warns against being lopsided or one-sided – this being an index of a lack of balance or harmony in one's living. Here we have a nucleus of related preoccupations: the centrality of movement to perception, the unity of the perceiving self (body/mind/spirit), and the need for balance and harmony.

Next he proposes that we experience and understand movement through the 'tension between forms and the transformation of forms'. As noted above, Laban's first training was as a painter, and this might explain his very plastic approach to movement – his gift was to be able to see the paths of movement we make in space, and to assign specific shapes to them. (The *OED*[14] defines plasticity as the capacity 'for being moulded or undergoing a permanent change in shape'.) Once pointed out, it is obvious that movement must have a spatial form – all movement involves a change from one place to another and a definable pathway between those two places. Laban insisted that we do not think of a specific movement in terms of its end-point, the goal or destination, but rather of the pathway (he also uses the word 'trace-form') by which it has been achieved and that we understand movement in general as a process of transformation, and not in terms of snapshots (a distinction that was central to Henri Bergson's philosophy of time and space). This explains why rhythm (which you might call the form of time) is such an abiding concept in Laban's writing.

Forms of movement

Laban understood the form of movement from three perspectives: first, the shaping of the body and its limbs, second, the pathways those body parts make in space, and third, the correspondence between these natural movement pathways of the body and the geometry of regular solids such as the cube. It seems an incredible leap to go from the observation of

EDITOR'S INTRODUCTION

natural movement to finding correspondences with abstract geometric shapes, but this is one of the challenges and difficulties of Laban's thinking. The matter is made more difficult in that many of us are unfamiliar with the four other regular solids that Laban refers to: the tetrahedron, the octahedron, the dodecahedron and the icosahedron. (They are 'regular' because each face of the solid is a regular shape: triangles in the tetrahedron, octahedron, and icosahedron, squares in the cube, and pentagons in the dodecahedron.) Plato made much of the significance of these solids in one of his last dialogues, *The Timaeus*. Laban's genius was to see a connection between these solids and movement.

Unfamiliar as these solids are, their inner structure is the stuff of everyday experience. Take the example of kicking a ball: this involves balancing on one leg, kicking with the other leg and using our two arms for balance – these four extremities are the four points of the tetrahedron (he mentions this in *The World of the Dancer* [1920]). We cannot avoid being tetrahedral in our movements. Turning to another solid, if you joined up the points of the six directions, up-down, side-to-side, forward-back, you would get an octahedron (illustrated with Figure 0.1 taken from *Choreography* [1926]).

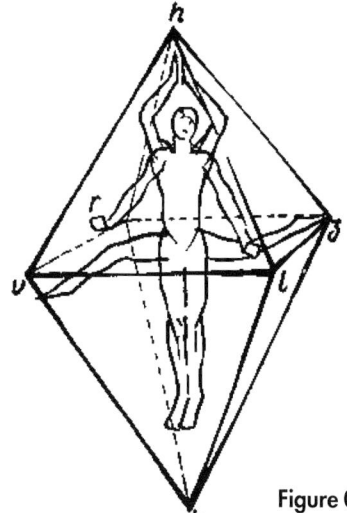

Figure 0.1 Illustration of the octahedron from *Choreography* (1926), p. 20

11

If you considered these directions as two-dimensional planes, one which goes forward–back (Saggital or what Laban calls the Wheel plane), one which goes up–down (Vertical plane: imagine standing in a door frame), and the last which goes side-to-side (Horizontal plane: imagine reaching to the corners of a table). If you then joined up the corners of these planes, you would have the icosahedron (Figure 0.2).

We are all familiar with the diagonals of the cube. Try to make a movement following the line of a diagonal and you will realise that it is quite a challenge to keep your balance. Compare this with going up and down, side to side and forward and back – these are much easier because you always come back to the centre. Already we are talking about movements within these perfect solids (or call them 'models of space'), and about different qualities of movement – those that are centred and those that make us off-balance (what Laban in the 1920s will call 'stable' and 'labile', or mobile). So, although it seems that Laban's thinking is esoteric and beyond our experience, in fact, there is much that is easy to grasp. As he suggested, we have to think with our *body* (the feeling of being off-balance or being centred), with our *mind* (the geometry of the movement) and with our *soul* (the emotional tenor of the movement, the fear of falling, or the comfort of solidity). In his preface to *The Mastery of Movement on the Stage* he suggested that we engage in a 'mobile reading'. It might be helpful to take this kinaesthetic approach when reading all of his writings.

Figure 0.2 Illustration of the three planes of movement from *Choreography* (1926), p. 23

Inner and outer tension, inner and outer form

There are three more interrelated themes to tease out of these two short paragraphs. The first is tension. The human being perceives something in the world and reaches out to it – the tension between the perceived object and the self becomes an actual movement, literally an 'ex-tension' towards it, a physicalisation or externalisation of the inner tension. It could be a movement reaching out towards the object, or one shrinking away from it: 'The polarities of this perceptive power are sympathy, indifference and antipathy.'[15] Thus tension for Laban has two meanings: first, the sense of an inner urge, and second, a degree of muscular contraction in the corresponding movement response. Humans share this outward urge with other living things such as plants whose upward movement is limited to following the heat and light of the sun and which depends on them having sufficient turgic tension in their cells (a plant that lacks turgor, or cellular tension, wilts). This example explains that 'tension' has the sense of both force and structure, both movement and form:

> In any case, through the forms surrounding us we are in the middle of a formidable book of magic from which we read about the nature of its creative forces and which we are able to render through imitation and reconstruction. All forms live. They are changing constantly, ceaselessly. They are in constant movement and proclaim through their image of tension the directions which determine their nature. Their *turgor*, their tension strives in these directions. The result, the form, is a harmony of strivings of force, which impress us sensually, teach us intellectually, touch us aesthetically, move us in sympathy or antipathy or leave us feeling indifferent.[16]

We have already touched on the second theme which is the necessary relation between the inner and outer form. The inner tension is like a vector: both a direction and a force. Laban offers a useful image for understanding the mutually dependent relation between outer and inner form: 'The outer form of a wheel is the rim, the inner form are the radial tensions of the spokes.'[17] Laban insists: 'One cannot separate mental tension from the respective form-tension (the form of a three-dimensionally arranged combination of inclinations of forces which are related to each other in very specific angles and dimensional ratios).'[18] The outer is the visible form, the inner is that which supports and accounts for the outer form. Returning to the regular solids, where the outer form is the cube, the inner tensions are the diagonals: for the octahedron the six cardinal directions are its inner tensions, and for the icosahedron the inner tensions are the three planes of movement (door, wheel, table). Another way of conceiving of these two tensions is that the outward is conscious and the inner unconscious, one the subject of Choreutics (the study of the forms of movement and their significance), the other the subject of Eukinetics (the study of the dynamics of movement, or what Laban will later call Effort). In *Choreography*, Laban describes these respectively as primary and secondary or auxiliary tensions. His thinking about inner and outer reaches its greatest subtlety when he proposes that we consider movements which take the form of the Möbius strip or lemniscate, a twisted ribbon whose surface defies the classification of inner or outer – it is both.

The third and final theme that we can find in these two sentences from Brandenburg is Laban's claim that we can call these inner tensions 'thoughts, feelings, acts of volition, etc.' (again, his trinity of body/mind/spirit). For Laban, thoughts have spatial form; they are 'thought-movements' which are directed out towards the world. This explains more fully how he conceives of movement – an ex-tension – being the development of an in-tention. The final point to make is that the shapes of these movements (which are thoughts and emotions) are already symbols, both 'gestural and graphic'. Although Laban did create an abstract notation for both Effort and Dance, he actually saw the shapes of movement forms as symbols in their own right. Their shape is the actualisation not a representation of a thought:

> To the dancer a symbol is not a mimetic image of an event or an image of a thing, but the appearance, the realisation

of a process of tension in gestural power. But dancing is not imitating compressions (as, for instance, name, word, sound are copies of compressions) but intellectual form itself, tension formation.[19]

We are all dancers

This explains why Laban insists that we appreciate and respect the art of the dancer, because in his conception the dancer is someone who can understand and celebrate the world through the way they move within it. We are all dancers:

> We all carry a dancer in ourselves. Even if we do not know anything about this dancer within us, we have the urge to awaken him within us. In this sense the budding joy of movement in our time is to be understood; even the much-maligned film owes its success to the reawakening of gestural understanding.[20]

Laban believed that although this figure of the 'dancer in ourselves' (later, in *The Mastery of Movement*, this figure would become the 'mime') had remained dormant for centuries, he was living in an era when Western civilisation was on the threshold of a new age of movement. There was indeed a flourishing of movement studies in the 1910s and 1920s[21] and part of his quest (in *Gymnastics and Dance* and *Gymnastics and Dance for Children*) was to situate his own vision of movement education within the context of the different kinds of gymnastics and dance of his time.

To summarise: one of the great challenges of Laban's thinking is that he invites the reader to consider moving as having a mental dimension. In *The World of the Dancer*, he seems to suggest that by moving according to specific spatial patterns, the dancer can access states of mind that would otherwise be inaccessible to human experience. Following Pythagoras' idea of the material universe being constructed according to certain geometric proportions, Laban claimed that the dancer could trace these divine proportions and thus experience their architectonic harmony. References to Choreosophy (the philosophical discourse of dance) are included in Roderyk Lange's section on movement notation (Chapter 9) and Valerie Preston-Dunlop's selections from *Choreutics* (Chapter 11). When writing in English in the 1940s and 1950s, Laban would refer to people being lopsided, that is unharmonious, in their movement. We can trace this preoccupation with harmony and balance throughout his writings: it appears in a functional dimension when he encourages workers to find a more harmonic way of working (where their own way of moving is matched by the demands of the job); it appears in a therapeutic dimension when he encourages patients with mental health problems to explore certain kinds of movement. This Sourcebook ends with Laban's meditation upon the connection between harmony in movement and music.

Dance as celebration

Central to his notions of movement culture and individual liberation through movement was the Festival. This introduces the last big theme in Laban's writings – *Fest*, or what we have translated as 'celebration'. This is the means by which mankind can rejoice in their new-found sense of movement: 'Man is becoming conscious of the inner festiveness of all natural events. These phenomena are the sign that we should strive towards and reach a new cultural level. Our time stands in this sign.'[22]

In the quotation above, *Fest* is presented as a kind of inner tension which finds its expression in movement, maybe in the huge movement choirs that Laban would create in the 1920s. Laban's vision was of a society that would be happier and healthier and people more in harmony within and between themselves if they all moved together. The educational purpose of festive celebration is

> to encourage and practise the inner outlook and the outward ability, to express in the sense of the plastic

experience. The framework of the ritual is the festive celebration. Preparations for ritual festive celebrations in the past were physical, emotional and intellectual exercises.[23]

Here we see an echo of Wigman's passage on the Dervishes quoted above.

In these few quotations we see how Laban's thoughts wheel through the same themes: education, health, harmony, celebration, form, the unity of mind, body and spirit. His very writing is a round dance or *Reigen* (he called *The World of the Dancer*, a book in five *Reigen*). A round dance is a collective celebration of life, it is the actualisation of a community through movement and it is a community because the shape of the circle defies sides or hierarchies, each person being equidistant from the centre: the shape of the circle is the meaning of the movement. While Laban's ideas are couched in idealistic, romantic and poetic terms, at the same time, much of his writing is grounded in the concrete experience of everyday movement, and sometimes his social critiques can be trenchant. Laban was immensely practical as well as visionary. He was aware that his thinking straddled two camps:

> For the majority of people – and thus also for the artist, who is the condenser of general human experiences of tension – there is no rift between these two views. They can equally consider the process both from an intellectual point of view (scientific) as well as from an emotional point of view (religious). The thing itself does not become clear to them through these theories of the intellect, of the spirit or the mind, but through experience, action . . . Action is the expression of the will and feeling through dance, integrating desire, feeling and knowledge into a unit.[24]

Finally, a note about Laban's influences: throughout this Sourcebook you may detect echoes of, or parallels and connections with, other thinkers. In his work of the 1910s and 1920s, there are references to Laban's interest in Rosicrucian thinking,[25] and you may detect connections with the theosophy of Rudolf Steiner. Equally, in his writings of the 1950s,[26] you may notice his use of Carl Jung's schema of Thinking, Feeling, Sensing, Intuiting. However, Laban makes few explicit references to the writings of other thinkers, so it is difficult to be specific about his intellectual sources and influences. Possibly Evelyn Dörr's plan to publish Laban's collected letters will answer some of these questions, but until then we can only guess at what Laban absorbed and adapted from his cultural environment.

Translation and Laban's writing style

Rudolf Laban was a great fan of Nietzsche's *Also Sprach Zarathustra* (the text of *Vom Tauwind und der neuen Freude* was drawn from it) and his early writings share its rhapsodic style. Laban comes across as a supremely confident writer, and, as I've noted above, few of his books contain references to support some of his more unlikely claims and facts. The German language allows one to make new words by joining up word-elements together and Laban took this to quite dramatic limits, creating words that are challenging to translate into English. When Gordon Curl commissioned translations of Laban's German books, this is the letter he received on 9 August 1966 from the translator W. Brooks:

> Perhaps a few comments on this work may be of interest. As a whole it has proved extremely difficult: partly due to the mysticism of the author which led him to considerable impression of thought, and hence of terminology, and partly due to an unorthodox use of the German language. His writing is not that of a well educated mind, but he appears to have had a passion for exuberant expression – and for seeking out the most unusual words for this purpose. Considerable delay was caused by the extensive dictionary searching which was necessary for evaluating the unusual noun-compounds that Laban used – and also to the fact that our original translator gave up the task. I must admit that upon taking over the work myself, I felt some sympathy with him.[27]

Mr Brooks was possibly not someone who knew much about dance and movement and therefore would be unaware of the difficulty of the task that Laban had undertaken, which was to give a written explanation of a kinaesthetic experience. Even today we still do not really know how to talk about the experience of movement, and about the shape and nature of the movements that we make in space. That said, Laban does not make things easy for either the translator or the reader.

The selections from *The World of the Dancer*, *Gymnastics and Dance for Children*, *Gymnastics and Dance*, *Choreography* and Laban's texts on film were translated literally by Dr Stefanie Sachsenmaier, and finally worked into fluent English by both of us. The aim has been to achieve a translation that makes sense in English but which remains faithful to the meaning of the original. Where it has been difficult to establish a single meaning for a German term, we have put the German in brackets after the English translation. We refer the reader to the Glossary of German terms on p. 359 for a fuller discussion of some of the terms. The materials from the John Hodgson Archive (abbreviated in the notes as 'JHA') in the Brotherton Library, University of Leeds, have been translated by a variety of different people and it is not always clear who has translated which particular text. The named translators are Richard Ellis, Vivienne Bridson (who also helped Hodgson gather the collection), Marianne Luddington, and Lisa Ullmann (who donated a substantial amount of material to Hodgson for his planned but never completed biography of Laban).

Notes

1 By Lisa Ullmann in 1975.
2 Such a book does exist: *A Vision of Dynamic Space* (see Bibliography for full details).
3 Mary Wigman, 'Rudolf von Laban's Theory of Dancing', *Die Neue Schaubühne*, Vol. 3, Nos 5–6, Sept. 1921 (in JHA, Box 29, Folder 39, Item 1).
4 JH interview with Lisa Ullmann, 7 June 1971 (in JHA, Box 31, Folder 45, Item 13).

5. Preston-Dunlop (1998: 193). Translator unidentified.
6. JH interview with Perrottet (undated) (in JHA, Box 30, Folder 40, Item 10).
7. JH interview with Lisa Ullmann, 7 June 1971 (in JHA, Box 31, Folder 45, Item 13).
8. In JHA, Box 23, Folder 23, Item 1.
9. Bartenieff, in Johnson (1995: 224–225).
10. Preston-Dunlop (1998: 186).
11. Ibid., p. 196.
12. A copy of this is in JHA, Box 12, Folder 16, with a spoken translation on Tapes 9 and 10.
13. Letter from Stuttgart, 29 April 1920 (in JHA, Box 26, Folder 23, Item 1.34).
14. *OED*, DVD, 2nd edn.
15. *The World of the Dancer* (henceforth *WD*), p. 126.
16. Ibid., p. 126.
17. Ibid., p. 14.
18. Ibid., p. 37.
19. Ibid., pp. 120, 219.
20. Ibid., p. 24.
21. For example, Emile Jaques-Dalcroze, Bess Mensendieck, Elsa Gindler, as well as those developing the approaches of earlier movement pioneers such as Henrik Ling and François Delsarte.
22. *WD*, pp. 68, 127.
23. Ibid., p. 32.
24. Ibid., pp. 130, 235.
25. We know that Laban was involved with Rosicrucians from an interview with his second wife Maia and from the programme of a meeting of the Order in August 1917 (both cited in Chapter 1, 'Dance activities and schools, 1912–1917, Ascona and Zurich').
26. *Effort and Recovery* (1952–1953), and 'A Glossary of Movement Psychology' (1954).
27. In JHA, Folder 23, Item 6.

Chapter one

Dance activities and schools, 1912–1917, Ascona and Zurich

Introduction

Dick McCaw

Although Laban did not publish his first book until 1920 (aged 41), he was incredibly active in the second decade of the twentieth century – creating schools, initiating artistic communities, summer courses and festivals, giving inspiring lectures and making his first dance works. The texts below give a flavour of this activity. I have focused on two areas of activity: first, the temporary artistic community that he established in *Monte Verità* near Ascona in the Swiss canton of Ticino, in the five summers between 1913 and 1917, and then the schools and projects that he established in Zurich in the same years (he moved winter operations to Zurich from Munich after World War I broke out in August 1914).

The first thing to note is how difficult it is to draw a line between some of his activities and institutions. He created festivals which are in effect temporary communities that spend time labouring, dancing, studying, rehearsing and performing. Suzanne Perrottet, his companion and co-teacher in both Ascona and Zurich, describes a day in *Monte Verità*:

Figure 1.1 Laban School in Ascona (1913)
Source: From *Der Moderne Tanz*, Hans Brandenburg, Munich: Georg Muller, 1921.

Figure 1.2 Laban School in Ascona (1913)
Source: From *Der Moderne Tanz*, Hans Brandenburg, Munich: Georg Muller, 1921.

DANCE ACTIVITIES AND SCHOOLS, 1912–1917

Figure 1.3 Laban School in Ascona (1914)
Source: From *Der Moderne Tanz*, Hans Brandenburg, Munich: Georg Muller, 1921.

> We worked together in his *Monte Verità* cooperative. Until eight in the morning we worked in the garden, then from eight to nine we learned to make sandals and from nine to eleven we danced, outside in the open air. We were only with Laban from nine to eleven, the three or four people who knew him there. In the afternoon we had our music and our speech hour. The speech hour was quite new. Laban made the rules. He gave a theme and we had to improvise around it, keeping our improvisation short. With Laban directing, these speech improvisations were full of meaning. He was the only person doing this sort of thing at that time. I was quite good at it but Wigman found a way for herself with words.[1]

When Perrottet talks of 'the speech hour', she is referring to Laban's pedagogy of the 1910s which was called *Tanz Ton Wort* (Dance Music Word) which formed the basis of his teaching both in Ascona and Zurich. He describes his operation in a letter of 9 May 1914 to his friend and collaborator, Hans Brandenburg:

> You know, of course, what my own plans for the summer are. Headquarters at *Mte Verità*. Initially I shall be very

busy with 'politics' down there. The reorganization of the 'individualistic co-operative' will take up a lot of my time to begin with. Besides, I [am] giving chiefly beginner's courses in dance, music and the spoken word. Apart from minor performances and celebrations every week there'll be nothing on a larger scale till the end of August. Then and in September, at the start of the autumn tourist season on the Italian lakes, I hope to organise a number of larger festivals. But more important than all these matters is the formation of our school, which, as you may know, may possibly be somewhere other than *Mte Verità*.[2]

This interdisciplinarity was but one facet in a much bigger drive to unite life and art in both an artistic and a spiritual sense. An example of this is when an artistic and festive event in 1917 was combined with a congress of the Masonic order *Ordo Templis Orientis*, of which Laban was a member. His second wife Maja (later Maria) Laban explains:

> He was most deeply interested in Freemasonry when he was in Zurich between 1915 and 1919. He told me that when he was younger, when he was in Paris, he had studied *Rosenkreutz* [Rosicrucians]. He was not interested in small religious sects but in the relationship between different spiritual philosophies, and how these affected people's thinking and way of life.[3]

At its most general, Laban was seeking out all forms in which one could celebrate life (a theme that runs throughout his career). The same breadth of artistic and pedagogical activity can be seen in the description of the activities of the different departments of the Laban School.

The excerpts begin with letters from Laban to Suzanne Perrottet from Summer 1912, when they met in Emile Jaques-Dalcroze's centre for Eurhythmics at Hellerau (where Perrottet and Mary Wigman were students) to Summer 1913. In these, he explains his approach to training, and how it differs from the music-led movement exercises of Dalcroze and gymnastics, and how he wants to shift from an impressionistic dance (where one reacts to music) to an expressionist one which comes from one's inner impulses. A prospectus for his Art School gives more detail about developments in his approach to training, and an article by his early collaborator Hans Brandenburg explains Laban's pedagogy even further.

Next come two programmes from Festivals in *Monte Verità* in 1914 and 1917, followed by Laban's recollection of the second festival and a Swiss newspaper article about the same event. These programmes and descriptions will give a flavour of his activities in these years. Finally, there is a programme for a series of lectures given in Laban's school in Zurich in June 1917 which gives a detailed description of the curriculum – taught across four different departments – and the teaching staff which included Laban, Wigman and Perrottet.

LETTERS FROM LABAN TO SUZANNE PERROTTET[4]

September 7th 1912

I assure you that too much knowledge is not necessary – No theory! One works according to one's soul! The harmony and the system of Jaques-Dalcroze is very good for the mechanical development but later one needs one's soul, in combination with the brain – I have arrived approximately at the same theoretical results as yourself. You also feel the need of 'expressive gymnastic' called dance – do not get too wrapped up in melodies – they do not have so much to do with dance – rhythm plays the most important part in dance – melody gives only the feeling – any gay melody will go with any gay movement, if the rhythm agrees – it is even better if the melody is not like the movement. But all this theory is quite stupid, I never do it, or as little as possible. It spoils or hinders the creative force. All the same, in learning and studying one must understand, know etc. . . .

September 14th 1912

Now I want to talk to you about my musical experiments. I have seen that, before all, one must add to rhythmical gymnastics, not only chorus work but also studies of 'psychic gymnastics' – this would lead from representationalism to expressionism. I have found the details for these studies in my work with music. My friends, having listened to some of my experiments, have been astonished, among them my old friend, the sculptor Obrist, of whom I talked to you.

October 5th 1912

I have now launched to the great surprise of the 'bourgeois' and the professors of gymnastics (don't worry, I am not counting you amongst them) 'free dance' new social dances. I shall send you a prospectus etc. . . . I am editing a marvellous one.

February 22nd 1913

If gymnastics plus rhythm = impressionism (you know from your own experience the faults of such an education), the Dance which follows the rhythms of music is purely impressionistic and furthermore influenced by something totally foreign to the human body . . . I can't and don't want to theorise too much. It would take too long to write to you, the way through which I am trying to develop in a very individualistic manner, the body and its artistic movements. The poetry of tensions, the counterweight, the equilibrium, the constant changes of these tensions, as well in soloists as in a group – the exuberance of dimensional feeling, the brutality of feebleness, of the driving force and the struggle between time and spatial dimensions.

PROSPECTUS: LABAN COURSES FOR DANCE, SOUND, SPEECH[5]

It is our aim to further all means of human expression equally, to give the dancer insight into music and speech, beside the study of movement, to acquaint the musician with speech and movement and in the same way to help the speaker (orator) to a necessary, not only theoretical, but practical knowledge of music and movement.

Hans Brandenburg (Munich) the author of *The Modern Dance* says, amongst other things, of Laban: 'Laban aims at works of art which on the whole have their roots in those expressions given to man directly without the help of outside material, just in the trinity of dance–sound–speech. It is impossible to let students only play and sing, but it is natural and most important for him to let them speak as well. Out of the art of movement there springs a whole complex of movement-arts which embraces music, the fine arts, poetry as far as they belong here.'

The gap between body and intellect is being bridged and so the original aim of man comes into being, the only aim of the future: 'the whole man'.

The Laban Courses are serving this aim as they offer the opportunity not only to the artists and those who wish to become artists but also to the non-professionals to get to know and learn to master the three main fields of movement, sound and speech. The furthering of the whole organism is of great value as well to the artist as to man in general. Our present time teaches us that we not only need strong intellectual but also physically capable men. No more one-sided super-development but that of a whole human being.

A NEW SCHOOL OF DANCE

Hans Brandenburg[6]

The school for the art of movement which to date had held its Winter courses in Germany but the Summer courses in the

Kanton Tessin has now been transferred to Zurich for good and will here develop further according to the following outlines.

Recently Laban students have shown examples of their work in Munich in an over-crowded hall.

'The Free Dance' was printed on posters and programmes. 'What is that?', the uninitiated but curious would ask. Well, they soon found out. It was not what the police and others had suspected, mistrusting the splendid word 'free'; it was not dance freed from clothing and morality. But it *was* dance without music or rather not – in so far as it was not a thing to which the word 'without' belongs as if one should have to apologise for something missing – but it was indeed free dance, self-reliant and based only on its own law. An unusual and, for many people, challenging view! But the serious ones among them could not so easily protest because it was much too obvious that there was the most passionate work in what they saw . . . If the genuine dance cannot be understood by the eye alone – as if it was a succession of beautiful floating pictures – much less can Laban's dance where even the ear can't help.

Here we have one of the most significant points in which Rudolf von Laban differs from Dalcroze. Laban does not wish musical rhythms translated into physical ones, but he wants to bring out the physical rhythm within his pupils. He wakens in them the pleasure of movement, and when this pleasure is awakened, the student is supposed to produce the rhythm himself, rhythm with all its elements: swing, timing, beat, structure and order.

The human body expresses its character only in movement, and the most beautiful thing is that it is, at the same time, spatial and temporal. Through this dual function it is such an infinitely rich instrument that, for Laban, the highest and purest dance is in the forming of silent movement. In aiming much more exclusively at the pure dance than Dalcroze and – on the other hand – and this is the second point in which he differs from the creator of rhythmical gymnastics – he is striving for an art form in its totality. Not for such total art forms that consist of an accumulation of various aesthetic elements but for those that have their root in the totality of expression which are given to man directly without the help of outer material, in the trinity of dance, sound and speech. To him, it is quite impossible to teach movement like Dalcroze where they only play and sing: for him, it is natural and therefore of the utmost importance to let people speak as well.

All this is an apparent contradiction to my statement about his aim for the 'free dance', but it becomes clear when you learn more about Laban's undogmatic ideas: first, those about the significance that music nevertheless has for dance. Firstly, Laban uses music as rhythmical sound, as a help for awakening the joy of movement and, secondly, he uses it so that the body can learn from such infinitely and richly developed time-rhythm; but here Laban is very careful. The body should learn from music only after it has understood its own laws and its movement-rhythm thus avoiding the danger of learning and copying something that accords with the music but not with the body.

Thirdly, Laban recognises the possibility of a total fusion between music and dance. Thus, he is like somebody who sees in absolute music, in principle, the highest aim. He is an opponent of programmatic music but without denying the existence of perfect songs, oratorios and opera, and even cultivates these forms himself. Laban's position to the relation between movement and speech is a similar one. He is an opponent of the somewhat 'conceptual' dance, the mime, but besides aiming for pure dance he aims for drama, for demonstrations in which movement and speech are fused. Let's try to make this aim clearer which at first glance looks a dual one. What does the 'free dance' demand of those who perform it and of those who see it? It demands that you draw the utmost consequences from the movement possibilities; that you understand the body and its laws in its whole wealth; that you know and feel what is space and time arrangement; that you understand fully the 'idea form' of the dance; that you, for example, learn to use and note the symmetries, repetitions, reversals, refrains and the architectonic, organic tempo and dynamic shades even better than music can offer with its analogous forms.

The ethical and aesthetical value of the free dance rests – like that of the absolute music – in its consequence, strictness, concentration and purity. Nevertheless Laban now places – beside this idea of the 'free dance' – this other one: Dance, Speech, Sound, or he rather allows these two ideas to supplement, interchange, increase and penetrate each other.

Out of the art of movement there grows a complex of various arts of movement which embrace music, art, poetry, as far as they belong here, as there are stage, music, decorative arts, drama. Man as a whole being – whether he wants to become an artist or not – will be educated, formed, created, thus learning to cultivate all his natural powers of expression, and actually everybody ought to do so. . . .

FESTIVAL PERFORMANCES IN SUMMER AND AUTUMN 1914 BY LAKE MAGGIORE[7]

The Week celebrations

Every Friday (or Sunday) continuous, connected Life celebrations

Every Tuesday

Performances of plays, dances and songs

4 big nature feasts

The feast of fertilisation
The feast of germination
The feast of ripening
The feast of decomposition

The School of Art prepares festival participants, actors and poets for the big festivals.

The small festivals will be directed and acted by the followers who have already completed.

The School has the possibility, and the aim, of supplying all prospective actors, whether they want to take part in the new festival cult or other performing activities, both the technical means and the real evaluation of the intellectual heights, and responsibilities, which this profession demands.

Every human being who wants to go on stage should, even in its most modest form of influence, get to know and value the work, the technique of his expression, the form, tone and thoughts.

The festival participants – each of whom are deep-thinking, life-loving as human beings – will experience in the exercises of the School of Art, a strengthening of their bodies and a deepening of themselves. Within the circle of his fellow pupils they will get to know and cherish more of the value of life and will return to life's battle strengthened, with body and spirit happily united.

The creative artist will be led from his poverty-stricken solitude of egotistic existence, into the community of noble thought and he will be given the opportunity to put ideas into practice through continuous performances.

The School of Art will in no way use all the time for the spiritual or ethical exercise of its pupils – on the contrary, it will give life itself its due – as it of course wants to glorify the right to life itself.

A Meeting of The *Ordo Templis Orientis*, 15–25 August 1917, Monte Verità, Ascona, Lake Maggiore – Ticino[8]

15 August

Reception of Congress Members

16–24 August

Congress Meetings – Amongst others, the following lectures, talks and discussions have been programmed:

1. About a-national social forms
2. About contemporary education
3. About the position of women in future society
4. About mysticism of Freemasonry
5. About new social forms and art

The lectures and discussions will be in English, German, French and Italian.
    Excursions are organized for the free days on 17–18th August.

'Sun' Festival – Laban School

18th 6.30 p.m. Initiation Ritual after Otto Borngraeber's, 'Song of the Sinking Sun'
11.00 p.m. 'Demons of the Night' Pantomime dance play by torchlight

19th 6.00 a.m. 'Triumph of Sun', Danced hymns

20th 3.45 p.m. 'In form lives the spirit': Lecture/demo by Herbert von Bomsdorff-Bergen
Demonstration by Laban pupils

21st 3.45 p.m. 'Musical Festival': Ensembles and solos for instruments and song-music by Bach, Gluck, Schubert and Mozart. Poems by Christian Morgenstern

22nd 9.30 a.m. Expressive culture in education, life and art. Lecture/demo in the open air on the art of movement. Speaker Mary Wigman. Demo by Rudolf Laban

8.00 p.m. 'The Miracle (or Wonder) Flower', Dance plays by Laban School: Pantomime and solo dance

23rd 8.00 p.m. 'Old Rites and Dances' from Old Mexico, Africa, Babylon, Egypt and the Orient. Introduction by Rudolf von Laban

If the weather is bad, it will be held inside.

LABAN'S DESCRIPTION OF THE 'DANCE OF THE SETTING SUN' AND 'DEMONS OF THE NIGHT'[9]

On a mountain meadow, enclosed by great clumps of trees on its south, east and north sides, and bordering a steep slope to the west, we had erected a fireplace of boulders. The audience sat on three sides against the groups of trees. On the fourth side, over to the south-west, an opal-coloured lake was visible far below the slope between towering mountains which gradually lost themselves in a range of blue hills. Here we performed the introductory scene of the festive play 'Dance of the Setting Sun'. After a solemn *Reigen* around the fire, a speaker, accompanied by attendants, came up the slope. The moment when his head appeared over the edge of the bank was exactly timed so that the lower rim of the setting sun was just touching the horizon. Standing there he spoke the first lines of his poem to the setting sun. Drawing closer and walking towards the fire, he was encircled by a welcoming group of dancers. He then recited the second passage of the poem, with the sun by now half hidden below the horizon. During the farewell *Reigen* addressed to the sun, women and children came out of the rows of sun, spectators and up to the fireplace to fan the flames. The steeply rising column of thin smoke was wafted this way and that by groups of people continually rushing towards it. Finally there was a poem to the twilight. It was accompanied by a solemn *Reigen* which in the end formed into a procession leading the spectators away from the meadow.

Shortly before midnight began the second part of the play, 'Demons of the Night'. A group of dancers with drums, tom-toms and flutes assembled among the spectators, and torches and lanterns lighted up the way to a mountain peak where bizarrely-shaped rocks looked down on a circular meadow. Here five blazing fires were lit and a group of kobolds performed leaping dances around and through them.

Then a group of masked dancers approached. The huge masks, made of twigs and grass, covered their whole bodies. Behind these diverse squatting, towering, angular and spiky shapes hid witches and fiends. Creeping up, they stripped off the disguises of the dancers in a wild scene and burned them. As a finale, around the dying glow of the embers, came the dance of the shadows. Then the torches of the attendants were rekindled and, with dancers in front and behind, the long train of spectators was led back to the starting-point.

'A LITTLE DIARY ON THE OCCULT, THE HIERATIC AND OTHER STRANGELY BEAUTIFUL THINGS'[10]

About two months ago there was a congress which took place in Ascona whose meetings attracted a very strange public. Nobody would have attributed this little mountain town with such an interesting invasion of strangers as here came together in the simple but elegant country houses on the mountain of *Verità*. But Ascona is today the main meeting place of the friends and followers of the occult sciences, and for this reason the congress of *Ordo Exempli Orientalis* took place here in August and guests came from England, Germany, Austria and even France in order to take their places in this extraordinary circle.

The aims of this Order of Eastern Examples are humane and clear: it spreads the teaching of the old Freemasons of the Memphis and Misarahine [Misraim] cult. Its intention is an intensive training of the heart based on love, goodness and joy. It has produced its own extensive literature whose purpose is to spread a greater life-fulfilment than the current materialism. As the order has no dogma at all with the exception of general brotherly love, so it has managed to attract to date many hundreds of initiates in the German-speaking countries.

In order to put the inclinations of this cult onto a human and timely path, this congress was blessed with a strengthening of their noble aims by a sequence of performances by the Zurich art school by Herr von Laban which gave great honour to little Ascona.

Since Herr von Laban transferred his school from Munich to Zurich in 1913, his institute has added much to the consciousness and range of its plan of study. From the necessary shaping of its basic principles, the Laban School has progressed far beyond what a dance college of the old school usually has to offer its pupils. It has in fact become an institute that not only trains the potential of the student but also educates him to become an artist. In the course of the training of the personality the whole range of eurhythmics is brought into play. No longer has it just to do with technique alone, but also with the whole range of art teaching of which the culture of expression in dance, and sound and word, is only the practical part. In the course of this practice of his mental and physical talents, the student should also take the opportunity to grasp the relationships and connections of the inner rhythm of his art and his cultural unity. He should sense himself not only as an individual, but also as a part of the cosmos and in the whole work of art. And so is revealed the theory of the two leading personalities, Herr von Laban and Mary Wigman. . . .

Such an education demands an enormous amount, not only from the teacher but also from the pupil, in terms of moral and physical work, and above all, of unreserved commitment. This is the basis of the gravity which characterises the performances of the individuals and the direction in the evening public demonstrations. Here we may see the publicity value of the school which today unites a great number of striking personalities in their diverse subjects of study: of dance, singing, drawing, film, scenery, pantomime, and so on. And it is precisely in this gravity and in the discipline of their efforts where the peaceful ideals of the Freemasons can be seen. One has seldom heard more convincing essays on the origin of the artistic rite of the mimic theatrical treatment of culture, and of the hieratic dance, than in the lectures given by Herr von Laban. And seldom has one seen the cult dances from ancient Mexico, Central Africa and from the East performed with more intuitive grasp of their essence than in his own school.

This leaves me thinking of the particularly high quality of the talents which, one can imagine, are to be found in this school.

THE LABAN SCHOOL: THE FINAL EVENING OF LECTURES, 27TH JUNE 1917, 8 P.M.[11]

Introduction

This evening is the last of our cycle of lectures on the language of art. . . . The necessary diversity of forms of activity, of serious education of artists and men, leads to an organisation into departments for the various fields. We consider that we can indicate the aims of our work in the best possible fashion if we talk a little bit about these individual regions. The teachers and participants who are particularly concerned with the work and aims of each department are named under each heading.

1. The Department for Dance, Music and Word.

Laban, Mary Wigman, Suzanne Perrottet, Sivon Langwarer, Klara Walter.

Dance is an inexhaustible source of rhythmic energies. The relationship with the other expressive arts has previously been ignored and thereby been restricted in its capacity for operation. We are trying to reveal and also to emphasise its own values. That much-used word is being lost today in unartistic meaning and in rather mechanistic brain-teasers. The spoken word, and even the properly-spoken and properly-understood word, can return the virility to language once again. The art of music must stand as an independent and as a subsidiary art must throw off the chains that bind it to other forms from other eras. It must once again serve the spiritual as a proper expression. Within souls stand things that are new and that have not been said before. . . .

2. Department for Pantomime.

Laban, Mary Wigman, Eve Moore

Pantomime stands between dance and word: original and entirely comprehensible to all as a visible recreation of will. The much-maligned film can take new art . . . into the widest possible spheres by means of a transformed artistic pantomime.

3. Department for Harmonious Education.

Laban, Mary Wigman, K. Wülfe, S. Bermel

Today's young man suffers from a one-sided education and vigorously strives for an enveloping, harmonic development. The adult who is often less narrow-minded must acquiesce in this search in order to be able to point his own children on the right road in the future. The arts of expression are an essential means of propagating an education of the entire personality. A modest beginning for the training for the modern age is the use of the rhythm of dance, music and word as well as harmony, as a means of education. This is the start of a path to a development that is fitting to the times. . . .

4. Department of Form.

Laban, S. Täuber, M. Nekrusias, Yvonne Ruchkeschel, K. Wülfe

The Department of Form has the job of providing all the necessary areas – clothing, props, etc. – to conform with the overall idea of any festival performance. It should also bring all the needs of our daily life, of the circles of pupils, into a harmonic form, and propagate artistic integration. Plans and models for appropriate festival venues are in preparation and are coming to completion. Increasingly one hears the complaints of spectators who have frequently been sitting in the rows of stalls of our local theatre and have only been able to see, for example, the top half of the actors' or dancers' bodies and have never been able to see their feet. It is quite clear how uneconomical and how inappropriate are the sight-lines in any large hall where only one or perhaps two rows of stalls have the possibility of a favourable view for the spectator.

5. Department of Organisation.

Laban, J. Scheiber, F. Höll

The principal purpose of this department is to bring the education, the life and the productions of the ranks of pupils into one form, which can serve the high interest of art and can also remain in touch with the practical demands of everyday life. A cultural approach casts its light ahead. It is guided and supported by its recognition of harmony and of beauty, in fact, of art. In this sense a proper education in organisation can work as an example for the general conduct of people's lives. We should also take this occasion to give our most especial thanks to the circle of friends, promoters and patrons who have been so useful to us and so helpful in our path towards our ambition in this last year.

Please note, during the summer months of July and August, if there is sufficient demand, some of the departments will be transferred to Ascona near Lake Maggiore. The other departments will take their summer courses in Zurich.

Notes

1 Interview with JH (in JHA, Box 30, Folder 40, Item 10b, pp. 8–9).
2 In JHA, Box 26, Folder 23, Item 1.

3 Transcript of an interview from 1973 (in JHA, Box 30, Folder 41, Item 10c).
4 All letters are in JHA, Box 26, Folder 24, Item 5.
5 In JHA, Box 29, Folder 39, Item 33.
6 *Badsiche Landeszeitung*, Munich, in JHA, Box 23, Folder 13, Item 10 (from a collection of Lisa Ullmann's handwritten translations in a document entitled: 'Excerpts from our collection of critiques and essays. From the many critiques of the press as well as from renowned artists and educationalists we copy here some parts that characterise our aims'; few of the articles have dates or publications).
7 In JHA, Box 23, Folder 12, Item 4.
8 In JHA, Box 35, Folder 45, Item 19/5.
9 In *LD*, pp. 158–159.
10 Author unknown, *The Bern Intelligencer*, 15 November 1917 (in JHA, Box 11, Folder 12, Item unnumbered).
11 In JHA, transcribed from Tape 6.

Chapter two

The World of the Dancer (1920)

Translation by Stefanie Sachsenmaier and Dick McCaw

Introduction

Stefanie Sachsenmaier

The World of the Dancer is Laban's first publication, dating from 1920. At present, there is no English version in print. The book gives the impression of a collection of thoughts reminiscent of notebook or sketchbook entries. It is made up of five 'round dances' [*Reigen*] with an Introduction and a Conclusion. In each 'round dance' we find numerous headings with smaller sections, which constitute comments or short abstracts and definitions on selected topics. On the (dis)organisation of the book, Valerie Preston-Dunlop mentions that 'hearsay has it that Laban confessed to Jooss that he had cut up the text into short sections and thrown them in the air, to land as the fancy took them'.[1]

The text has been claimed to be almost impossible to translate. We have to bear in mind that the German of Laban's time is now dated – it was written nearly a century ago – and certain terms will produce different resonances when read today. Laban's style of writing does not seem to aim for precision and indeed, in the Conclusion of the book, he states that his writing has not emerged from academic research but that it stems from his actual *experience* of dancing, and is the result of extensive conversations with dancers. An implicit value judgement in this statement is at the core of Laban's thinking that mirrors aspects of the practice-as-research debate that emerged in the 1990s in the academic sector related to the performing arts. Laban states the following in the Introduction of *The World of the Dancer*:

> The form in which I dress my insights gained from a thousand dances, conversations with dancers, writing about dance and movement, further from the teaching and rehearsing of dance, is the 'thought round'. Dance explains itself only in dance. To order thought motives in the sense of dance composition and to grasp thought as a physical, mental and spiritual [*körperlich-seelisch-geistig*] movement is the basic task of the person who creates a 'thought round'. The plastic relationship of concepts and thoughts to each other stands above logical connections. Logic is a sub-section of the dance-plastic thought-tension relationship, the basis of dance thought. [2]

The statement shows that Laban saw not only a physical, but also an intellectual and spiritual function in dance. More than that, he was concerned with how we can make sense of dance in terms of its 'experience', without imposing any sort of logical framework on the practice, which may distort it. His insights, as he states, have been gained in the act of dancing or of creating dance itself. In order to write about the practice of dancing and dance-making, Laban literally 'created' new words that would express his experience and *sense* of something perceived. The idea of a 'thought round', to which he refers, beautifully demonstrates how he combined the practice of 'round dancing' with a way of thinking that is akin to the dancer herself, and also how he maintains that there is 'thought' to dance itself: 'To the dancer all questions of psychology and the theory of cognition become a plastic conception of form tension through the experience of body–spirit movement. He interprets the world for himself according to the sense of dance experience.' [3]

This approach of writing with a 'sense of dance experience' is crucial to bear in mind when encountering *The World of the Dancer*, in that Laban shows a tendency to drift into the poetic rather than the scientific in his writing, despite at times claiming such an emphasis. What remains at the core of his work is the convergence of the practice of dancing with the practice of writing: 'One should also realise how difficult it is to limit this experience to words and systems of thought that are overlaid by science, philosophy or mysticism.'[4]

Laban hints here at a key issue of the practice-as-research debate, which is an acknowledgement that dance practice has its own logic that might not be rendered in writing, which is governed by a different logic, at least in the academic sector which outlines precise established conventions. What is interesting here is that at the time of Laban's writing a relevant debate was strongly driven by French philosopher Henri Bergson, whose conception of 'process'[5] continued later to inspire writing by philosopher Gilles Deleuze as well as the contemporary cultural theorist Brian Massumi, by way of example. The point that these writers seem to be making is that the established conventions in academic research and writing miss something crucial in practice. Typical notions that are debated are those of 'change' and 'transformation', as well as 'intuition' and 'judgement'.[6]

The overall themes of *The World of the Dancer* are, as the title suggests, Laban's conception of dance and its function for the individual as well as for society at large. Throughout the book, Laban keeps referring to the dancer as a person who actively engages body, mind and spirit. It becomes clear upon reading *The World of the Dancer* that Laban seems to have felt a 'mission': his dance research is more than research into 'dance' – it is research into life overall. At the core of his writing he addresses the question of how to live life 'fully' – his very specific conception of *dancing* is his answer.

The first 'round dance' focuses mainly on the concept of dance, in terms of body, mind and spirit, while the second chapter looks principally at physical and psychological phenomena related to the dancing body. The third 'round dance' emphasises dance in society – its function in work as well as public celebrations, followed by a fourth that seeks to identify the role of dance within the arts. The fifth and last section unveils thoughts on dance 'experience'.

The present selection of excerpts has been chosen from an informed perspective of hindsight. Certain themes that have proved to be key concepts in Laban's later and more elaborated thinking and writing are already touched upon and discussed in this first publication, hence providing a foundation for much writing to come. The selection provided here reveals his early developments of specific concepts, allowing the reader to trace the evolution of Laban's thought from these beginnings to the excerpts provided from his later publications.

The first point of focus in the excerpts provided in this chapter will be Laban's conception of 'dance', the 'dancer' and what he calls 'dance sense'. Second, selections have been made that illuminate his preoccupation with public celebrations [*Feste*] and the function of the 'round dance' [*Reigen*]. A third section draws together a range of excerpts in which Laban thematises his preoccupation with the human body in terms of its internal states when in motion as well as in relation to its spatial surroundings. The fourth and last section draws together a short selection of Laban's writing on work and rhythm.

Rather than a collection of essays, the book is aphoristic in style and does not follow any straight argument. Meaning is built through repetition and resonance throughout the book. Paradoxically, its small sections tend to entail very long and complicated sentences. While this is indeed a characteristic of the German language and could have been changed in this translation, I have attempted here a translation that is as literal as possible.

Dance, dancer and dance sense

> Dance lives not everywhere in each individual, but in the majority of people – dance which waits to be awakened.[7]

In the Introduction to *The World of the Dancer*, Laban sets out by drawing attention to his basic concepts of the 'dancer' and 'dance' as such. His quest is a renewed understanding of 'dance', and a different function of the practice within society at large. This notion of 'dance' still exceeds our current conceptions in the early twenty-first century.

Laban is mainly concerned with what we may call a person's 'way of life', and his emphasis is one of drawing together 'spiritual uniformity, humaneness, indeed an all-round affirmation of life'.[8] He states that terms other than 'dancer' might be found for such a person, yet he identifies that in his view 'the only pure full expression of this experience can be the art of dancing'.[9] Laban emphasises that 'dance' in this sense is rarely practised, and what is regularly called 'dance' does not correspond to his own conception: 'Such inherently different things are called dance and the art of dance, that no clearly defined term and no full evaluation can be found.'[10]

In Laban's conception, a 'dancer' is:

> that new person, who does not draw his awareness one-sidedly from the brutalities of thinking, feeling or will. He is that person who strives to interweave clear intellect, deep feeling and strong will into a harmoniously balanced and flexible whole whose parts are interrelated.[11]

Dance is here understood as a practice that engages a person's body, mind and spirit, which Laban continually refers to in his descriptions of dance experience. He identifies the 'physical-spiritual-mental educational power'[12] of dance and states that 'dance experience has its roots in the whole rather than a partial sensation of a person'.[13] His concept has hence a philosophical-spiritual emphasis, but is directly rooted in the practice of dancing itself. Stating that '[t]here is . . . no emotional excitement or intellectual achievement without body movement and vice versa',[14] Laban does not see the realms of body, mind and spirit as separate; instead they are inextricably formative of and dependent on each other.

The excerpts listed below are a selection of Laban's numerous small sections of *The World of the Dancer*, which specifically outline his conception of 'dance'.

INTRODUCTION

Every artist is a dancer, so are some thinkers and dreamers, and in his unrealised nature so is every man. . . . Of course there is some artistic skill alien to dance. Many writers, musicians and painters are devoted to earning a living without dancing. Likewise thinkers, researchers, organisers do not at all always create with dance faith. For the dancer, however, this segregates art from artistic skill, liveliness from staleness, where the former allows for an element of dance, that of a total experience, while the latter arises from a deviant mechanical or some other one-sided universal feeling. . . .

Only few realise that dance, this art that is so often seen as a secondary, individual phenomenon of life, has something in its essence that fulfils the whole of the physical, spiritual and mental being. In time, a more clear evaluation of dance thought and dance activity will result from the stimuli contained in this work.

There are very few dancers just as there are very few true poets, musicians and sculptors. Next to the art of dancing, there is dance technique. A lot of what is called dance is inartistic gymnastics, acrobatics, posing, pretension, eroticism and the like. We are at the beginning of an understanding of the deeper meaning of this art and thus may not judge it or even condemn it. We can only look with awe into the workshop of nature in which the dancers' spirit arises.[15]

DANCE AND LIFE

Dance is intellectual nourishment for man. Transference of essential knowledge and of enthusiasm can only be achieved by practice and application of gestural power. . . . Dance is not to be understood as a singular striving of man, but as something that permeates his whole being, his very essence, a unity which determines and organises all action and reaction in everyday life, rest and celebration.

The arrangement of the round dance of human life is the symbol in which we recognise the 'dance kernel' of all existence.[16]

THE EXPERIENCE OF THE DANCER

The experience of dance constitutes the meaning of the world for the dancer. What the researcher seeks, what the dreamer longs for, what is sought by a person with desires, is found and experienced by the dancer in dancing. Dance is the limitless possibility of comprehending and communicating. Art teaches the dancer to recognise the three-stranded tensions of desire, feeling and knowledge, not as limited powers, but as the results of countless gestural rhythms in which the world gives and takes itself.[17]

MULTIPLICITY IN UNITY

Dancing is not just ability, it is also faith and knowledge. It unites desire, feeling and thought as nodal points or chords of rhythmic changes of gestural power. The dancer knows that everything is dance and the infinite gesture of the world can be concentrated in discerning thought, structure and deduction. He believes that life can and should be serene and beautiful. Art to him is the round dance which changes and unites the inexhaustible wonders of the world into force.[18]

BALLET

A ballet salon. A bored, loose-limbed master demonstrates elaborate contortions of the body, praises elasticity of the legs as the only worthwhile ideal to aim for and to the accompaniment of soft music drills pathetically smiling girls and boys in exact pirouettes and leaps. The dancer leaves the room.[19]

DANCE SENSE

Whoever can transform impressions from the environment into a physical- spiritual- mental feeling of tension has dance talent. If the dancer perceives a form by means of sight or touch, if he hears a sound wave, if he thinks a thought, then a tension or a sequence of tensions arise within him from which he draws certain conclusions about the nature and character of the phenomenon before him. I should like to call this *dance sense*. Today this dance sense has atrophied because it is not practised enough – only the artist has it to the degree that it comes into the equation as a knowledge-bringing element for the world of his will, emotions and thoughts. This dance perception integrates the whole sensory, emotional and intellectual perception into a unit. The discerning spirit of man attains a full *impression* which then can be divided again into the rational *expression* of verbal gesture, the deliberate expression of physical movement or the emotional expression of the tonal gesture.[20]

REAWAKENING THE DANCE SENSE

The first task of the dancer is to awaken and activate his dance sense, the centre of awareness.

His whole effort is directed towards conquering this basis of complete human awareness for himself as for others; to pass it on and to preserve it.

The dancer does not thereby forgo the power of thought, language and the tonal expression of emotion in music. On the contrary, the true dancer will examine all perception of tension, fully experienced through dance sense, with awareness, feel it with his emotions and grasp it with his will.

It all depends on experience. If one should try to understand knowledge gained through dance sense by reason alone, where it is written down in words or spoken, then again one could only attain partial knowledge based on reason. When the emotions are roused and enraptured by the discovered insights and images, and are thus in agreement with them, then an emotional understanding becomes possible, but no full understanding in the sense of the plastic idea. Note also, a pure physical grasping of a sense impression is not a total experience. Only when the intellect, emotions and the will of the dancer are combined as plastic tension, does this affirmation of the world arise within him which without mystery or doubt guarantee the inner balance of satisfaction which one can call total experience.[21]

DANCE VISION

Perceptive dance sense can read far more from a gesture than the distinction between two opposite component parts of a gestural chord.

With acute receptiveness it is possible to grasp, to experience the full content of consciousness of a phenomenon from the first gesture, from the first sound, from the first thought which swings towards us. In certain circumstances one grasps even more in this extraordinarily short space of time: the whole content of consciousness of the whole environment, yes, even of humanity. Such 'enlightenment' is certainly rare. It only occurs when the ability to experience impressions of the receiving person and the expressive ability of the communicating person in themselves and in the sense of dance knowledge are fully developed. The artistic experience of a process is sometimes of this nature. The two- and three-dimensionality of all phenomena is perceived as the symbol of the endless manifold variability of the unit and activates effects that are inexplicable and incomprehensible to reason and other partial knowledge.[22]

THE DANCER'S POWER AND THE DANCER'S DUTY

No being on earth has the power to release demons like the dancer. But along with the power of gesture he is also given dance conscience. He seeks self-realisation through a plastic sense; mastery of his abilities and powers. He ennobles their being when he only places them at the service of dance spirit and does not use them for selfish ends. The impulse of selfishness breaks the power of the gesture. Selfish desire results in a momentary glitter but never a lasting effect. The dancer knows that it is a basic law of gestural power not to allow oneself to be constantly misused for selfish purposes. The dancer also knows that the selfish initiative of many people who are dancing and those dancers who make wrong steps create that poor opinion of dance and dancers which we encounter everywhere.

One should contrast the symbol of 'dance' that is living in the dancer with the general view on dance. One should admit openly and clearly how our culture judges dance and dancers; which role and what status in our public life it gives to this dance approach. It is the dancer's duty to preserve freedom for his individuality through the tightest scrutiny of his own desires and actions, as well as by the sharpest scrutiny of alien impositions, while at the same time gaining the understanding of the ignorant.

How many people are secretly dancers? How their wishes, fantasies, thoughts, feelings are dancing! How many people dance, jump, exercise secretly? Yes, one could ask: 'Who – in their most inner being – is not a dancer?'[23]

DANCE AS ART

The ideas about the art of movement, dance and dancers are today still completely unexplained.

Within the concept of dance, a range of colourful conceptions are blended which range from the sensual display of beautiful bodily movements, via profound artistic stage presentations, to the round dance of the stars in the cosmos.

The various distortions of dance exercise and dance play must not be taken as artistic achievements. Dance practice or gymnastics has a pure educational value. A piece is not danced for the spectator. Each kind of round play is related to the personal sensation of being moved which has arisen from a heightened feeling for life, and is satisfied in itself. Artistic dance aims at expressing a finished artwork.

Art is not a refined work of nature as, say, the well-educated person who portrays himself in the round dance. Art is self-denial, to transform oneself in the service of the artwork.[24]

THE ROLE OF AGE

A further organisational difference is that the age of students and practitioners is not as important as in the acrobatic performances of the ballet. Naturally, as in every profession, there exist certain limits for the beginning of study and the capability for training, but these are considerably more broadened than before. Well-formed, supple and agile adults can still successfully begin study, because it is only a matter of the natural suppleness of the limbs and not of artificial contortions and distortions, which can be forced upon the sinews and ligaments of the body only when growing up. Even people who are healthy and agile, who live naturally, can perform on stage into their later years because it is not youthful beauty that is shown but movement, floods, waves, spiritual expression of human movement.[25]

Celebration [FEST] and round dance [REIGEN]

The notion of *Fest* is central to Laban's concept of dance. *Fest* is here translated as 'celebration', although there is more to a *Fest* than the act of celebrating. Related terms are 'festivity' and 'festival'. A *Fest*, as Laban outlines it, is closely tied to the round dance [*Reigen*], it is an occasion where such communal dances could take place. It might be described as an event where the community gathers and celebrates, which was common practice in the early part of the twentieth century in Germany, where Laban spent much time living and working – a time when artistic culture was strongly sought and supported.

Martin Gleisner, one of Laban's contemporaries, refers in his book called *Dance for All* to a 'deep dissatisfaction' of people in the 1920s with the traditions of bourgeois festivities that had become the norm. He describes these events as 'beer-drinking' gatherings in which speeches and at best choir-singing would take place. Instead he recognises a wish for a 'new form of celebration', which people perceived, according to him, as more meaningful and having a larger purpose. Gleisner approves of a growing occurrence of such events, where not only the watching of performances but also the act of 'performing' itself is central.[26]

For Laban, this form of 'celebration' has a key function in his concept of the role of dance in society. As is evident from the previous excerpts on 'dance' and the 'dancer', Laban writes with a vision for a psychophysical engagement with creative movement specifically for the common person, the amateur, rather than a dance elite that is trained in specific skills.

As Preston-Dunlop mentions, Laban referred to what he called 'the will to celebrate' [*Festwille*] as a 'natural drive, combining enjoyment of splendour and play', and she further describes how

> Lonely people, people denied communal cultural activities of any significance, epitomised the longings of modern man to participate together in symbolic activity, for the will to live is bound up with the will to live together, . . . and is given form in community action, whether in family, religious or political groups, as children and as adults.[27]

The form of celebration that Laban advocates is not merely a space for enjoyment and coming together, but more than that, an opportunity for the development of inner expression and growth of people fostered by movement. A celebration in this sense also has an educational function in that it combines enjoyment with instruction. Hence, for Laban, a celebration [*Fest*] is an event where body, mind and spirit are engaged at once and can be furthered, where 'dance' in the way he understood and sought to foster it could take place.

INTRODUCTION

It is dance that speaks to us from the thought-round of the poet, the sound-round of the musician and the pictures of painters, sculptors and toolmakers. Dance is all culture, all sociability. Dance is the swinging force which relates intangible conceptions to religion. Dance is all knowledge, perception and construction, which fulfils the researcher and the man of action. But the purest image of the dance of dances, of universal happening, is the round dance in which the human body swings.[28]

THE RHYTHMIC ORGANISING POWER OF THE FESTIVAL

What is the desire for celebration? Desire for celebration is man's longing for eurhythmic beauty, to unite with others in beauty, to be released, strengthened, exalted and ennobled by beauty. Like the will to work, the desire for celebration has its inherent law, its rhythmic basic idea.[29]

RHYTHMIC CULTURE, BEAUTY, FESTIVE CULTURE

From the very depths of his being, the individual feels the desire for harmony and beauty for himself as well as for his environment. Man dreams and longs for the objects and forms in his environment to be equally harmonically and eurhythmically shaped as his own ego, his fellow men and his being together and working together with them.

People must be educated in celebration. They must learn to see beauty, to understand and enjoy. Then the longing for rhythm shall become so powerful in man that he can no longer live without this basic element of dance. Then the human world shall automatically shape itself out of its festive wish into an artistic cultural formation.[30]

RITUAL

Rituals are symbolic actions. Their educational value and purpose are to encourage and practise the inner outlook and the outward ability to express oneself in the sense of plastic experience. The framework of the ritual is the celebration. Preparations for ritual celebrations were in the past physical, emotional and mental exercises.[31]

DANCE AS A WAY OF EXPERIENCING AND SHARING THE WORLD

Dance does not only have artistic and scientific value. There are important educational forces hidden in dance since it leads to a plastic experience of the world of visual appearances. One can hope that the understanding of the world experienced through dance will spread out into the widest circles. In this way, the general approach to life can only be enhanced. The role of rhythm in all kinds of work and organisation is known. Many emphasise the necessity of a newly blossoming culture of celebration, which provides the human being with relaxation, distraction and instruction. The dancer hopes for its emergence out of the art of the round dance, which itself is a synthesis of all human impression and expression. Its strongest and purest expression is the dance of the human body, which is purified of all intellectual, mystic and intellectual prejudices.[32]

UNIFORMITY OF DANCE KNOWLEDGE

Form and animation are partial aspects of gestural power. The sum of the gestures, the round dance, is the unit which embraces everything. We become conscious of the round dance, recognisable in the changes of gestural power in the animated form, in experience, life. From the spatially immeasurable infinity of the solar systems to the equally immeasurable swinging play of the most minute spatial particles, the same order, the round dance, prevails. The gestural change is the mirror which allows us to identify the law of the round dance.

In the chain of gestural changes, one gesture is followed by another. A release from the rigid, motionless state, which our language often one-sidedly calls at times form, at times excitement, it is always the same continually swinging gesture, this apparent partial dance of the round dance, which itself releases and revives as it transforms into a new gesture.[33]

DANCE CELEBRATION CULTURE
[TÄNZERISCHE FESTKULTUR]

The dancer sees the celebration as a sea of petals, having emerged from a wish for beauty. In the variety of flowers he distinguishes groups, forms, colours, and points of calmness of their movement. He recognises their relations, their harmonies and sees most of all how their derivations relate to man's original forces. He sees the different tensions and movements of body, spirit and intellect. Works of art can be matters of a celebration or can exist next to a celebration. The celebration itself is the height of cultic dance schooling, education of manners, conscience and freedom through dance. The means of celebration is the diverse expression of gesture in dance, without any theatricality, decoration and disguise. For a dancer, the pleasure of art and the joy of celebration are two very different things. Only a lively and very expressive person can exist in the medium of celebration without any mask, without disguise and transformation. Only the glory of their own rhythm adorns the person. He does not participate in the celebration in order to show himself as the professional artist, but in order to elevate himself as well as his fellows who swing with him.[34]

EVERYDAY LIFE AND FESTIVAL

We live an existence full of struggle and work, which reaches into our recreations, high points and distractions. But at the same time, however, there exists a constant profound exaltation as soon as we recognise within the depths of our souls their steady blossoming, growth and awareness as an inner celebration, which permeates everything we do.

Starting from this point, the dancer, the artist, the intellectual worker, or whatever we like to call him, should create his pleasing, elevating and instructive works. He should remember that the illusion of complete harmony and beauty separated from life makes his work as feeble and unpleasant as the common intent to serve only the requirements of necessity as in functional art, cult and similar things. The knowledge of the relationship between celebration and work should cause each person, but particularly all organisers of public celebrations, festivals and amusements as well as all national and youth educators, to occupy themselves fully with the nature of festive elevation. It is a sad sight to see how the festive urge of man seeks nourishment in the gutters of superstition and tasteless artistic offerings.[35]

FESTIVE THOUGHT

The thought that the whole of life is a celebration has an extraordinary attraction to the dancer who wants to fathom the meaning of existence. Perhaps this was the general conception in earlier cultural epochs when man limited himself in his work to the production of the most necessary functional objects, held in beautiful forms, and for the rest lived a festive and cheerful life. Present-day man, however, believes that he can discover nothing festive in everyday life, in his celebrations, distractions and recuperations. He thinks: work is done only under the pressure of economic necessity and its essential meaning and purpose is to earn money. He fills his free time with activities, studies and pleasures which are intended to help him to forget the unbearable thought of the aimlessness of his efforts.[36]

Space [*Raum*], crystal, gesture [*Gebärde*], tension [*Spannung*], compression [*Ballung*]

A major part of Laban's writing is concerned with a very detailed observation of the human body and its relation to space. In this the first of his publications, Laban had already identified specific key notions that anchor his emphasis in the spatial-dimensional, with a focus on the dynamics of movement – an investigation which he would keep developing for many years to come. His observations of the body and its relationship with its immediate surroundings and the universe at large seem at first to have a scientific basis. However, Laban himself refers to what he calls 'artistic wisdom', stating that '[t]he artist relays to us intuitively and without scientific basis the laws of harmony that govern our cosmos. He is even capable of communicating these laws to us more intensely than it can happen through science.'[37]

It is again the actual experience of the practice of dancing itself that Laban is mainly interested in, at times at the expense of scientific accuracy. Nevertheless, Laban was greatly concerned with the significance of numbers, conceiving of numerical concepts as symbols: 'A number is not only a measure, it is pregnant with concepts. From this results a symbolism of numbers, proportions and forms.'[38]

One should not forget here that Laban initially trained and was active as an artist. The drawing of a human body necessarily entails a preoccupation with spatial direction and dimensions, and the question of what positions are naturally 'possible' for a human body is readily at stake in the practice of drawing. The expertise Laban will have gained in painting and drawing before being directly concerned with 'dance' and movement possibly led him to view what he experienced in spatial-dynamic terms.

Laban dealt specifically with the concepts of space [*Raum*], crystal structure, gesture [*Gebärde*], tension [*Spannung*] and compression [*Ballung*], all of which are interlinked in multiple ways. Further important notions for Laban in this context are 'rhythm' and 'harmony', as in the harmony of space as well as of movement, as well as the idea of 'swinging' [*Schwung*], which suggests a pendulum movement and a state of 'animation'. Generally Laban is concerned with 'plasticity' – a feeling for form, in terms of the experience of the dancer herself. Below are excerpts that draw together these concepts in a range of variations.

INTRODUCTION

The idea of tension must . . . be illustrated; the dancer does not imagine it in the form of a rope, a cord or the points of a star (although these are quite pretty symbols), but a harmonic awareness, feeling, touching, experiencing through the self of all the infinite changing forms and possibilities of change of the world. From this universal event springs something that is perceptible, a form of existence, which in this work I call compression [Ballung]. This compression begins, continues, fades away and creates through this play of tension the sensation of time–space–force or the like.[39]

PHYSIOLOGICAL AND PSYCHOLOGICAL EFFECTS OF THE NATURAL LAWS OF BODILY FUNCTIONS

The human body follows certain spatial laws in movement. Each movement consists of several directional tensions which mutually balance each other. The spatial inclinations of these directions more or less merge into each other and are related. When spatially related directional tensions swing together in the body, then a harmonic movement feeling occurs, a balanced movement of feeling and movement image. But if disharmonic directional tensions swing together simultaneously, then the movement is grotesque, distorted, awkward.

An emotional-intellectual event coincides with a physical event. Movement form and spatial image are not only symbol and image of inner event, but are identical to it.[40]

THE DIRECTIONS OF SPATIAL TENSIONS

For each movement there occur countless individual tensions in the body, which are conditioned by anatomical structure. . . .

It is not the individual directions that give tension to the body. Every primary direction has secondary directions which help to maintain balance, to let preceding movements phase out and to prepare for the next movement. If we capture one of these moments, then as in an image a motionless position emerges, in which a spatial tension becomes visible that clearly strives into several directions simultaneously.

Let us take a person who leans forward while walking, with the right arm pointing longingly at a distant spot, and freeze him in mid-stride. The right leg supports the centre of gravity, its direction is a downward vertical. Three further primary directions are noticeable, namely the aiming of the right arm and the directions of the left arm and the left leg which maintain the balance.

The connection of the end points of these four directions, the point of contact of the supporting foot with the ground, the fingertips of the outstretched hand and the fingertips and the toes of the left hand and foot, provide the edges of a tetrahedral shape, which is standing on one corner. The actual directional forces pass from the centre of the body, the body's centre of gravity, to the corner points of this tetrahedron.

The body is thus tensioned according to four directions which emanate from the centre of gravity. The transition into a different position of tension via countless intermediary positions is a movement.[41]

FUNDAMENTAL MEANINGS OF INCLINATION

The body raised forward and upward is a symbol of man's independent directional striving. The senses are collected to the front in the face. Grasping arms, striding legs and torso move forward more easily than backward. A firm stance, which shows courage and defiance, is only fully upright through pride, while arrogance already produces a backward inclination directed upward. Stepping forward is a demand, an attack, sympathy. Stepping backward is revulsion, fear. Bending, crouching are humility, subjection, sorrow. Stretching is pleasure. Greedy lust is crooked, free cheerfulness is elevated. Turning to or away from something is strengthening or weakening sympathy or antipathy. Strong emotional excitements pull a whole side of the body backward or forward. In a strong demand the right foot and right hand move forward simultaneously. The head, too, follows this striving forward, if the inclination is called love or anger.[42]

TOTAL TENSIONS

With the dance gesture a change in the balance of the whole body takes place and thus a change in tension of numerous, perhaps even all, muscles of the body. The slightest change in the position of the arm involves the whole body, even if this is hardly noticeable.

(We are talking about harmonic tensions and their consequence, harmonic movements. The nature of disharmonic movement means that slackness or rigidity of individual limbs becomes necessary through the manner of directional application. Think of a clown strutting with his arms hanging loosely like a stiffly strutting dandy. In contrast to this, as an example of harmonic movement, a cat, whose whole body is in constant, flowing motion.)[43]

BODY SENSE AND TENSION SENSE

The dancer does not only see pictures in his mind and compare them, but also strives to experience their tension values in copying the positions and movements being portrayed. To his surprise, after lengthy practice, a feeling and understanding of movement grows in his body, according to which all these positions are ordered systematically. He senses body tensions which are constantly repeated. He calls a number of these body tensions 'basic tensions', because all others are merely variations of them. He realises that in combat and work, where there is the greatest need to conserve energy and where the best possible achievements, even health and life, are dependent on absolute certainty of movement, these same basic tensions always recur. From this, he gains the insight that in these tensions, which come from different individual directions, a kind of harmony of movement is fixed by nature.[44]

THE NATURE OF DANCE KNOWLEDGE

Dance knowledge is newly created and born again and again from the individual conscience freely developed through the exercise of gestural power. Everywhere the dancer sees the rhythmic sequences and counter-movements of the regularly, symmetrically, proportionally or eurhythmically arranged processes of tension.[45]

DISHARMONIC MIXTURES OF GESTURAL COMPONENTS

There are two forms of sensations and communicative swingings which seem exaggerated or mannered to us and they are: first, the 'saturated' expression in which the parts of gestural chord linked to the will, the emotions and thoughts occur as equally strong, as is, for example, the case in the dramatically overburdened solemnity. Second, the almost complete separation of a single factor of expression, whereupon the bodily form, the emotional form or the thought form becomes so predominant that the other two almost disappear. The third possibility is harmonic balance. Here the three basic components of the gesture maintain their balance within a chord of expression by emphasising the main form and setting the other two less emphasised forms against each other. In life, just as much as in art, both disharmonious possibilities of saturation and lopsidedness are justified: however, they will always demand a painful solution and for this reason they should not be applied blindly.[46]

HARMONIC LAWS OF FORM

A further remarkable discovery is that formation, growth and movement of all natural things, from the crystal to the plant to the animal, are subject to the same spatial laws of tension, which man uses in his harmonic body movement. The dancer's way of observing form has been confirmed by modern crystallography. It explains that the construction of crystalline forms occurs according to the same basic rules as the construction of artistic harmonies in dance, music, speech, poetry and thought.[47]

THE CRYSTAL LIVES

The process of crystallisation is excitement and movement. These two parts of the phenomenon can be proved here as elsewhere. . . .

'Understanding' means basically to follow excitement, a force by means of movement, growth, etc. There are alien impulses which seek to be followed, like the gesture of throwing a stone, and there are innate impulses like the strivings into certain directions within the crystal, or the impact of human fantasy in the manifold directions of thought, drives and feelings. But 'understanding' remains always a process which we have been used to calling 'intellectual'. If we stick to this term, the wonderful construction of the crystal is also an intellectual process. The driving force everywhere is the power of gesture. The plastic sense of the dancer can never refuse to accept the impression that all things speak to him by means of the gesture.[48]

Rhythm and work

Laban's specific focus on the human body in terms of its capabilities created a concept in which the individual being is central. As stated earlier, his conception of dance as a practice for all people meant a shift away from the dancer as a conservatoire-trained and technically skilled practitioner, and instead he sought to foster an engagement of an individual's body, mind and spirit in the act of dancing.

'Dance' for Laban is largely a metaphor for an activation of those aspects that for him make up a human being. 'Dance', in his view, can and should occur anywhere, everywhere, and it is the experience of dancing itself rather than a performance of dance to a viewer that is key for Laban. His concern with 'dance' in this sense extended even into the work sphere, where workers, according to his point of view, should strive to perform tasks and actions that were in themselves meaningful and furthering of their physical, spiritual and intellectual being.

His later work on Effort finds its beginnings in *The World of the Dancer*, where Laban already included sections on rhythm in work, the use of tools as well as an overall philosophy of the role of work in everyday life. At the heart of this thinking is a quasi-socialist position which constantly negotiates between individual and communal experience, to the level of society at large. A small selection of indicative excerpts is provided below.

DANCE-LIKE WORK

The mastering of every job of work demands a rhythmic order and a rhythmic interweaving of actions. The worker must be deeply connected with his work. He must be familiar with the sources from which the idea came for the work to be achieved. He also wants to know the aim towards which the result of the work, the finished work, is directed. In work, a physical-spiritual-mental exchange of forces must take place between the creator and his creation. Then work shall not torture, kill, exhaust, but invigorate and exalt.

Every factory should maintain a dance-like rhythmic approach in terms of its overall organisation of the work forces, time, right down to the simplest operations.[49]

THE MANUFACTURED ARTICLE

When the dancer looks at an object – be it an instrument, a container or a roof – then the image of movements and thoughts, even the feelings of the people who created the article, becomes immediately alive.

Some objects – for example, those of today – lack any expression of movement. Compare a typical stiff chair of today with a Rococo chair. Here excessive stiffness, there excessive movement.

The leg of the Rococo chair curves itself, as if to accommodate the mobile calf of the person sitting on it in all those poses which are connected with his mental leaps and emotional turns. It seems as if the chair leg wanted to disappear completely and carry the seat merely like a curved bracket.

(The seat supported in the form of a bracket has been known for a very long time.)

Dance power is charmed into the object. One sees it as part of the person; it is not only in itself organic but also in relation to its surroundings. The chair back narrows and produces a contour which looks like the harmonic movement swingings of the human body. It makes space for the elbow which wants to circle freely. If the arm of the seated person runs along the back of the chair down to the ground in order to pick something up quickly, it follows with naturally harmonic arm action the outline of the tool. The chair is mimo-plastic, it mimes the mobile plasticity of the human body.[50]

ECONOMIC DISADVANTAGES OF PHYSICAL NEGLECT

In the final understanding and consideration of the decline of human capability, the determining factor was that it brought about an incapacity for work and thus economic disadvantages. The care of the sick cost money, the age of those unemployable through disability sank lower and lower, workers of every kind were becoming less efficient and willing to work. The whole of the overstretched enterprise could then only be held up with great efforts and sacrifices.[51]

ATTEMPTS AT REGENERATION

Here are some attempts to awaken our body sense: lessons in gymnastics were increased in schools, factory exercises were introduced and children were sent to courses in rhythmic physical training. Finally our youth pulled itself together and took up hiking, sport and games. There was an interest in the body, form, beauty. The eye was trained; pictures, dance shows, slides, films were viewed. One got to know again the power and depth of the gesture and soon was part of a movement striving towards health, which was supported and advanced by artists and craftsmen of all kind.[52]

Articles manufactured through unpleasant work have a slavish, deadly feel. One sees in each piece the number of hours which were needed to produce it. Next to the price tag hangs an invisible list of the hours of torment during which a person was rhythmically dead. Any cultured person should turn away from these products in disgust. . . . Happy workers are dancers, masters and not slaves of work.[53]

NEW EVERYDAY FORMS

Industry will no longer disappear from our lives. Its refinement shall bring about cultural human work in its factories and deepen the value of their products. In everyday work and the related organisation of life, as in celebration [*Fest*], in recreation, in art, it is a matter of forming the necessary innovations simply and naturally in the sense of a dancerly view of life. Everyday work must not control but serve life. Work on the cultivation of the ego and the community is the most essential thing in human life.[54]

THE HEALTHINESS OF BODILY SENSE

There are everlasting rights in economic life and in art, in everyday life and in celebration [*Fest*]. These rights always succeed when the whole organism is endangered by their suppression. One of these unchangeable rights is: the right of bodily sense, the right of dance mobility and plastic sensing. For decades we have seen in our cultural circle a movement which is pressing towards physical health and physical improvement through sports, gymnastics and dance.

This pressure is one of those protective measures which, like fever in a sick body, causes revolution and rebellion in order that something new and refreshing can arise from sick life.[55]

BASIC IDEALS

Cult and the practice of free human community do not have as their aim to create laws but instead to awaken conscience and insight. Policies and actions of professional associations and the economic–social relations with each other will be solved of their own accord as soon as the individual has been ethically schooled. Communal education through exercise, cultic play and festive togetherness guarantees this unified basic ideal. This ideal is designed by nature as eurhythmic behaviour of the parts towards each other and to the whole. The importance of the cultivation of conscience through combat and games, as well as through the economic–social insight and festive togetherness makes it necessary to direct all these strivings as festive cultural tasks to a professional group. It is hard to give a name to this professional group without being misunderstood. As pioneers they are warriors, as educators they are teachers, and as artists they are free dancers or gymnasts. They oversee and lead this great dance, so to speak, strategically, pedagogically and artistically.[56]

Notes

1 Preston-Dunlop (1998: 66).
2 WD, pp. 14–15.
3 Ibid., p. 42.
4 Ibid., p. 12.
5 In *The Creative Mind: An Introduction to Metaphysics*, Bergson identifies the problem of conventional acts of reasoning in the theorisation of creative processes, stressing that retrospective reasoning merely provides an account informed by aspects that, at the time of their creation, were not yet known and identified. See Bibliography for details.
6 For a discussion of the relationship between writing and performance practice, and specifically the notions of 'intuition' and 'judgement' in performance-making, see various texts by Susan Melrose; for instance, 'The curiosity of writing (or, who cares about performance mastery?)', published on her website URL http://www.sfmelrose.org.uk/curiosityofwriting/, 2003 (accessed 2010).
7 WD, p. 16.
8 Ibid., p. 9.
9 Ibid., p. 9.
10 Ibid., p. 9.
11 Ibid., p. 9.
12 Ibid., p. 10.
13 Ibid., p. 10.
14 Ibid., p. 20.
15 Ibid., pp. 14–15.
16 Ibid., p. 128.

17 Ibid., p. 48.
18 Ibid., p. 44.
19 Ibid., p. 176.
20 Ibid., p. 27.
21 Ibid., pp. 127–128.
22 Ibid., p. 61.
23 Ibid., p. 105.
24 Ibid., p. 157.
25 Ibid., p. 184.
26 Gleisner (1928: 133–136).
27 Preston-Dunlop (1998: 72).
28 *WD*, p. 14.
29 Ibid., p. 132.
30 Ibid., p. 132.
31 Ibid., p. 58.
32 Ibid., pp. 65–66.
33 Ibid., p. 42.
34 Ibid., p. 148.
35 Ibid., p. 119.
36 Ibid., p. 118.
37 Ibid., p. 244.
38 Ibid., p. 207.
39 Ibid., pp. 12–13.
40 Ibid., pp. 143–144.
41 Ibid., pp. 24–25.
42 Ibid., p. 80.
43 Ibid., p. 33.
44 Ibid., p. 30.
45 Ibid., p. 119.
46 Ibid., p. 53.
47 Ibid., p. 32.
48 Ibid., pp. 63–64.
49 Ibid., p. 129.
50 Ibid., p. 149.
51 Ibid., p. 141.
52 Ibid., p. 142.
53 Ibid., p. 130.
54 Ibid., pp. 153–154.
55 Ibid., p. 140.
56 Ibid., p. 123.

Chapter three

Gymnastics and Dance for Children (1926)

Translated by Stefanie Sachsenmaier and Dick McCaw

Introduction

Dick McCaw

Gymnastics and Dance for Children (GDC) begins with an almost elegiac look back to childhood, a time when we could take pleasure from life. Laban is not simply mourning the loss of childhood but of a way of looking at life which he argues is healthier than that of adults. He echoes William Blake's *Songs of Innocence and Experience*, when he compares a child's cheerful impression of 'the humming of bees' with the adult's more prosaic preoccupation with the 'inconvenience of insects'. Why is it that adults have to see the sorrowful and negative in everything around them? Why do they have to sully that 'inexhaustible spring which can always astonish and delight us anew'? For Laban, the child possesses something that the adult has lost – he calls it different things: 'Life' with a capital 'L', a connection with our true nature, the source of our happiness, the source of a 'properly functioning body', and he advises that we 'guard this source jealously'.

In much of its content, tone and certainly in its rhapsodic structure, *Gymnastics and Dance for Children* looks back to

The World of the Dancer. The preoccupation is much broader than the title would suggest – it does not propose a curriculum for teaching Gymnastics and Dance to children. As we have already seen, the author has a very specific notion of the child: Laban (again like Blake) starts from the assumption that children have an intuitive sense of right and of ethical behaviour which adults then destroy with an education system that privileges the development of the intellect over bodily movement. Society's problems, Laban will argue, result from restraint and repression of a child's desire and capacity to move – and this starts with insensitive and coercive education. The teacher should follow rather than lead the child.

Education of younger children should be through the exercise of natural movement in order to encourage the harmonious development of body, mind and spirit, rather than through the abstract concepts of language. And 'free' gymnastics is the means to deliver this education of the whole person. In *Gymnastics and Dance*, Laban wrote about 'free' gymnastics and here the word assumes much greater resonance – it is the opposite of educational 'drilling' and 'constraint' which limit and stunt the child. The child that is allowed to continue to express itself through movement rather than language is one that will retain his or her ethical purity, and sense of goodness towards others.

In *The World of the Dancer*, the dancer was a Nietzschean philosopher; here the dancer/movement teacher is responsible for the child's entire education: moral, spiritual and intellectual. Rather than being someone who drills and bullies, the teacher is a gardener who helps children grow, according to their individual potentiality. Laban operated on the assumption that humans are born inherently good and that the correct educational system – i.e. one that is focused on movement – will foster that goodness. This is achieved by adapting the education to the child with the teacher-gymnast being able to 'play with children as if one were a child oneself'. Many of his sentiments may seem hopelessly idealistic or naïve to many readers. But it is clear from descriptions of Laban playing with children how the rapport he was obviously able to establish with young children was based on a delight in their imagination and a respect for their feelings. He got results through empathetic engagement with children, by being a child himself.

Late in this book, he notes that Western philosophy 'knows compassion towards misery or a feeling sharing guilt, but knows nothing about communal happiness'. Laban sought to promote communal happiness through the education of movement and through the continuing practice of movement with the aim of creating a more harmonious and happy society. A worthy aim, surely.

This book does not only deal with movement education but also touches on his developing ideas of space harmony and dance notation, and these I shall include in my selection of passages from *Choreography* to indicate the development of his thinking. Here, I have chosen to begin with some simple definitions of Gymnastics, Dance and the Child before citing the first eight pages of the book. After that I shall pursue the themes of ethics and pedagogy.

INTRODUCTION

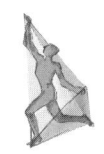

Who has not experienced, in their earlier years as a child, the deep impression made by the humming of a bee, the play of light in the branches, the neighing of a horse or the gambol of a kitten? Also the spinning of sunbeams, the moving cornfield in the wind and the broad, blue sky, which always left everything appearing very grey after staring at it for a long time – it all held us enthralled. How curious we became about everything! We always experienced new impressions; but we did not yet grasp the meaning of everything that was going on around us. However, the impressions remained. Partly they continued to follow us in our later life, partly the impressions received in childhood asserted themselves in certain situations for years and decades, when you again faced the aforementioned events. Indeed, for us grown-ups, these small experiences merely constitute memories. For we look at these things with very different eyes. They are indeed the same eyes; but with the addition of knowledge and experience. Thoughts about the purpose or use of objects or their uselessness and futility play a role. Apart from childhood recollections, other memories play a part. We think of walks in waving cornfields, of conversations which stirred the soul, which agitated our inmost being, and the sky above us often weighed on us with heavy clouds, threatening our existence. As children we perceived the humming of the bee as a special impression, without it triggering any other thought in us. Only later on as grown-ups did we connect it with the idea of the inconvenience of insects. Many other shifts have changed the childish happy amazement into a recognition of suffering, which permeates the world.

We ask ourselves – is the sorrow in the world really so predominant as it seems to the grown-up? Is there not in us an indestructible, strong spring, which can always astonish and delight us anew? The main cause for turning away from the serene world view that we have in childhood is an inner melancholy, and this inner melancholy is to a large extent the result of our inharmonious physicality. One would not disagree that necessity alone, the incomplete satisfaction of our life necessities, are the cause of this sorrow. . . . Happiness does not lie in external circumstances, happiness lies in us. Happiness lies in the strength which we can gain and foster in ourselves. It is certainly not easy to evoke this happiness in oneself, when leading a life of worries, without air and light. It is not easy for the very reason that this life of worries, without air and light, weakens and stifles the source; the source of health, the source of a properly functioning body. There is only one way out: to accustom man from earliest youth to guard this source jealously, and to nurture and preserve it with greatest care.

It is not the purpose of this work to criticise our entire way of bringing up children. But in observing what nature demands in a human being, through observation of a growing child and its spiritual needs, we can at least form a picture of how this 'body–soul' [*Körperseele*] can be kept both alert and healthy, for as long as possible, perhaps throughout its life. It is without doubt the case that children today witness the distresses and worries of grown-ups too early. All efforts for reform in this respect have been without effect, and indeed, it is not an easy undertaking as long as social circumstances form an obstacle. Educators believe that a child should learn that life is a difficult matter. Life, to a child, is without doubt already just as difficult as it is for us grown-ups, but the child experiences it in quite a different way. We should, therefore, not make it more difficult. It is only too easy to confound the requirements of education, to change the nature of a child into an unhealthy culture, and to lay the foundations for later practical life, with the result that a false, insecure and unhealthy conception of civilisation is fostered in the child. . . .

It is a paradox to say that in order to bring up children well it would be best to arrange a thorough gymnastic discipline for grown-ups, but it is true. It is obvious that a man who has purged and liberated himself of all the dross of his sufferings and has become stronger through calm, rhythmic development of his body, is much closer to the child, and would hence be able to handle the care of a child in a sensible way. In a nutshell, if we say that the rhythmic, free-moving, well-trained adult organism resembles more closely that of primitive man, that of the child; and if we then try to strive for this grown-up to see the child not as an apprentice, but as a teacher, from whom he can copy nature's intention, and who will help him lovingly to fulfil this – *then* we have a picture of a rational education.

Now unfortunately it is not the case today that all men come into the world as children; very many of them come into the world as old men. They have inherited the clouded blood and sick nerves of their forefathers, they are little old men, sad, reflective and unfree. With such children, the fresh, primitive sense of life has to be awakened at first. This is an enormously great art. It can of course only happen by observing healthy children and aiming to bring the development of sick children along similar tracks, as seen with healthy children. The educator – be it mother, father, teacher or any other grown-up – who deals with children in any form, is a gardener. He has before him a plant given by Nature, which he cannot force into blossoming in a way that is out of the ordinary. He will never be able to turn a buttercup into an orchid; but he can give the buttercup its place in life, just as much as the orchid, where it can grow and bloom properly, and where the heart rejoices in its presence. So it is with all human children. Let us say that the educator of human beings can ennoble the human 'plant', in the same way as a gardener can ennoble a fruit tree. . . . The educator is a gardener, not only in his selection of the means by which he fertilises and cares for his plants, but also in the patience with which he allows his plants to grow without demanding any distortion of form, which would run counter to the natural growth pattern of the plant itself.

How then should one learn from a child? Above all, those of us who have seen many children grow up, see that the life of a child passes through quite curious phases. We know that, ideally, up to school age the child should be relatively untouched by life; it should simply receive impressions. . . . The child constantly receives new impressions, it tries to orientate itself in its environment. But naturally the child does not have the least intention of orientating itself in the manner of an explorer; it does not search for objects by which it orientates itself – they are simply there, and catch its eye. The most wonderful harmony of the world becomes visible when one observes how children of different natures react to different things, when they are not influenced in any way, and how they extract from these things that original similarity and association of ideas which make us grown-ups laugh so much. . . . One can of course try to familiarise oneself with this world of childhood. But this has to be done with the heart and not with the intellect. One has to play with children as if one were a child oneself. And why should one not be one? It can only have a good effect on the life of our soul and on our spiritual health if we become children among children once in a while. . . .

In the second life period of a child's life, its schooldays, the actual inner spiritual life is completely independent from what is taking place in school in terms of formal instruction. The teaching at school seeks to bring order into the experiences that the child has accumulated throughout its earlier years. The child is taught slowly and gradually that in no way does the sun intend to hide behind the roof-top in order to play with the child, but that it is a heavenly body like the moon and the stars. It is told that these various heavenly bodies shine down on earth, which again is made up of land and water, the latter in the form of seas, lakes and rivers.[1]

The child

There are several kinds of reference to children in Laban's book: to actual children he has observed and played with, the three ages of children he deals with – he categorised them as pre-school, school-age and adolescent – to the 'child' as an idealised figure, and finally to Youth with a capital 'Y', as a rather different, more political idea of the spirit of change in Germany. In many respects, the Child is Laban himself, ever fascinated by the three realms of Nature and imagining himself 'in the character or being of an animal, a plant, or even an inanimate object'.[2] At the heart of Laban's notion of ethics and education is the idea that the child is the human in its purest state, a similar state to 'the noble savage' who has not been polluted by Western society and its life-denying values and practices. Two passages below also indicate how Laban believed that this natural instinct for ethics is best awakened through movement rather than intellectual endeavour, and because free gymnastics helps develop a child's sense of movement, so it also helps them become more moral beings. The matter is self-evident in Laban's mind: 'It is impossible to arouse the minds of people today to deeper ideals which will maintain the flowing out into Life, in any other way than by Gymnastics.'[3]

THE CHILD

Observing a child with its intuitive kindness, its impulsive cordiality and many other fine qualities, reveals acutely that we cannot speak of a rational origin for these things. We can conclude rather, that a hiding and suppression of the body, of physicality and movement, is also a suppression of the origins and sources of essential virtues. Those drives, however, from which vices are thought to arise, are actually unhealthy and repressed drives. The dark demonic forces which govern mankind find a natural outlet in the lighter, clearer forces, when the life of movement [*Bewegungsleben*] flows according to its own logic. The adolescent has more logic in his body than many a grown-up has in his mind. The collision of the natural and healthy forces with the ordering of the outside world, with the customs and moral notions which are part and parcel of our civilisation, is another matter. True morality does not lie in these customs, but in the foundation of mankind, and there are all too often false, abstract conceptions of morality, which distort and spoil the life forces within young people.[4]

It seems a wretched thing to me that ethics has to be preached as a law, and hence as prohibition or commandment. Would it not be better to refrain from these abstractions and to keep young people healthy in such a manner that they find their bearings in the world of drives and forces which exhibits just as much variety and richness as the world of feelings and thoughts, if we were to help them to understand and to organise this world of drives and to guide them to that maximum capacity which is present in the minds of young people?[5]

The child knows what an ethical action is, not only from the praise of adults, but also its own soul has an urge to apply the forces and the drives working inside it, in a way that is somehow proper or right. The concept of what is proper and right is a concept of direction, as the word itself indicates. It is a concept of striving. It is a concept of movement. It is the concept of a properly directed movement, of a rhythmic movement in the sense of some kind of higher law, and not just a utilitarian approach to the environment. Out of this urge for movement a child experiences a metaphysical inclination, and seeks to fulfil itself in this metaphysical inclination, to find its bearings, also through feeling, as it does in the environment. But a child goes even further. Both in its judgement as well as in its actions, it tries not only to connect with the environment and everyday life, but it also makes ties between the environment and everyday life. It judges the actions of the environment according to that purposeful sense, of which the child has become conscious as a way of judging ethics, and it even tries to act upon its environment accordingly, hence to stimulate such actions which in its view properly accord with the rhythm of everyday life. How better can these aspirations be explained than by the child gymnastically feeling their inner order progressively more clearly and thus slowly becoming conscious of true values? The complete harmonisation of these feelings and aspirations certainly cannot be attained by the kind of gymnastics we have today.[6]

GYMNASTICS, DANCE, SPORT AND EVERYDAY MOVEMENT

One always has to bear in mind the basic concept of gymnastics. Gymnastics is neither game nor art, it is a controlled functioning of the body, whose objective is to awaken and stimulate dwindling vitality, to preserve and nurture existing life energies [*Lebensenergien*].[7]

The passion for movement, which we all have, cannot be explained alone by speedy motorised transport on the ground, in the sea and in the air. There is something else present, which is a drive for regeneration, and machines should finally only serve the purpose of relieving man of wearisome labour, so that he can come closer to his inner mental and spiritual becoming through a liberated physicality. This coming-closer is quite definitely not being sought solely in the intellectual fostering of the mind or emotions that can be expressed in words. This coming-closer is based on our understanding that only with a body whose soul and spirit are in harmony can we provide that measure and conscience towards which we inwardly aspire as the ultimate aim of the cultured whole man. The practice of our children is the path towards this ideal.

One thing cannot be repeated too often; that is the fact that the new means of gymnastics which we are rediscovering today in the child's being neither speaks only to the body nor exclusively to the mind and spirit. It is movement, for our times a newly conquered means and freshly discovered field. Only knowledge of movement, the grasping of the nature and meaning of movement rhythm and movement harmony, only the feeling and experience of this very curious means of expression and centre of life can guide us so that we truly attain the objective of gymnastics.[8]

There is, above all, a fundamental conviction that life does not exist just to be endured. Furthermore, culture and civilisation do not have the purpose of binding and breaking everything that is original, but of creating a free life, which in itself contains the urge to balance inner and outer life beautifully and harmoniously. In order to introduce young people to gymnastic experiences one should not work simply with theoretical concepts and a cold utilitarian approach, no more than one could allow oneself to do this in earliest childhood. One has to smooth the way for the instinctive strivings of these children and to show them the joys and sorrows of human destiny in the constraints and possibilities of body movement.[9]

[L]et the child try out everything, so to speak, so that it can measure its abilities against its dreams and desires. I consider this a very important task of gymnastics and think that all exercises of an adolescent movement choir are centred around these objectives. In turn, however, one should not present children with anything preconceived. The richness of their unspoilt nature allows the release from their own inner life and they can often hardly manage the abundance of ideas and possibilities that flow towards them. The growing child becomes aware that the realisation and application of benefits of a gymnastic education are an urgent requirement for the health of the population and of culture as a whole. They see and feel in their own bodies, in their school-fellows and, above all, in the no longer critically observed adults – whom they watch much more acutely than one would think – what damage has been done, and how much this damage is rooted in a physical-spiritual-mental stagnation.[10]

The individual can recover, can centre and educate himself mentally when alone; but true celebration [*Fest*] requires the element of conviviality. In the celebration of free gymnastics, vocalisation and thought are from time to time implicated in group and combat games; both are physical processes and are conceived as movement expression just as much as gymnastically-trainable expressions of the mind and the spirit. Free gymnastic exercises do not teach specific laws of movement but they awaken the plastic, harmonious sense of physical conscience. . . . All expression originates from physical movement, all impressions are of physical, and therefore of moving nature.[11]

Education

Late in the book, Laban reflects on how he has taught children: 'I cannot recall ever having given any kind of stimulus. . . . At the most I told the children a little story and we began to play. All the rest came from the children themselves.'[12] Once again, we see him stressing his child-centred, child-led approach to education and it is one where there is no 'persuasion, no cramming, no pressure, no drilling!' Drilling, forcing knowledge into the child, is the antithesis of his approach which follows and feeds the child's interests and capabilities, and which insists upon respecting the child's freedom to learn in his or her own way; that is, through play, games and the exercise of their imagination:

> Of course our mechanically-oriented culture has robbed man so much of his freedom that he cannot imagine any more a life without drilling, prohibitions and regimentation. ...A prematurely regimented body–soul [*Körperseele*] becomes inefficient with regard to its own decisions, and drilling and training, that is, mastery, are only valuable if they can be summoned up and applied by an autonomous will power.[13]

In the language of today's cognitive science, the teacher's responsibility is to create a 'stimulus-rich environment':[14]

> [B]ut the child must be guided into higher levels; it must be guided to unsullied authority. To be guided there is the aim of the child. It seeks and finds this way by itself. One only needs to provide it with the necessary surroundings and the opportunity for play and to ensure that the play does not get bogged down in the sand.[15]

In the following passages we can see how the child is taken as an autonomous, 'free' learner, and simply needs help in this self-driven task.

EDUCATION

The initiation of the complete young personality can only be achieved if this personality is free, and this freedom, again, is present only if the sense of movement is developed in a manner appropriate to the respective age.[16]

One has to break the habit of considering instruction, memory and imagination as properties exclusive to intellectual concept formation. Only then will it be possible to apply the art of movement in the service of true education and the healing and advancement of human potential.[17]

On the whole, we can be satisfied with the common concept that the child, right up to late adolescence, playfully practises a mastery of life. Hence it will also be necessary to present gymnastics to the child as a playful practice in the functions of the body and the mental and corporal attitude that goes with it.[18]

Thus, we see already in the small child the presence of an urge to give form to its inner life and its expressions through movement. We do not wish to overemphasise here the beautifully measured harmonious shaping, which is arguably more accentuated in the gymnastic intention of adults. No, to the child, spatial shaping in itself is important, corresponding to its development, which is directed by the unconscious guidance of the child's soul. And we must adapt to this unconscious guidance, we must listen to the expressions of this unconscious guidance, if we want to help the child and the adolescent – which is the only thing education can do – to ease the journey leading to the fulfilment of their inner drive, if we wish to partly clear the obstructions out of the way.[19]

Hidden in our deepest soul under much dross, we can still find the originality of the first age of life as well as of the richness of imagination and the depth of mind. Especially in the evaluation of gymnastics, of being moved, an exuberance is actually often being expressed. All those who know the present-day youth movement are aware of the ways in which young people of their own accord tried to overcome the spell of long-standing prejudices and malpractices. Youthful enthusiasm here is a much deeper human wisdom than the dusty old precepts of the elderly. . . . Not a few of the hopes for the future and insights have been found in the inner life and questing of this youth. Above all, we grown-ups, who have cared for our bodies and our human freedom from the beginning, are more flexible in our minds and have remained closer to pure human thinking as can be seen in a growing child.[20]

Notes

1. *GDC*, pp. 7–13.
2. Ibid., p. 110.
3. Ibid., p. 78.
4. Ibid., pp. 52–54.
5. Ibid., pp. 73–74.
6. Ibid., pp. 126–127.
7. Ibid., p. 22.
8. Ibid., pp. 47–48.
9. Ibid., p. 117.
10. Ibid., p. 120.
11. Ibid., pp. 130–132.
12. Ibid., p. 112.
13. Ibid., pp. 67–68.
14. For example, John H. Flavell's *Cognitive Development* (London: Prentice-Hall, 1985), pp. 185–189.
15. *GDC*, p. 80.
16. Ibid., p. 79.
17. Ibid., p. 96.
18. Ibid., p. 17.
19. Ibid., p. 72.
20. Ibid., p. 117.

Chapter four

Gymnastics and Dance (1926)

Translated by Stefanie Sachsenmaier and Dick McCaw

Introduction

Dick McCaw

Gymnastics and Dance (*GD*) is divided into five chapters: Fundamental Ideas of Gymnastics, Movement Culture and its World View, Anatomy as Basis of the Laws of Movement, Social Possibilities, The Art of Movement, and Conclusion. As in *Gymnastics and Dance for Children*, the focus is on the philosophical and spiritual dimension of gymnastics and the art of movement or rather the lack of a culture of movement in the Europe of the 1920s. Once again, Laban explains his notion of Free Gymnastics, and its relation to Free Dance, and emphasises that his ultimate aim in both gymnastics and dance is celebration: 'Freer than the art of education, the art of thinking, the art of working, an understanding of the world is the art of celebration.'[1] The ultimate end of education is *Fest*, the celebration of Life.

The excerpts below begin with passages from 'Fundamental Ideas of Gymnastics'. Whereas in *Gymnastics and Dance for Children* Laban's definitions of Gymnastics emphasise play and freedom, here he offers a more detailed definition of 'free' as opposed to 'gymnastics with equipment' (Laban uses the German word *Turnen* for this kind of gymnastics) and its relation to dance. His first definitions are of the dynamics or qualities of movement, the territory he will later cover in *Effort* (1947). As I note in the Introduction to Chapter 5, *Choreography*, Laban made no categorical distinction between Effort and Shape in his books of the 1920s.

The discussion of Gymnastics is followed by excerpts from the second chapter where Laban outlines a Philosophy of Life (or *Weltanschauung*) that is rooted in movement and this complements his reflections in *Gymnastics and Dance for Children* on ethics and movement. Again and again, Laban emphasises that his gymnastics – both for adults and children – is not about keep-fit or body-building but is a practice, by means of which someone can experience him- or herself as a balanced and harmonious whole of body and mind. He aims to teach what he calls 'harmony of movement'.[2] Later in the book, after a very sophisticated reading of Lucian's dialogue on Dance, Laban turns to Nietzsche for an example of the dancer-philosopher:

> It is a fact that a valuable dance performance can only be presented by a person who is equally well-educated in terms of body, mind, spirit [*Körper, Geist, Seele*]. What the ancients called a dancer and what in our times might live up most closely to Nietzsche's concept of the dancer in his *Zarathustra*, is a complete picture of human culture and not a clown or an acrobat, and certainly not that marzipan doll, which we were allowed to admire on the stages of our faded court theatres.[3]

Laban's books of the 1920s were written at what he considered to be a turning point in European culture – 'Today we live in a time of cultural revolution' – where movement promised to be more central in everyone's lives.

This leads on to passages where Laban describes the nature and art of movement both in terms of their spatial harmony and their dynamics – what will later be known as Choreutics and Eukinetics. (The Greek preface 'eu' means harmonious.) As noted above, this book is a more detailed account of gymnastics and dance, and although it cannot be described as a handbook, he does give examples of his approach to movement training. Thus, the final three sections consist of three practical explorations of Laban's ideas: first, Creation and Scattering (what will later be known as 'Gathering and Scattering'), then the Dimensional Scale, and finally the Movement Choir. None of these are exercises: the first two are principles of movement and spatial orientation that can only be understood through actual practice. When Laban refers to 'swinging', this is the very embodiment of a 'free' movement, in the way that it suggests ease and flow. The Movement Choir (*Bewegungschor*) is something between gymnastic practice and dance, between education and celebration – a means by which lay dancers can experience each other's company through harmonious movement. It is not about 'purely gymnastic physical education' but 'leads to those human values which to strive for bring us joy'. He continues that the choir is 'not just one of the many ways that modern artistic body culture takes, but today it is *the only possible way*'.[4]

In the section on Motion Factors (a term used in Laban's books of the 1940s and 1950s), in addition to Strength, Time and Space, he introduces a fourth term, 'Flight' which later will become Flow – here it is defined in terms of balance, whether one is Stable or Labile (i.e. off-balance and thus 'flying'), and according to the polarity of Bound or Loose (what will be later called Bound or Free Flow).

FUNDAMENTAL IDEAS OF GYMNASTICS

The number, measure, weight, form and proportion of movements can be measured. There is a whole array of numbers, forms and measurement ratios which, as ancient and unbroken traditions, have an almost religious character. If we take a closer look, then we can see that these are the cardinal numbers with which we are obliged to classify the areas of our sensory perception.[5]

Movement is concerned with spatial displacements which are carried out in a particular temporal rhythm with a very specific muscular force. All the thousands of spatial directions into which a person can 'swing' are fast or slow, strong or weak, long or short. They become measurable in relation to the initial and succeeding movement. The relation of one movement to another establishes their spatial-rhythmical value, their spatial-rhythmical distinctiveness. For instance, I could perform a movement in which I throw myself far forwards, projecting vigorously into space with a great emphasis on force and speed. Anyone will recognise that this movement is a sort of energetic thrust or blow. Likewise it is possible to perform a different movement which is in complete contrast to the one just mentioned; moving forward slowly with a weary and dull, sad movement; the movement remains very narrow but the direction is the same. In between these two poles, the numerous rhythmical possibilities swing back and forth and branch off into the thousand-fold formations which we call human gestures. Becoming acquainted with the most distinctive form of gesture will be just as useful for the practitioner as the experience of the primitive basic form, from which this individual form has emerged. A feeling for differentiation is developed. It is clear that the different shortcomings inherent in the practitioner's being, such as slowness, inertia, hastiness, weakness, brutality, etc. can be moderated, regulated and brought into awareness through continuous practice of spatial-rhythmical gestures. The physical-mental-spiritual influence is thus made apparent.

We have spoken about artistic dance and about gymnastics as a form of functional dance [*Zwecktanz*]. If we wish to mention all of the human body's forms of movement, then we must not forget everyday movements, from basic locomotion and walking to any variety of work. The same rules and forms of movement also occur and operate in work and in all daily movement, as they do in dance and gymnastics, training and practice. The specificity of gymnastics is that certain basic orders and sequences are systematically singled out, brought into awareness and cultivated from these pervasive features of movement. The bodily strength and spatial control resulting from this selection and its application can serve various purposes and aims. In short, gymnastics can be of use in work and daily life, and can further serve the art of movement, especially dance, and also games, sport and exercise; in the case of dance, of course – particularly arranged and shaped – it has the purpose of actual expression, of communication. Perhaps the appropriate term here is festive work or work on a holiday – as opposed to work on a workday.

The lawfulness of forms of movement can be subsumed in a type of grammar, which lists the forms of movement, discloses their harmonious and disharmonious possibilities of connections, i.e. their relatedness and unrelatedness, and teaches us how corresponding movement formations can be created from these similarities and differences. Artistic dance further expands this law of movement. Here we find certain measures, such as letters, words and phrases of expression; the grammar thus develops into a syntax, into a theory of harmony and also a poetics of the form of movement. In conventional gymnastics these combinations do not occur. It is also not necessary for the participant in movement choirs [*Bewegungschöre*], or the gymnast, to study this science in all its depth. He intuitively adheres to these rules. In the same way as the naturally gifted singer or the extemporising orator do not need to immerse themselves in every last detail of the technique and philosophy of their means of expression, likewise the gymnast draws from his natural sense of rhythm in movement.

A fundamental difference between artistic Gymnastics and Dance might perhaps be noted here. In general, 'free exercise' [*Freiübung*] will only produce movements that are somehow related to harmony. Strength, suppleness, openness, courage, health and joy are cultivated. These forces also find expression in artistic dance. Art can, however, speak of everything that fulfils human life, and not just of a selection made for reasons of idealistic purposes. It can also speak of suffering and displeasure, mourning and disharmony, the grotesque and confusion, to the point of insanity. Art portrays human life with its various polar opposites and contradictions. Art is not an exercise, which gives preference to any particular aspects of life. Another difference that exists between gymnastics as such and games and sport still has to be addressed here. Games and sport, like everyday life, have no grammatically-ordered basic forms of movement.[6]

We still have a considerable amount to say about gymnastics which uses equipment. (The connection between the word gymnastics/exercise [*Turnen*] and the word tournament [*Turnier*] gives us food for thought.) Are 'free' gymnastic exercises that do not use equipment, not equally beneficial or even more beneficial for our health and for the educational purposes that gymnastics pursues? Was this form of exercise not known or recognised in former times? In order to answer these questions, we must again go back to the fundamental idea of gymnastic education. The human inclination to practise gymnastics stems most of all from the drive to move in a useful and harmonious way. Exercising, by means of overcoming natural obstacles or by use of gymnastic equipment, certainly encourages functional and harmoniously balanced movement. But as soon as the equipment is abandoned, a person only too easily slips back into the instinctively bad and non-harmonious forms of movement, or imitates the strong, rigid body tension which is necessary when working with equipment, and which in due course leads to debilitating tightness that counteracts the intrinsic harmony and value of movement. It has often been said that gymnastics without equipment marks a shift towards dance.[7]

Even if dance is indeed not a form of gymnastics, then at least it contains something that allows people to make well-formed and harmonious movements. In general, people fail to recognise the deeper meaning of dance classes and lessons in social behaviour, which nowadays indeed have become rather superficial. In order to reassert the general validity of dance education, this importance must once again be stressed. Today it is no longer common in ballroom dance classes to focus on those elements which are recognised as lessons in social conduct. Dancers experience a complete spiritual [*seelisch*] reversal which elevates them above everyday attitudes of life and harmonises their mind in a similar way to gymnastic movement.[8]

It is clear that the most simple exercise combinations are of great advantage to the beginner and for highly specialised applications. But it is equally apparent that in the exclusive practice of such simple exercises, again only certain parts of the body are strengthened and included, whereas combined practice undoubtedly tends to involve larger areas of the body and trains them more thoroughly.

In these simple exercises and exercise sequences, the body is effectively regarded as an apparatus, in fact, as a very primitive apparatus. Inherent in this form of exercise are some of the drawbacks of gymnastics that uses equipment. It is mechanical. The more complicated a movement becomes, the more the mechanical is lost and a mental-spiritual [*geistig-seelisch*] element emerges that favours particular forms of conduct. In these preferred forms of conduct both something very personal and impersonal is expressed.[9]

The form of an artistic dance performance can resemble basic functional dance [*Zwecktanz*]. In terms of content, they often have the same spiritually concentrated notions. But from a simple step to marching in step to a small jump, in artistic dance, tension is bound in a different way to functional dance [*Zwecktanz*]. There are movements which appear in the form of mutually contending waves where we cannot do justice to our notion of human gracefulness. We find gracefulness in the natural world: inanimate nature, the surge of the sea, masses of clouds driven by the wind, human and animal bodies moving freely, swaying trees in a storm – all are characterised by flowing lines which constitute the essence of that which we call beauty or gracefulness. Artistic dance, however, gives this beauty a further and more profound meaning. It reveals something about this beauty. It is no longer goal and function, but a means of expression for the communication of the hidden secrets of the world. Artistic dance comes full circle from everyday movement to the whole wealth of everyday movements. What distinguishes artistic dance intrinsically from, on the one hand, social dancing, and, on the other hand, the functional dance of gymnastics, is the diversity and precision of spatial positioning and differentiation.[10]

MOVEMENT CULTURE AND ITS WORLD VIEW

It is a remarkable phenomenon that the gymnastically oriented person has a completely different approach to life and to all aspects of life than a person who feels hatred, animosity or indifference towards physicality. The corporeally sentient person has no liking for the exclusive intellectuality of those who relish its emphasis. He perceives this form of intellectuality as degenerate, as an illness. After all, man is not on this earth simply for his intellectuality. This combination of contemplation, which in the course of millennia has gained such outstanding value and such outstanding importance, indeed has a completely different source. Man has his intellect in order to navigate his environment, to master material life and savour it appropriately. The mind is not there for us to set up principles, orders and systems for all manner of things, especially when these phenomena lie outside our sphere of experience, outside that which we can be and the impact which we can have. That does not mean to say that philosophical and logical matters should remain alien to Man, but that he should be wary of using these two resources which nature has bestowed upon him to reveal the world to such an extent that no healthy core remains. The gymnastic outlook is also a world view. It has its own means of allowing the intellectually incomprehensible to be actively grasped and evaluated. With these more natural and healthy means, it engages in the struggle for the advancement of life. The abstractions of thinking, which lead to notions of self-destruction and the destruction of everything around, have no place in the mind and senses of a person who moves with vitality. An excessive use of mind and sentiment, which can lead in this direction, is alien to movement. This emanates from constraints which are rooted in precisely this unfamiliarity with movement.[11]

We have to look more closely at our body and its possibilities for movement. We must examine how this instrument of our mind and soul actually works. We must comprehend how our mind and our soul are connected with this instrument and where the focal point is from which we can develop our vitality. That is the gymnastic longing; that is the aim which we strive for. Deflated by the immense consequences of the adoration of the intellect, one tries to return to the formerly common forms of instruction, of life and education.[12]

Everyone knows that the basis of all things and all perceptions is movement and humanity can only communicate through movement. And yet one disregards just this movement, which is the basis of all things. For instance, one calls the human body's expressiveness primitive and unspiritual. This is so because a man who does not know his body is not able to grasp the enormous spiritual depth which becomes evident in the expression of movement. The desire and intention of the dancers of our time are to bring back into gymnastics the sense of inner experience. The dancer has the most complete order of movements; he knows all the laws of space and physicality like nobody else, and all gymnastics must turn to the knowledge of the dancer.

What we find in gymnastic exercise [*Turnen*], designed to simply regulate health and strength of the body, has of course nothing or little to do with an artistic body culture. The latter is about a sensitive exploration of a highly developed mental-spiritual potential [*Hochspannungen*] through the use of a sixth sense, the sense of the body or the sense of movement. Those who have observed a terrifying lack of a sense for movement in primary schools, colleges, elementary schools and courses for children and adults, and who are convinced that this mistake, this lack of one of the most natural and beneficial powers of man, must be corrected, can reach for no other means than the choric art of movement.[13]

GYMNASTIC MOVEMENT

Between natural movement and dance a third term has to be included, which is gymnastic movement. Here the intention of purposeful movement is the training of the body, bodily experience, the identification and mastery of movement. The movements executed for this purpose are not natural, but are geared to fulfil in different ways certain aspects of gymnastics. Some stretch muscles, others are designed to help build up muscles, others loosen the joints, others still lead to general suppleness and agility, while finally some sharpen the sense of balance. Next to this central aim, gymnastics also has the possibility of getting close to dance movements in that gymnastic exercises are thought out which take place in a kind of flight-dance [*tänzerischer Fluchtablauf*]. Hence spiritual purposes accrue.[14]

TENSION AND RELAXATION, STABILITY, LABILITY

All bodily movement affects our experience by the degree of its departure from the vertical. That does not only apply to the audience, but also to the person who is moving. Man feels a certain lability in movement. This condition is similar to a swing, a flight, a fall. The body is for a moment released from gravity. This only happens in very specific inclined directions and body positions. Further, these body positions develop according to certain laws within the body and here we find a new series of exercises which have nothing to do with choreography or the mechanics and expression of movement, but which are connected to balance exercises, although with an added element, which is a fleeting quality [*Flüchtigkeit*].[15]

MOTION FACTORS

We mentioned that there are mainly three modes of movement which everyone can identify and these three modes have a specific means of measurement. We called these three basic modes the measures of strength, time and space. But now we see a fourth mode: the fleeting quality [*Flüchtigkeit*] which we want to simply call flight. While we could watch in fine detail the contrasts between force, time and space as strong and weak, slow and fast, wide and narrow, in fleeting quality, we have the contrast of bound and loosened. For the bound movement we can of course adopt a stiff and firm position during which the whole of the equilibrium is distributed directly over and around the centre of gravity. For the most fleeting movement we have the jump, which leads away from the ground, that is into a slanting direction (naturally during its upward movement, that is, from the moment when the stiff position is left behind through impetus until the moment in which the ground is approached in the fall). But now there are a whole number of fleeting movements in which the ground does not have to be left at all. In order to explain this better, we must discuss the peculiarity of flight more exactly. There are two laws of movement which regulate the body with regard to this fleeting quality in movement. These two laws are the law of countermovement and the law of succession. One can carry out a movement in such a way that one raises first the extreme end of a limb towards its intended destination, that is, the hand and the fingers, and then only lets the arm, shoulder, body follow. The other possibility is the contrary, that is, to let the movement stream from the centre of the body, where an arm movement has the sequence: an impulse in the trunk leading out to the shoulder blade, upper arm, lower arm, and lastly the hand. This movement comes from the centre of the body and ensures a fleeting quality, whilst the first movement needs a tremendous stiffness of the body in its execution, meaning a strongly bound condition.[16]

THREE EXAMPLES OF 'TRAINING'

Gathering ('creation') and scattering

As the basis of these exercises let us consider a pulling towards and pushing or directing away of arms and legs. We can best begin with the arms. When we hold both arms diagonally in front of our body and lead them into a semicircle in front of our centre, while bending our body so that the arms are coming close to the chest in a gathering action, then we have found a characteristic basic movement, which we want to call 'gathering' in the context of fleeting movements. In contrast to this, if we return outwards, with both hands stretching out, coming together in front and above our heads, via two semicircles into the open inclined position that we started out from, then we have a movement which pushes, shoves away from the body, and in this particular exercise we want to give this movement the name 'scattering'. This gathering and scattering are of course never merely a pure arm movement; the whole body follows. This movement begins as a wave from the centre of gravity, through the spine into the torso, the throat, sideways into the arms up into the fingertips. Downwards this wave of movement reaches into the pelvic musculature, and from there into thighs, calves, feet, into the tips of the toes. Of course it is much harder to imagine this gathering movement in which the whole body is involved through a description than through an appropriate exercise involving simple muscular tension. Perhaps a description of an expressive action will bring us more closely to the execution of this form of movement.

Let us assume that a person, stepping forward with his right leg, picks up a large ball with gathering arms, that he keeps repeating this movement, of course only symbolically, without really picking something up, until the best possible lightness and the most harmonious line has been found, maybe then the sensation of a light gathering, as it can be applied as a basis for these exercises, may be grasped. Scattering can perhaps best be elucidated through a proud, upright, dismissive gesture. This movement must of course have the quality of pushing something away in its arm movements and gait, let us say as when a person steps slowly and upright through a heavy curtain, the narrow gap which he is forced to part with his arms, all the while maintaining a calm, majestic posture.

Dimensional scale

There is a swinging scale [*Schwungskala*], which a person can easily perform swinging with his arms. Elsewhere it is discussed how these swinging scales are applied in different martial actions, for example, in fencing, as a basis for self-defence. Here we want to briefly describe the directional exercises without going any further into its connection with the martial arts.

One ought to stand on the right leg, the left leg extended backwards. The entire right side of the body, especially the right arm, swings in the main dimensional directions in the following sequence:

high
low right
left
right
left-backward
right-forward

Then one can easily add the first swing 'high' again. The continual pendular swinging in these directions will slowly educate the body in a more precise feeling of space, which means that a basis will be provided through this swinging scale [*Schwungskala*] from which our consciousness can form complications and combinations of spatial directions.

What remains important in our present field of observation is that the singular structure of this movement always has spatial movement as its aim and purpose. These spatial movements are not only to be found as the ground rules of basic locomotion, but also in other phenomena of movement, for instance, in the growth of the human being.

The movement choir

The swinging together of men must aim for a refinement of spiritual contact and further the sense and desire for harmony. The poet, and hence likewise the dance-poet, is not entitled to ask about the moral and ethical impact of his work. He presents it and either it has an impact or not, and if it does, then it is a work of art and it is ethical. The most meaningful and deepest feeling that we can experience, the awakening of the will within us, the awakening of that force which gives us the capacity to constantly swing together with the original dance of being, is aroused in the spectator through the swinging of the genuine dance artwork.[17]

Notes

1. *GD*, p. 168.
2. Ibid., p. 121.
3. Ibid., p. 156.
4. Ibid., pp. 133–134 (my italics).
5. Ibid., pp. 15–16.
6. Ibid., pp. 17–20.
7. Ibid., p. 22–23.
8. Ibid., p. 23.
9. Ibid., pp. 26–28.
10. Ibid., pp. 28–29.
11. Ibid., pp. 30–31.
12. Ibid., pp. 39–40.
13. Ibid., pp. 130–131.
14. Ibid., p. 80.
15. Ibid., p. 67.
16. Ibid., pp. 67–68.
17. Ibid., pp. 162–163.

Chapter five

Choreography (1926)

Translated by Stefanie Sachsenmaier and Dick McCaw

Introduction

Dick McCaw

Divided into 29 chapters, whose titles correspond very accurately to their contents, *Choreography* (CH) is one of Laban's more systematic studies of movement. The title refers to Feuillet's *Chorégraphie, ou l'art d'écrire la danse* (Choreography, or the art of writing dance) published in Paris in 1700, and Laban gives examples from this script in his book.[1] *Choreography* could well be '*Die Schrift des Tänzers*' (The Dancer's Script) which was mentioned in *The World of the Dancer* as its forthcoming companion piece. He refers in a letter of 1 February 1920 to 'the two books Seifert [his publisher] are going to produce':

> My 'Choreography' is completed, inasmuch as I have only the necessary ordering and transcribing of the manuscript to undertake, if I can only get a few weeks peace . . . a person cannot create a form of written notation, he can only display those natural laws on which written notation as a convention can be based. My 'Choreography' will be

> greatly enriched by the research that I have undertaken since my earliest youth into written symbols, hieroglyphs as well as formal logic. I intend to publish this research, at least in outline, at the same time as the notation, as I believe that our era is ready for these things and has an urgent need of them.
>
> The new choreography must not only show the position but rather the tension of the whole body which automatically produces the attitude of the limbs. This can only happen through a knowledge of 'Dance' instead of 'dancing'. I would be pleased if someone had relieved me of the labour of 'creating' choreography. I would then have time for better things. But there is, sadly, no prospect of this.[2]

The fact that the appearance of this volume on script took a further six years, and that the dance script (or notation) used in *Choreography* was superseded in 1928 by his *Schrifttanz* (dance script) in Vienna, indicates the struggles he had with finding a means of notating dance. The problem is that Laban did not want to notate static postures and floor patterns, but the *spatial form* of actual movements. More than that, he also wanted to grasp the 'tension of the whole body which automatically produces the attitude of the limbs' – this is more than muscular tension, but the inner structure of the movement. To notate these forms you first have to understand their nature – which explains why there is as much in this book about the nature of movement in everyday life and dance as about its notation. In fact, Laban's dance was conceived of as a 'more natural kind of movement' than the formal and prescriptive Ballet:

> While in old ballet the various spatial directions appear separately as scale-like movement sequences for the legs and arms, in the new dance the spatial directions combine together into scales which are not divided according to body parts. In this more natural form of movement the entire body takes part in the swinging.[3]

But while he wanted to go beyond Feuillet's notion and notation of dance, Laban was keen to stress the continuity between traditional Ballet and his Free Dance; thus many of his innovative ideas about space and movement are expressed with reference to the vocabulary and the five 'positions' of ballet. In this, he was unlike Mary Wigman who saw modern dance as a complete break with tradition.

Many of Laban's major themes were already present in *The World of the Dancer* but in *Choreography* they are cast in a much more practical way, and look ahead to later works like *Effort* (1947) and *Choreutics* (1966). Jeffrey-Scott Longstaff notes that Space Harmony (i.e. Choreutics) and Effort were not separate concepts in Laban's early thinking:

> In modern-day analysis, the concepts of 'effort' and 'space' are generally used to refer to the two general categories of 1) movement quality and dynamics versus 2) movement form and shape. While *Choreographie* is primarily concerned with spatial attributes of movement, at this stage in the development of Laban's analysis, effort and spatial concepts were thoroughly integrated. The effort/space distinction may be related to another distinction which could be referred to as functional movements versus expressive movements.

Longstaff continues:

> It appears that Laban encountered an inevitable conflict between analysis and synthesis. On the one hand there is a need to distinguish and separate effort and spatial attributes for the sake of notation and analysis, while on the other in the phenomenon of actual movement these are thoroughly integrated and inseparable, they always function in tandem.[4]

This theme is picked up in Chapter 2 where he notes that movements consist of primary tensions – i.e. their spatial direction or inclination from the vertical – and auxiliary tensions – i.e. their dynamic quality – which can transform the movement. In passing, he introduces the notion of the 'trace-form', the imaginary 'vapour trail' that a movement might leave in space. So, while he describes the points in space of an octahedron and a cube, he is more interested in the journeys *between,* rather than *to* them – Laban is exploring the nature of dance movement, not Newtonian physics or Euclidean geometry. But equally he sees these movements (the diagonal tensions within the cube, or dimensional tensions within the octahedron) as their inner structure. Thus there are inner and outer shapes. The third element he explores in this chapter is the way in which the limbs and torso are organised in movement – note particularly how he addresses the fact that we narrow ourselves by turning to the side when reaching, or when boxing.

The excerpt from Chapter 7 returns to the simplest of his movement scales – the Dimensional Scale – (the inner structure of the octahedron), which has already been touched on in the excerpts from *Gymnastics and Dance.* He refers to its connection with the martial arts, and Irmgard Bartenieff comments:

> his whole space harmony work resulted from studying the martial arts. In the martial arts he saw that in the situation of survival you have to make use of space and energy. You are forced to. From there, he developed the interrelationship of energy and space to what we call our Effort. It was then called Eukinetics and was developed for the dancer.[5]

Bartenieff continues:

> The use of space and movement was developed from the core of the defense scale which is a scale of how you successfully protect yourself. The up is protecting the head, the down is protecting the lower quarters, the across is protecting the heart, the out is protecting this flank, the retreating is protecting the belly . . . it's all over the body, so the order is important.[6]

The book also introduces some of the movement forms that will form the heart of his choreutic studies: three and four rings, the A and B scales, and the Axis and Equator scales, all of which are regular pathways through the icosahedron.

Chapter 25 continues the exploration of Primary (spatial)

and Secondary (dynamic) Streams of Movement and describes the four motion factors which will later be called Weight, Space, Time and Flow, but here are called 'force', 'time', 'space' and 'lability'. Lability, the precursor to free flow, is described as 'flight' and 'volatility'. Lability is opposed to Stability, and this opposition in turn relates to the difference between the stability of the dimensional scale which always comes back to the vertical, and the lability of the diagonal scale (that is, the 45° diagonals within a cube). The vertical dimension is important for establishing equilibrium, but dance requires the thrill of movements which deviate from the vertical axis before returning to it to regain balance. Looking ahead to *Choreutics*, Laban relates the three axes of movement (up–down, wide–narrow, forward–back) to movement factors qualities (respectively weight, space, time) in a diagram that presents both Space and Dynamics as three parallel bipolar ranges. This is an excellent example of how space and effort are related in Laban's thinking in the 1920s.

The final excerpt comes from Chapter 27, which offers a sustained reflection on the differences and similarities between everyday, functional movement and dance movement. Longstaff offers the following note on these 'two kinds of movement':

> The effort/space distinction may be related to another distinction which could be referred to as functional movements versus expressive movements. Here two kinds of movements are distinguished, though also inextricably tied together:
>
> Everyday movement (*Alltagsbewegung*) or purposeful movement (*Zweckbewegung*[7]); so-called substantial (*stoffliche*) or concrete (*gegenständliche*) movements. Though it is pointed out that this type of movement can also be part of artistic expression.
>
> Artistic movement (*künstlerische Bewegegung*, or *Kunstbewegung*), or formal movement (*formale Bewegung*) which has outer features of artistic intention. Though it is pointed out that this always returns to substantial movement as its source.

Ultimately, dance is more interested in the spatial form than the everyday function of movement. In this chapter there are passages which reveal the incredible subtlety of Laban's understanding of the nature and meaning of human gesture.

INTRODUCTION

An account of the world of dance forms can not only consist of a list of fixed states. This world must be regarded as a surge of actively varying transformations of states. The area of activity in which the processes of form transformation can be observed in practice is body movement in everyday life, gymnastics and dance. Theoretically, movement and dance studies, theories of gymnastics, etc. have dealt with this matter.

More is known than one thinks on this subject, in practice and theory – even if there are enormous gaps. Research can be undertaken into how a form is composed, how it can be decomposed, in what way it can be transposed into related forms, and how, via related forms, it arrives at different ones.

For this purpose a primary basis from which forms are made must of course be known but this knowledge and system is only a subordinate help. An observation of the basic form transformations which simple body actions (gripping, locomotion, standing, etc.) consist of, without doubt, constitutes the basis.

These actions have differing states and conditions in which again particular form transformations prevail. All quantitative and qualitative differences of actions are to be traced back to the particularities of the form transformations in movement. . . .

It is by no means easy to observe and account for the presence of a form or even a simple form element in a movement. It can be sensed a) according to specific methods and b) through practice. Only a careful study of human movement can enable us to describe it clearly and unambiguously.

Fundamentally one ought to begin with the description of the movement, and mention incidentally the individual spatial forms, form transformations and their laws. The objective is for us *the mastery of the movement through explanation.*

But the basis (the form transformations) is unknown to the general public, not only theoretically, but also practically in our era in which dance is alien. Hence one must choose a way of introducing an elucidation of these problems, one which seems to foreground something which is foreign to the essence of movement, namely a study of space that is based on fixed positions. In the same way the practical and theoretical ballet instruction begins with the learning of positions and attitudes, and of the most economical movement; that is, with the study of posture instead of a study of movement.

In these writings the attempt is made to portray the elements of the study of posture, the 'conditions', if possible directly in terms of their dynamic values and their correlations with the action, the event.

The intended result of obtaining a way of notating dance movement in its present-day freer and richer form, has thus been attained.

ELEMENTS OF FORM THEORY[8]

A static study of forms [*Formlehre*] describes conditions; a dynamic study of forms describes processes, events. The following questions emerge: In what way do rhythms of forms come about? How will the continuously present tensions of shape and balance transmute before they become expression or action, or before they subside? There are:

1. Primary tensions which serve particular actions,
2. Auxiliary tensions which help to build up or destroy primary tensions.

Of further importance is the observation of:

1. the paths of the form elements relative to one another in space,

2. the distribution in the body, i.e. the answer to the question: Which forms are most suited to which limbs?

The movement process is to be followed from its initial to its final stage. The phases lying between these create the actual movement.

The dynamic study of forms [*Formlehre*] is superior to the static study of forms. However, it has too many gaps in its structure. We know too little.

One must begin with the static study of forms [*Formlehre*]. When we observe a movement, we notice above all its *bodily engagement*. One of the two symmetrical halves of the body leads. We distinguish:

right leading and
left leading

streams of movement. There are movements that are mirror-imaged. These can also occur at the same time (asymmetrical and symmetrical movements).

Furthermore, we observe a spatial and directional orientation, which we judge by the angle of deviation in relation to the upright body position.

The most external – but most important – observation appears to us to be the *form image* [*Formbild*] which the body inscribes in space. This moving form has particular properties. It is *always* plastic, i.e. tensions of counterbalance take place in the body, which, next to the vertical, arrange the mass of the body in the sideways and sagittal planes in space.

The plasticity can be markedly stable or labile, depending on whether one aims at more stillness (equilibrium) or more movement (falling, pushing, swinging).

The moving form has *components*, namely beginning, middle, end, each of which, again, has its own basic form. Very many (but even so only a finite number) of mixed forms are possible.

Form is characterised:

a) in flight (degree of lability) by its kinetic content,
b) in force (degree of tension) by its dynamic content,

c) in time (degree of speed) by its rhythmic content,
d) in space (degree of size) by its metric content.

SWINGING SCALES[9]

The natural swinging scales of a human being, which have been known for ages, reveal themselves from a variety of considerations as extraordinarily functional. They have their basis in the nature of our body's construction. Especially in fencing, that is, in sabre fencing, one sees movements performed which have such characteristic spatial directions that can be used as a basis for our analysis.

With regard to all kinds of martial arts the following has to be noted: every higher organised animal has the following vulnerable parts:

> the face with the sense organs,
> the two arterial sides of the neck,
> the two soft areas between the hips and the ribcage,
> and the abdomen

thus six vulnerable parts in total, which need to be protected particularly in fighting. An attack on these vulnerable parts presupposes a defence with arms and shoulders, etc. As in fencing, so in any other kind of self-defence,

> the face is protected by an *upward swinging*,
> the soft side which is turned towards the opponent by a *deep swing*,
> the sides of the neck by a *sideways warding-off motion*,
> the kidney area by a *backward* thrust,
> and the abdomen by a *forward* thrust.

A person who is attacked always presents to his opponent the smallest possible target which is his side, since the human body is narrower at the sides. The right-handed person, when fighting, will present his right hip and his right arm towards the opponent, in order to protect his vulnerable parts.

He will raise the right arm in order to protect his face,
he will lower the right arm to protect his right flank,
he will bring the right arm across to the left for protection of the left side of the neck, and will lift the right arm outward to the right to ward off a danger coming from this direction to the right side of the neck.
He will meet an attack endangering the left hip with a backward thrust of the right arm, and endeavour to push forward any attacks threatening his abdomen.

PRIMARY AND SECONDARY STREAMS[10]

Every movement has a *primary stream* (basic direction, basic form). In addition, *secondary streams* occur which influence its development with regard to its degree of lability, or its lability fluctuations. Furthermore, the secondary streams give a temporal, dynamic and spatial-metric nuance to movement.

For instance, to be speedy means to eliminate the resistances which counteract the drive of reaching a goal suddenly. The temporal development and the duration of a movement are defined by the type of secondary stream that helps to override resistances. There are four regulators of intensity. They govern:

1. The range of intensity of force
2. The range of intensity of time
3. The range of intensity of space
4. The range of intensity of flight (lability).

> The polar opposites of these ranges are:
>
> Force: weak – strong
> Time: fast – slow
> Space: close – far
> Flight: tense – mobile (flowing, swinging).

All *gathering of force* occurs through a drawing together of the body (or of individual muscles) towards the centre. The primary direction here leads downward (gravity). If the body stretches upward, it finally loses the capability to move further; tension is exhausted and a state of non-tension, of *weakness* arises.

If a person wants to reach an object lying at a distance, then he will always have to turn one of the sides of his body towards it, since in this way he can produce the greatest, *furthest stretch*. A *narrow movement* will always be turned towards the opposite side.

Width and narrowness are thus influenced by a *sideways* expanding or inward-turning, that is, *narrow* secondary directions, whereas the gathering of strength and relaxing ('untensing') will occur in the area of steep inclinations.

When dealing with spatial positioning we also need to refer back to the element of time. Every fast *movement* will be a kind of narrowness, a narrowness which is characterised by a *backward* jolting of the centre of the body. *Slow movements* are linked with *forward* protrusions and extensions of the body.

In so doing we obtain a way of establishing the spatial-temporal-dynamic nuance of a movement through the application of particular secondary directions. It should also be noted here that lability and stability play a large role in all these quantitative manifestations, which means that it is important to know whether these secondary directions are more dimensional or diagonal. For the dimensional directions are promoters of stability while the diagonals ensure a labile flow. The degree of a diagonal inclination of a form will thus govern its intensity of flight.

Stillness is a dimensional balancing of the body mass around the centre of gravity. Movement is a diagonal lifting-out from this state of equilibrium.

Every movement has its *beginning* in *stillness*, a journey leading to a new stillness, with this second stillness being its conclusion. The new journey can be performed:

a) with increase or decrease of force
b) with increase or decrease of the speed
c) with increase or decrease of the spatial opening
d) with increase or decrease of stability.

The initial intensity (in force, time, space, flight) can be conceived of in relation to the preceding or following movements, also as an increase or decrease. Movements which are performed without an increase or decrease, thus always remaining at the same distance from the body, or which without emphasis retain the same muscle tension and speed, appear to be mechanical, lifeless. Harmonious liveliness of movement requires a continuously flowing change of nuances of intensity. . . .

Deep			High
←――――――――――――――――――――→			
Strong	half-strong	half-weak	Weak
Back			Forward
←――――――――――――――――――――→			
Fast	half-fast	half-slow	Slow
Out (right or left)			In (right or left)
←――――――――――――――――――――→			
Far	half-wide	half-narrow	Narrow
Labile			Stable
←――――――――――――――――――――→			
Diagonal Fleeting	half-fleeting	half-rigid	Rigid

The contribution of the secondary streams occurs in the body posture at the beginning of a movement, as a kind of preparatory swing, which is visible in space. The spatial visibility so to speak *dies off* and transforms into degrees of intensity, whereas the primary stream emerges as victor from this dichotomy and tends towards a purely spatially definable directional aim. The end of course again constitutes a reversal which transforms into a postural stillness. This postural stillness can be short and non-intense, scarcely noticeable, for example, those moments of balance which occur inbetween fast steps, but it is always present. These moments of stillness divide a movement into clearly distinguishable phases.[11]

ON EVERYDAY, FUNCTIONAL MOVEMENT AND DANCE MOVEMENT[12]

With regard to the conceptualisation of dance notation the following remains to be observed: There are two kinds of movement; *everyday or functional movement* [*Zweckbewegung*] and *artistic movement*. These are not so much two forms but are better conceived as two different coexisting contents.

Functional movement and everyday movement can also be called substantial or concrete movement, but in doing so we commit an error as substantial movement is in no way totally excluded from artistic expression.

The opposite pole to *substantial movement* could be called *formal movement*, which on the one hand does bear the outer features of artistic intention, while on the other it must always return to substantial movement in order to make it into an artistic movement, to ennoble it to some extent.

In dance, as in all art, the *balance between substance and form* is without doubt essential. But we must nevertheless observe both *forms* of movement separately, in order to better arrive at our aim of identifying the formal distinctiveness of dance movement.

If we examine movement closely in terms of its content, we see that fundamentally it has two purposes in everyday life.

One is to communicate, that is, to make a statement. In movement it is naturally always only a matter of expressing things which cannot be conveyed literally in words, and which render the exact essence of a movement content.

We can mention in broad terms that this is a matter of expressing the will, the drives and the powers which reside in Man.[13] The drives and powers, the will, do not always express themselves only as imperatives, as appeals, as demands, as one might assume. On the contrary, one can communicate a great number of the correlations of power that are expressed through movement as instruction or as entertainment, one can enhance a speech in everyday life through movement, or say in gestures something for which we lack words. A questioning and astonished gesture of the body will, with its other powers, communicates to us much more clearly and exactly the context, this astonishment, than the mere cry 'I am astonished'. The astonishment in the gesture can include a mixture of shyness, aggressiveness and of a thousand other things. Even the tone of the voice will not be able to render these nuances in such great detail.

As already stated, in artistic dance this communication is mainly dependent on teaching or entertainment. The imperative movement, the incitement, the appeal is the second form of movement, which is characterised by a purpose with regard to its content. If I incite or demand something, then I can also feel this content clearly. I can even express it with words.

The simplest functional movements of this kind are without doubt gathering [*Heranrufen*] and pushing away [*Wegstossen*]. One can also curse or bless, conjure, one can stimulate sensually, awaken curiosity, can motivate the aesthetic or philosophical sense of the body, one can sanctify or profane (all movements with a certain tendency). Even these purely functional movements naturally have their place in art. They have nothing to do anymore with communication taking the form of instruction or entertainment, they lead in a certain direction.

We have many more conventional movements than we think. Even if these can fundamentally also occur as mimed expressions, they are always connected to purely formal action. For example, calling someone to come closer happens with the same gesture as pulling an object towards oneself. Or take a more spiritual affair: someone rejects something according to all the rules of old-fashioned etiquette. According to the old rules of decent behaviour, this is depicted approximately as follows: 'The rejection occurs by gently raising the shoulders with a simultaneous outward rotation of the arms, while the inner surface of the hand has to become visible.'

In this way a shyness is expressed in the drawing-together of the body; a timid apology. At the same time in the turning-out of the hands a certain helplessness is indicated, something inactive, hence it is also a mime. The hands are in a position which communicates that one would like to gently push back one's counterpart. A brusque rejection will rather have a pushing away or sudden defensive movement as a by-product (that is, a negative response).

But all these movements are to be grasped as purely formal, and thus we come to the next substantial point in our investigation. What is formal in a movement? Is it the specific body posture, which shapes the muscle, as in our example perhaps the raising of the shoulders, the bending of the arm towards the body, or the turning of the hand? Artistic dance has answered this question as follows: It tunes into a train of thought which essentially leads to a position where one only needs to consider the *spatial directions* or combinations of spatial directions, and that the performance of these spatial directions, the entering into it with particular limbs, only takes place and is considered secondarily.

The essential aspects are always the *dimensional* or *diagonal directions*, then the *pathways* in which these directions are performed, that is, round, spiral, straight, and then at the most it has to be considered in what way the body maintains its *balance* while it fulfils these spatial directions or spatial forms, and which limbs are employed for that purpose, pushing or swinging.

The dancer has always been uniquely interested in this spatial language as a means of expression; how he has applied it, to what extent he wished to fill it with substantial forces and thoughts, is a very different question.

We have already mentioned that in dance also the *time rhythms* are fundamentally nothing other than images of *spatial rhythms*. Indeed, we also have time rhythms conceptually, which we absolutely do not comprehend as time concepts; this will introduce us very soon to the concept of those movements, which dance seeks to differentiate in terms of time, without thinking in the least of any time units or time proportions.

Notes

1 On pp. 54–55.
2 In JHA, Box 26, Folder 23, Item 1.
3 *CH*, p. 12.
4 In Longstaff's notes on his draft translation of *Choreography*, which is lodged in the archive at library of Trinity Laban.
5 Bartenieff, in Johnson (1995: 224).
6 Bartenieff, in Johnson (1995: 225).
7 Stefanie Sachsenmaier and I decided to translate *Zweck* as 'functional', thus *Zwecktanz* is functional dance and *Zweckbewegung*, functional movement.
8 Chapter 2, pp. 3–6.
9 Chapter 7, pp. 19–23.
10 Chapter 25, pp. 74–77.
11 *CH*, pp. 74–77.
12 Chapter 27, pp. 80–85.
13 Laban's note: 'Here one must briefly mention that drives and powers have of course two poles. The internal impulses, which lead to virtuosity, are likewise drives and forces, just as the impulses which lead to vices. It is necessary to say this, because the concept "drive" has been misunderstood because of our decreasing ability to move.'

Chapter six

Texts on Laban's choreographies

Gaukelei (1923) and *Titan* (1927)

Introduction

Dick McCaw

While this is a sourcebook of Laban's writings, it is important to give some idea of Laban as a ground-breaking choreographer, and thus in this short section I have selected some passages that describe him at work, first, in *Titan* which was a piece for movement choir, and the first piece to make use of his dance notation. Fritz Klingenbeck describes the process:

> My first job was with *Titan* which was for eighty male and female dancers. I was involved in writing the score which had to be sent to Albrecht Knust in Hamburg. When he received it, he had to learn the script and teach the dance to the people there. Laban came the week before the performance to see how his employees had managed. Through this collaboration we were presented with the first practical problems arising out of the use of dance notation.[1]

THE LABAN SOURCEBOOK

The first extract is from a review of *Titan* and this is followed by an article by Laban that was included in the programme from that performance. In it, he describes his ideal model for a dance theatre – one where every member of the audience has an equally good view of the stage – and his use of dance notation. The third is an extract from an interview with Rita Zabekow who had danced with Laban when he was Ballet Master at Berlin Opera House in 1930, and describes how he reworked one of his earlier pieces, *Gaukelei* (1923).

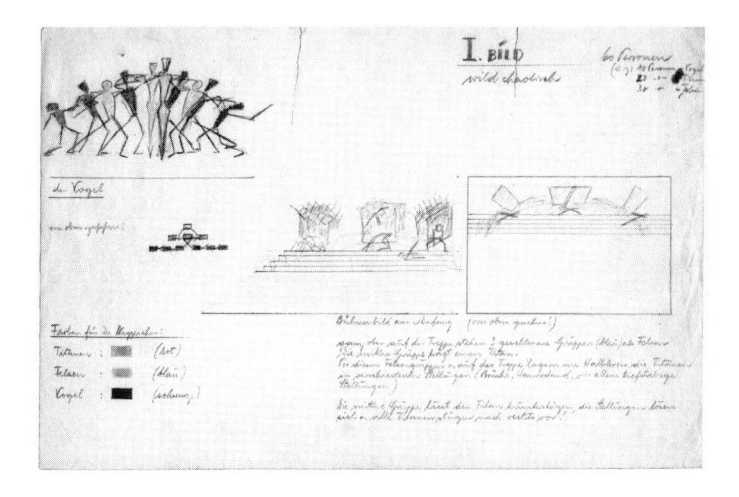

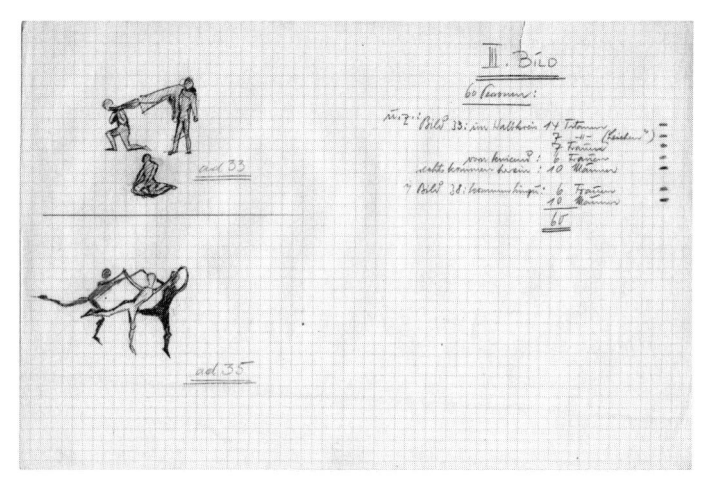

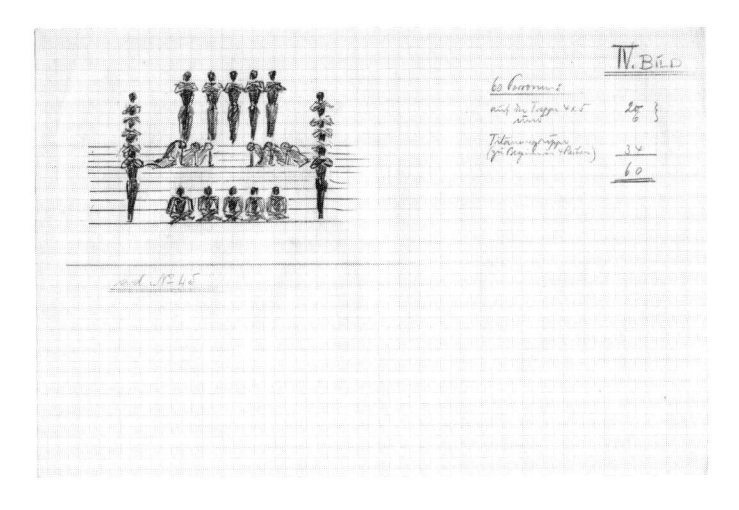

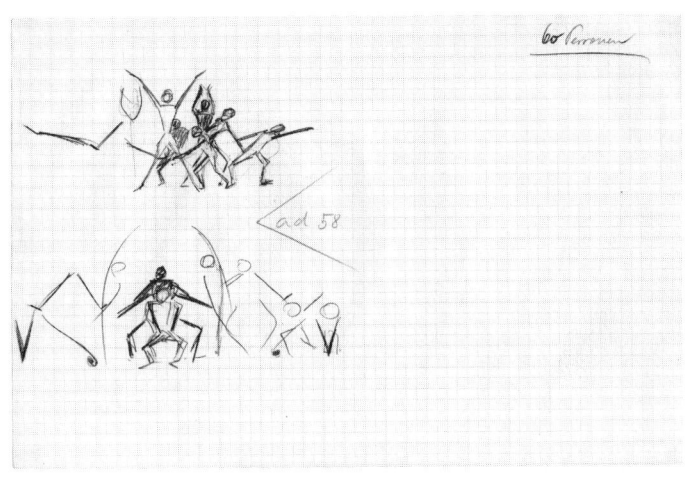

Figures 6.1–6.4 Images from Laban's stage-plan of *Titan* (1927)

TITAN, THE CELEBRATORY CHORUS OF THE HAMBURG MOVEMENT CHOIR[2]

Titan is a choral work, so the theory has it, and it is certainly a very good choral work. The individual dancer has disappeared. Only groups move together and against each other. They offer the regularity of an ornament or perhaps rave in

THE LABAN SOURCEBOOK

Dionysiac chaos. The whole in its clarity and its penetration, has an extraordinary effect as if it had its roots in the Apollonian intellectuality of a Greek ritual, or rather as if it was the mystical feasts of the Pythagoreans who also worship measure and number. As far as this choral work, *Titan*, is concerned, the choral works must appear as if performed by the laity. This work is rooted in the general flow of the movements. It is not a dance performance of an individual and no pantomime talent is required. Apart from a certain technical

Figure 6.5 Hamburg Movement Choir
Source: From *Tanz Fur Alle*, Martin Gleisner, Leipzig, 1928.

skill the Laic dances need above all a sense of precision and tempo: that means the ability to move in the rhythm of the others in the general group. Unfortunately, this was a serious stumbling-block in the choral celebrations on Sunday morning. Laban is proud of the fact that this choral work was studied from his own written descriptions in dance notation, but somehow these choral celebrations have something a bit frosty about them, and this one cannot escape even if this has arisen from some roundabout digression on the way between the dance composer and the actual performance, or simply from the awkwardness of the laic figures themselves. The choral work itself was good, but the choral celebrations seemed like a good piano piece played by a laic figure who is pleased if he can at least get the technical difficulties over and done with properly. Nevertheless the large building of the Busch Circus resounded with loud applause.

A CHORAL MOVEMENT WORK AND A CHALLENGE[3]

The dance work for a large group has nothing to do with a work for dance theatre or anything of a similar nature. Its meaning and aim is the choreographic experience of the dancer's choral movement work. The participants are amateurs. The dance inventor and the dance leader are more concerned about the group entrusted to them than about themselves. The play is plastically conceived and can be seen and experienced from all sides. The open space, the ring, the circle in the middle of the community is the place needed for the performance. The ideal dance space is the arena. The model which I showed at the theatrical exhibition at Magdeburg shall suit the purposes of the great choral work.

The spectators sit in rows in a dome above the dance arena. Each is an equal distance from the dance area, about 18 metres. Thus the dance movement is clearly seen and the overall impression can be taken in. In our halls the spectators in the front rows are too near the dancer. From the gallery at the back no details can be seen at all. Even in the circus building the rows of seats are arranged progressively further and further away from the dance, while the lower rows are too close to the stage.

Dance script, movement choir and domed hall are the challenges of the new dance experience in the community. *Titan* is a challenge. I have been able to create the work, and have also found a dance script. Both have arisen from the urge of youth to form movement choirs. The space, the venue, is lacking. Perhaps our enthusiasm shall produce it!

The forces of Nature express themselves in dance, what they are and what they do can only become evident in animated form. These forces are difficult to describe in words. Of course mythical literature has created the characters of gods and superhuman beings, which basically are personifications of these forces. One such character is Titan. Embodying the might of a group of creatures, he is the spirit of this unit of many. Titan is the demon of enthusiasm which inspires a community. Titan is the common spirit which produces civilisations and culture. Titan builds and demolishes. Titan prays and rages. Titan is the phenomenon which reveals itself in group rhythm.

It was my intention in *Titan*, my dance work for a large group, to show this phenomenon in its various phases and in a quite definite line of development. In the first scene the group is representative of the alarm which grips it when it experiences the power of its titanic qualities. Linked together the group feels the rigid and transient and surging principle. Later it experiences an urgent impulse which is inexplicable and which is faced with hostility from that which is rigid. In uniform rhythm these two forces work together in the second scene. The rhythm rises to harmony which fades away. In the third scene the formative wish is awakened which leads to the suffering of conformity. Then there is an intermezzo in which the group possessed of restless movement becomes relaxed and cheerful. The fourth scene passes over the peak of rigidity to the cry for personal liberation.

The ritual of the fifth scene could be an entreaty of the inherent force which seeks to disregard the law of rhythm to which everything is subject. But the eternal pulse tears open the old wound and the rhythm of life exists anew.

In the sixth scene this rhythm wins and results in the originally 'de-forming' forces of transience and rigidity becoming the companions of grace and pride.

Titan was written down in movement script, first shown months ago and is now being rehearsed anew. (See the example of the script from the fifth round which scores simultaneous movements of several groups alongside each other.)

Only now do I dare attempt to indicate its rhythms with words. The vision of this work arose from movement sense. Its experience is also only possible by means of this sense. Whoever studies the written version in movement signs can perhaps come up with similar analogies to those which I have set down here. The title *Titan* is probably also a result of this abstract interpretation, and one which seemed to me to be representative of the total content of the work.

RITA ZABEKOW REMEMBERS LABAN[4]

When we worked on this project, on *Gaukelei,* it was naturally the libretto which was first ceremoniously given to the whole ballet company by our ballet master, our dear 'Papi', Rudolf von Laban. Many ideas had been followed and discarded when one day he said, "Yes, today we must sort out what we want to do, and I feel that this should be *Gaukelei.*' Then came what we had been longing for. Everyone was given their parts. He gave some instructions to the dancers who were to dance the parts of the princesses, and I think it was Kurt Graf who was to dance the prince. Then we had to improvise. He loved improvisation. First we worked three or four times with the music, then he said, 'Princesses, you do not play your parts well, improvise.' The prince also had to improvise to communicate his love. Sometimes in this way the parts came together, sometimes they did not. 'You are on your own, you bring no warmth, this poor maiden loves the prince and he does not know it.' Laban drew a picture of the parts, writing in details from people in our own lives, and then we would work again. So, we came towards *Gaukelei.*

We worked for three to four years in the same way as I have described for *Gaukelei* with our 'Papi' von Laban, Rudolf von Laban. He was a father to us. He was not only an artist, I think it is better to say that he was chivalrous. You could go to him with all your problems whether they were trivial or serious. He would always listen to us and we had no fear of him. I can still remember that he was rarely angry with us. Because of these things I still have respect for this great artist who we called 'Papi', who would listen to our private and professional problems and help us to solve them. . . .

He saw choreography evolving and he moved himself, allowing people to improvise. I was pleased that he expected me as a special dancer to take a lead in this although it meant that I had to accept his criticism as sometimes I have too simple an idea of the songs and did not anticipate the unfamiliar movements with which he led the ensemble. . . . Sometimes he would say that the ideas of the ensemble were much too scattered but that it would pass for that day and that consequently it would probably work out better. He left us with a certain amount of freedom. The way he worked at the Festival was to select good assistants. He showed them the way which he wanted to work and they helped him to realise it. He had an absolute inferno of ideas, one came after the other without stopping and at times they would be with him writing the ideas down in his dance script.

Notes

1. Interview with JH in 1973 (in JHA, Box 30, Folder 41, Item 10e).
2. Author unknown, *Hamburg Echo*, 30 July 1928 (in JHA, Tape 3, translated by Richard Ellis).
3. By Laban, from the programme for the performance on 29 January 1928 in Hamburg (in JHA, Box 29, Folder 36, Item 13f).
4. Interview in JHA, Box 30, Folder 41, Item 10a.

Chapter seven

The Choreographic Institute Laban (1926–1929) and Laban's presentation at the first Dancers' Congress, Magdeburg (1927)

Selected and translated by Vera Maletic

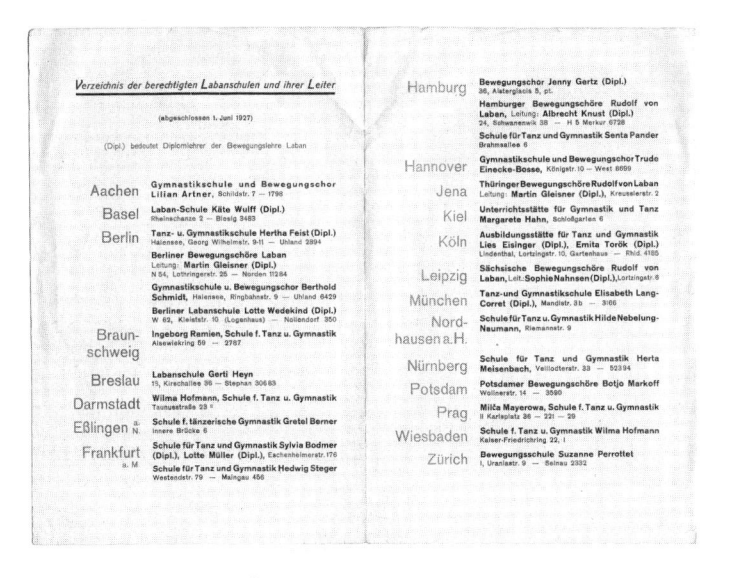

Figure 7.1 Directory of Laban Schools in 1927
Source: John Hodgson Archive, Brotherton Library, University of Leeds.

Figure 7.2 List of Laban vocational training schools
Source: John Hodgson Archive, Brotherton Library, University of Leeds.

Introduction

Vera Maletic

The period from 1926 until 1929 was among the most prolific phases of Laban's creative life. In 1926, he published three significant books: *Choreography*: Volume One, *Gymnastics and Dance*, which has an enclosure entitled 'Practical exercises' with outlines of his movement classification including references to punch/hit, press/pull as some of basic types of expression, and *Gymnastics and Dance for Child*ren.

In 1926, Laban also founded his first Choreographic Institute in Würzburg. In spite of some initial uninformed local reticence to Laban's ideas, the Institute was located at the Theaterstrasse in the vicinity of the Würzburg theatre and potential collaborations with the theatre and the university were anticipated. However, in 1927 the Institute transferred to Berlin-Grünewald, and in 1929 it would join the Dance

Department of the *Folkwang* School in Essen directed by Kurt Jooss.

The text and the format of the Würzburg Institute's small brochure can be seen as an imaginative example of artistic promotion (see pp. 124–125).[1]

The pamphlet speaks directly to the potential 'consumer' and he or she, of course, 'belongs to us' as they have been practising some kind of movement and dance and are interested in several of its aspects. It outlines succinctly its multifaceted function and its complex sources. The gist of it was to form a new dance aesthetic and theory of dance within a two-part framework of theory and practice.

In an article that was published in 1929,[2] Laban states, 'the Choreographic Institute Laban was created in the beginning of 1926 because of the need to obtain a place in which central problems of the art of movement could be clarified and fostered.' It was motivated by the insight:

> that fostering of the art of movement has become a basic social phenomenon;
> that in contemporary dance there is a desperate struggle between a new view of the World which finds influential supporters, against an old, fading view of life.
> that the old static art no longer suffices as an expression and means of enlivening of our time, and that a new rhythmical-dynamic, and labile way of life and art should arise.

Laban discusses the *Aims of the Choreographic Institute* by considering the following questions:

> What are the *foundations* of every contemporary movement education and the art of movement?
> How best to *summarise* the achievements of attempts and groundwork to date?
> How can *principles* follow from various areas of work that belong to it?
> What *development* can the art of movement gain on the basis of such principles?

CHOREOGRAPHIC INSTITUTE LABAN

WHAT IS IT?

WHERE ARE ITS SOURCES?

WHO BELONGS TO US?

Office Würtzburg. Theaterstrasse 24

CHOREOGRAPHIC INSTITUTE LABAN
WHAT IS IT?

A place for research and collecting choreographic knowledge.

A place for the transmission of this knowledge to the growing generation of dancers and choreographers through clear contemporary practice.

A place for collecting and publishing modern theatrical dance works.

A place for creating exemplary performances of old and new works of the art of dance.

Dedicated to the memory of great dancers of the **past.**

Dedicated to rising forces in the **future.**

Operating in the **present** as a master's laboratory of the art and science of dance.

CHOREOGRAPHIC INSTITUTE LABAN

WHERE ARE ITS SOURCES?

In the innumerable Eukinetic writings of all races and periods.
In the contemporary elaboration of dance notation and dance knowledge.
In the dance technique and the teaching of composition based on choreographic research.
In the expectation that our time brings to the art of dance of the future.

The language of movement is
present in our subconscious.

We have to bring this means of communication to the awareness of all nations and races.

We have to create an art form corresponding to our time, that uses the language of movement as a means of expression.

CHOREOGRAPHIC INSTITUTE LABAN

WHO BELONGS TO US?

All who are mastering movement.
All who observe and understand movement.
All who write down movement.
All who want to learn movement and its notation,
> as dancers or teachers of dance,
> as researchers and dance writers,
> as dance inventors or directors.

All professions can participate in the choreographic science and practice. It is a means for and supplement to the education of viewers and lay persons, and a means and aim for the vocation of dance artists and scientists.

Choreography is an age-old order that has always been apparent in the arts, sciences, and philosophy. This ordering has been rediscovered in the visible music and visible language of movement. Choreography provides a new branch that offers those that are in it enjoyable pioneering work, giving individuals and collectives an opportunity to advance.

The Choreographic Institute should not elaborate on an answer to these questions solely in the form of theoretical investigations but should provide a practical foundation for the various areas. This brings about a division into a theoretical and a practical department. The former will deal with the development of a general movement science, and the latter will foster all the areas of the art of movement.

While the theoretical department investigates the laws of Choreology, the development of dance notation, and the recording of old and new dances, the practical department trains dancers and dance teachers. The curriculum is divided into partly separate and partly common movement seminars.

Common subjects for dancers and choreographers:

Elementary choreographic movement training
Introduction to the theory of space and expression
Lectures about the history and aesthetics of dance
General dance knowledge.

Only for dancers:

Dance technique
Choreutics and Eukinetics (practical dance theory about space and expression)
Rehearsing, performances.

Only for choreographers:

General movement theory
Notation
Choreographic theory of harmony

Complementing his own teaching of dance directing, composition and theory, Laban had an excellent staff consisting of his disciples and collaborators. Gertrud Snell, a gifted theoretician, published several articles on the science of movement and on fundamentals of a general dance theory, including Choreutics and Eukinetics. She would also teach movement notation.[3] Performer and choreographer Dussia Bereska who, already in 1920, co-founded the Laban's Dance Theater (*Tanzbühne Laban*) and had led the Chamber Dance Theatre Laban (*Kammertanzbühne Laban*) since 1923, taught Eukinetics; various movement/dance expressions would be experienced through improvisation and composition. Bereska also taught Choreutics, dealing with the spatial structure of movement, which she shared with Gertrud Loeszer. (Laban had toured with Loeszer in 1925 with a series of dances without music inspired by some Wagnerian personalities.) Hermann Robst, a member of the Chamber Dance Theatre Laban, conducted dance training and assisted Laban with classes in choreography.

Among various strands of the rationale for the Institute, such as fostering the art of movement and contemporary dance, Laban sees movement notation as a significant component. His Kinetography Laban was published in 1928 and presented the same year at the second Dancers Congress in Essen. He argues that: 'The quest for the laws of this new art leads to a new *Choreology*, the ordering of circular flowing movement, in contrast to the law of a picture, stillness, stiffness.'

The identification of this flowing can only be recorded in *Movement notation*.

This knowledge and art can become known through *dance works* that can be produced from written records.

> Only such a dance literature (in dance notation) will be able to educate viewers, critics and theoreticians. The current lack of critics, who are not confused, is a real hindrance for creating necessary prerequisites such as schools, stages, festival halls. . . .
>
> Kinetography Laban is a simple alphabet of symbols with the single aim of recording dances and movement sequences in an easily readable manner. Any harmonic, psychological, choreological or any other notions are *consciously* eliminated. *Every* child should be able to simply observe movement, simply write it down and read it.

Laban's aim of making Kinetography an objective and universal movement notation is here expressed.

Not unlike in his subsequent talk at the first German Dance Congress, Laban is critical of the status of the *dance theatre*:

> It will only become possible after some clarification of works. Today the public, as well as the private dance scenes are only a *compromise* between old methods and new persons or new methods and old persons.

Laban also questions the existence of a *dance academy*:

> Only a unified view, that was prepared through untiring clarification, about the value and the essence of movement, can serve as the basis of a place that we would consider worthy to be included in establishments which have long existed, such as, stadiums, sports schools, conservatories, etc.

He envisions new dance professions of the future, such as:

> The dancer as stage dancer, concert dancer, dance teacher, dance leader for lay persons' choirs, for the theatre of word and sound, for the dance theatre; the dance scientist as choreologist, kinetographer (dance writer); the dance-composer, the theoretical investigator and dance critic; the sociologist who deals with this new world and its manifestations.

In stating how the work of the Choreographic Institute is preparing the foundation for the future of dance, Laban lists the departments that have been established in the Berlin Institute:

- The department for a general movement investigation.
- The department for informative lecture tours with slides, film projections, and demonstrations with dance performances.

- The department for recording dances, movement-choir works, directors' annotations for operas and plays.[4]
- The department for instruction in Kinetography, training of teachers of Kinetography.
- The department for directing and the study of group and solo dances.
- The department for projecting choral celebrations and dance performances of celebrations.
- The department for composing dance programmes, including dance directing and dancerly production.

The January edition of *Schrifttanz*[5] brought a chart entitled 'What is necessary?', demonstrating all the major concerns of the Institute (Figure 7.3). It is an example of an informative slide that Laban used in his lecture demonstrations.

'The Dance Artwork or the Very Image of Itself': Laban's presentation at the first Dance Congress in Magdeburg

The opening statements of Laban's presentation at the first Dance Congress in Magdeburg in 1927 entitled 'The Dance Artwork'[6] surprised some audiences. Contrary to general expectations that the reformer of the new dance would not be a supporter of the ballet tradition, he called for a link with the tradition:

> The dance artwork requires as any other art form the connection with tradition. What arises from improvisation is nature – not art. Fostering of natural movement grace belongs to the care of body and soul, not to art. A complete work of art should be formed on the basis of artistic laws; sheer intuition is not enough; all man's active forces, such as willpower, feelings, and intellect, are drawn together in forming a work of art. Not only theatre dance but also social dance is bound to established rules in their structures.

WHAT IS NECESSARY?

Practically and Theoretically

A clear differentiation of dance areas of work: Dance for Layman Science of Dance the Art of Dance

The balance of instinct and knowledge in				THE SCIENCE OF DANCE			THE ART OF DANCE	
DANCE FOR LAYMAN	and	DANCE PEDAGOGY					Possible communication by means of:	
Plays of lay-persons	Training of teachers	Training of professional dancers	Choreosophy	Choreology	Choreography	Pure Movement		Movement in association with the art of speech and sound
An approach to presenting gymnastic experiences as a rhythmically organized play. (Gymnastic experiences surpass the area of body-building. When we consider all basic movement occurrences, all understanding, feeling, and activity, the entire view of the world is integrated. In play, the education through dance is possible in all areas of experience.	An approach to such a playing, and the art of transmitting it educationally	To put aesthetic-formal elements in relation to the knowledge of the ethical effect of all art.	The theory of ethical and aesthetic influences on fostering movement and the art of dance in the service of a new communal culture and education.	The theory of the laws of dance events manifest in the synthesis of spatial and temporal experiences.	The theory of an effective articulation of a movement event, as well as for the purpose of the notation of educational exercises, and of works of the art of dance.	As structures of spatio-rhythmical speech in the sense of an European experiential culture. (Appearing as quantitative but qualitatively ingenious: individual dance – chamber dance – group dance.) Predominance of spatial structure, predominance of rhythmical properties.		Movement expression in gesture (pantomime), play and opera.

Forming of works – composition

In the sense of Choreosophy, Choreology and Choreography. The predominance of laws. Predominance of free intuition. Connection

Figure 7.3 What is necessary?

> The fundamental laws regulating the dance artwork have been known for a millennium. They are at the present time forgotten or ossified not unlike laws of poetry, music or other arts that fall into oblivion from time to time or are not observed. The logic and order of dance is called Choreology that deals with balancing relationships between the movement force and its unfolding in the space. Choreology should not be mistaken for Choreosophy and Choreography. Choreosophy is the science addressing the spiritual relationships between contents of the art of dance. It helps us understand that dance can convey other things than for example poetry and music. Choreography is the dance form itself. Firstly: as dance, and in the second place: as notation or the drawing of the dance artwork with relevant movement signs.

In reading *Choreography*, one can see his debt to the theory of the ballet's five positions as one of the fundamental means of spatial orientation. Further, his explanation of Choreosophy, Choreology and Choreography is synchronous with the concerns of his Choreographic Institute and its endeavour to develop a general movement science. This was also the period when Laban intensified the research on his movement and dance notation to be published in 1928 and presented at the second Dance Congress in Essen.

Laban further differentiates between Choreology and Choreography:

> The analytical choreology articulates the dance ornament into spatial directions that are dynamically differentiated, out of whichever returning spatial waves and spatial forms are constructed. The latter are words of the language of dance that can be in part translated into concepts. A gesture of worship, a bacchantic turn, among other motifs are about such dance words. The study of choreography shows how sentences and poems can be built from such words creating a dance sense. Dance structures that the viewer receives with devotion, pleasure or enthusiasm, are for him obviously dance-like, in other

words, they speak to him clearly of an inner motivating power and developing driving force that is anchored in a universally human experience. A simple quiet walking can be breathtakingly transformed into chaotic maenad-like racing or the other way around. Here too there are approximating explanations in words given to a thousand dance contents. However, in spite of this facility of being explained, the work doesn't need to be an everyday action, or mime or drama, but can be a dance.

He also discusses different types of movement that can bring a variety of dance forms and contents:

The form of the dance artwork is first of all characterized by the type of movement that is used as a means of expression in a particular piece. We know of essentially different types of movement, on one hand, the everyday movement or functional movement – to which by the way belongs also the health-promoting gymnastics – and on the other hand, the artistic movement. The pantomimic form of the dance artwork arises from the use, as well as stylization of functional movement. Pure dance speaks through purely ornamental fluctuations of balance. However, the impression remains arabesque-like if the inner urge is missing. The emergence of dance contents ruled by one's physical urges is of a creative nature and cannot be learned or forced. There are no persons who are without an initial natural urge for dance. Look at a child. The task of dance pedagogy is to grasp, understand and order these drives and their ornamentally-rhythmic forms of expression.

Regarding performance spaces, Laban argues:

Today a dance piece, among others, does not have a site of its own where it can be performed effectively for the audience. Perhaps in a circus. In any case not on the proscenium stage. The dance arabesque is three-dimensional and can be clearly perceived from above. The dance theatre firstly as a space, and secondly as a well trained ensemble that does justice technically and spiritually to the composition and the dance creator, and to an audience with an educated sense of form and movement as well as motivation – all these are prerequisites and phenomena that are so far completely missing in creating a dance artwork.

It is as though his statement about the shortcomings of the proscenium stage echo his early attempts in designing a theatre in the round that he proposed between 1916 and 1922. They can be found in his *A Life for Dance*[7] and in *The Vision of Dynamic Space*.[8]

Though Laban had an equal proportion of male and female collaborators, the social tradition of patriarchy at times dominated his views. This can be seen in statements such as:

> The dance artwork has nothing in common with body culture and harmonious movement. Those who view body culture or even giving expression of sexuality as the purpose of dance, are dance enemies. Those dance critics and writers, such as Fred Hildenbrandt, who appears to promote dance through flowery descriptions of predominantly feminine bodies support dance illiteracy, missing out on any inner relationship with the language of dance. The cause for this inability is the uncultured nature of one's own driving force. Here is evident a cultural need for pure dance artworks in which foremost male dancers should participate. . . . The design of a dance artwork will incidentally – as all building – remain predominantly an activity of man.

Granted, Laban was promoting dance for men but it is as though in these statements he neglected to acknowledge the works of some of his talented female students and collaborators, such as Wigman and Bereska.

In outlining the current status of dance artwork, Laban shows some pessimistic views with regard to the development of dance in the last quarter of the century, and offers several unfavourable observations:

A clear composition and interpretation of the dance work are a *conditio sine qua non* for further development of dance. Until today there has been no art of dance in the true sense of the word. We have barely differentiated social dance from the art of dance. And in the art of dance or even more in studies and attempts of several centuries that should mark the start of this kind of art, we are still struggling in form and content against the overtones of music and drama. The art of dance is the most differentiated of all arts. It does not stand – as it is often falsely stated – at the beginning of each development of art, rather it creates its peak (see China and India). Only mature cultures produce dance artworks. Our race approaches the cultural stage in which the dance artwork will become an existentially essential mirror of our driving force. Dance is perhaps the art of the future.

In spite of the complaints about the overtones of music and drama as well as his conjecture that dance may be the art of the future, Laban and his students and collaborators created several pieces without music and dramatic content within the realm of the art of dance, such as in the 1925 *Choreographische Tänze/ Tanz-Compositionen* (choreographic dances/dance composition).

In addition, several works of the Laban Dance Theatre embodied the art of dance of his time (Figures 7.4–7.9).

Figure 7.4 Rehearsal for *Agamemnon* (1927)
Source: Photograph from the John Hodgson Archive, Brotherton Library, University of Leeds.

CHOREOGRAPHIC INSTITUTE LABAN AND DANCE CONGRESS

Figure 7.5 Gleisner Movement Choir (1927)

Source: From *Der Moderne Tanz*, Dr Rudolf Lämmel (Peter J. Oestergaard), Verlag, Berlin, 1926.

Figure 7.6 Herta Feist School, Berlin

Source: From *Der Moderne Tanz*, Dr Rudolf Lämmel (Peter J. Oestergaard), Verlag, Berlin, 1926.

Figure 7.7 Rehearsal for *Titan* (1927), photo given to John Hodgson by Albrecht Knust

Source: John Hodgson Archive, Brotherton Library, University of Leeds.

Figure 7.8 Rehearsal for *Titan* (1927), photo given to John Hodgson by Albrecht Knust

Source: John Hodgson Archive, Brotherton Library, University of Leeds.

Figure 7.9 Rehearsal for *Titan* (1927), photo given to John Hodgson by Albrecht Knust
Source: John Hodgson Archive, Brotherton Library, University of Leeds.

Notes

1 Brochure for the *Choreographic Institut Laban* is a photocopy deposited at the Rudolf Laban Archive that Laban bequeathed to Lisa Ullmann (1946–1973).
2 Article published in *Monographien der Ausbildungsschulen für Tanz und Tänzerische Körperbildung* [Monographs of Training Schools for Dance and Bodily Education in Dance], Volume I, ed. Liesel Freund (Berlin: Leo Altertum Verlag, 1929), pp. 11–14.
3 G. Snell, '*Tanzwissenschaft*' (*Science of Dance*), *Die Schönheit*, 1926, pp. 62–67; G. Snell, '*Grundlagen einer Allgemeinen Tanzlehre*' (*Foundations for a General Theory of Dance*), Part I in *Schrifttanz*, Vol II, No 1, January 1929, pp. 8–11; Part II in *Schrifttanz* Vol II, No 2, May 1929, pp. 21–24; Part III in *Schrifttanz* Vol II, No 3, August 1929, pp. 48–50.
4 In the footnotes to the article, Laban informs us that Universal Edition in Vienna publishes a periodical journal *Schrifttanz* that communicates to the German Society for Dance Script which in turn supports the aims of the Choreographic Institute.

5   R. Laban, *Schrifttanz*, no. I, 1929, p. 19.
6   R. Laban, 'The Dance Artwork or the Very Image of Itself', *Die Tat: Monatschrift für die Zukunft deutscher Kultur*, November 1927, pp. 588–591.
7   *LFD*, p. 186.
8   *VDS*, p. 53.

Chapter eight

The Pageant of the Trades and Crafts, Vienna, June 1929

Introduction

Dick McCaw

A Life for Dance was published in 1935 when Laban was Director of the *Deutsche Tanzbühne* (German Dance Organisation) in Berlin under the Nazi regime. In this autobiography he exercises his flair for descriptive writing, and although dates and names are not mentioned, and chronology is not respected, it is a vivid account of important moments in his life working as an organiser, teacher, researcher and creator of dance. His *Festzug der Gewerbe* (Pageant of the Trades) which took place in Vienna in June 1929 must have been an important event for him, since he returns to it in *Effort and Recovery* (written between 1950 and 1953) where he reiterates his belief in the value of active participation in movement:

> This shows very clearly that our modern trend to be a passive and critical spectator is an arch-enemy of the real recovery to be gained from the art of movement, in dancing as well as also in communal singing or speaking. There are obviously two kinds of movement, one is presentative,

made for an audience, and the other kind is made for the recovery value it contains which the performers enjoy by themselves. In adult civilisations there is, as it seems, not much place for the latter kind. . . . Thousands of people can now experience the benefit of the rhythm and flow of dance, not only as spectators but also as active players in the joy of moving.[1]

Public processions, parades and celebrations were central to Laban's career from an early age. When apprenticed to a scene painter in Bratislava (and thus probably still in his teens), he created *tableaux vivants* (literally, 'living pictures') to celebrate the arrival of the provincial ruler who was 'coming for the unveiling of a great monument':

> We were asked not only to design triumphal arches but also *tableaux vivants* which were to be put on at the city theatre. My pride knew no bounds when I was allowed to get my fancifully-dressed friends into the oddest positions. With one group, which was to be formed round the bust of the ruler, I had tried out all sorts of positions while my master was away and when he returned I showed them to him one after the other. When I gave the word, 'Now, ladies and gentlemen, position number one!' the pianist struck up a flourish. And so on for number two and all the rest. My master and the corporation who were also there found each new tableau more enchanting than the last, and finally it was decided to show all of them as a sequence, each one with an increasingly dramatic flourish. This was how my first moving *tableau vivant* was created, and it opened up a completely new field of activity to my imagination. . . . I designed hundreds of these sequences and gradually they developed into real group-dance scenes.[2]

Thus he moved from the still to the living image. Valerie Preston-Dunlop's biography notes how he made a living in his early life organising carnivals and parades in and around Munich:

His first full carnival season in 1911–12 consisted of arranging lavish parties and outlandish costume entertainments, word having got around that he was a capable movement director. . . . He also had to spend time in the winter of 1912–13 earning money through the Munich carnival celebrations which, as before, seemed to be an almost constant run of balls and events in November, December and January. . . . As carnival 1913 came to its climax on *Rosenmontag*, Laban wrote, 'It drives me crazy . . . they are starting to point me out as the "dancing master".' It would seem that his carnival performances were attracting more attention than in the previous season, but personally he was frustrated with having insufficient resources to ensure their success.[3]

She goes on to describe his preparations for a Munich festival in 1914 for which he created 'a burlesque, *The Birth of the Dance in Hell*'.[4] In his curriculum vitae, he 'advertised himself as a *Festspiel-Regisseur* (Producer of Arts Festivals)'.[5]

Throughout Laban's writings we find passages about celebratory dance and movement, and these parades and burlesques of the 1910s could be seen as forerunners of his movement choirs of the 1920s and 1930s. Preston-Dunlop makes this connection clear:

> His idea was to rekindle the interest of the urban workers in their own traditions by researching the movement patterns, and, if any, the folk dance material that included their craft. He intended that the workers should, so to speak, dance their own industry. He planned to present the different dances in the most up-to-date manner possible, including the use of the absolutely novel loudspeaker system for recorded music, also in its infancy. A marriage of tradition and modernity was his overall vision. . . . Laban's daily challenge was to turn the workers' minds beyond simply working for hard-earned financial reward to becoming aware of the work rhythms of their trade, for which there was understandable resistance. Why interrupt a routine to make conscious an unconscious automatic act?[6]

Here we have an example of many facets of Laban: his marriage of tradition and innovation, his vision of people isolated in their working lives coming together in celebrative movement, and his future involvement in factories in Northern England in the 1940s. What follow are descriptions of the parade in two specialist magazines, and then Laban's own description in *A Life for Dance*.

LABAN'S PARADE OF TRADES AND GUILDS IN VIENNA[7]

A movement choir of several hundred girls, prepared by Laban and his chief co-workers . . . in weeks of unsparing effort, was not noticed as well as it might have been in the super-human dimensions of the procession. In this it was shown how unbelievably difficult it is to work with people with little physical skill, which in this case – probably for good reasons – was necessary. The movement sequences practised to the specially composed music for the procession were really beautiful and extremely expressive but suffered a lack of precision. With organized groups of people used to movement (sports clubs, etc.), profound and lasting effects could have been achieved.

The publicity had promised a dancing procession, a creative, new shape of the processional idea based on movement rhythm, but during the preparations one piece after another broke away from the original plan, and what was left was a compromise which the good citizens had forced on the artist Rudolf Laban. The industries stifled the dance, not least by the massive physical presence of the committees of the different societies, who took the opportunity of moving, solemnly-robed and perspiring, ahead of their products.

LABAN'S VIENNA PARADE[8]

On Sunday 9th June a six-kilometre snake of colourful festively decked-out vehicles, rolled and danced along the *Ringstrasse* in Vienna to the *Praten*, accompanied by many thousand people, mostly young, mostly dancing along in rhythm. For the first time dance formed the basis for a folk festival of huge proportions in this festive pageant. It was estimated that there were one million spectators along the route and at the stopping places. A giant city had been made to participate. Laban, who was the designer as well as director, screen-painter and dance-master of this undertaking, had the idea of creating a dance festival of labour, which was to show the working rhythm of the various trades. It was apparent from the rhythms that this was not just a superficially observed simulation of the various work methods, but a bringing to light of an almost forgotten treasure of craft culture through profound and painstaking study. In this way extremely interesting motifs became apparent through Laban's intensive preparations, whose work psychology might be worth exploring.

Each group showed one trade. Since the motto of the pageant was 'Then and Now', the development from manual labour to machine production was inevitably stressed. It was pleasant to note that the 'up-to-date' elements were well received. So working conveyors belts, welding and riveting machines hissed past, their droning noise sometimes being the only accompaniment to the novel work dances.

The modern electric and radio industry supplied loud-hailers, which carried the music – especially composed for the pageant – for miles around. Cubist boxes mounted on the vehicles replaced the medieval heralds who are usual on such occasions. The grouping of the pageant was arranged according to human needs: clothes, building, food, entertainment, tourism. In the last category all nations were represented by their national dances. And indeed all manner of dancers were shown. Large movement choirs divided the procession into sections. The working youths of Vienna danced in their work-clothes. Like a revue appeared the umbrella, handbag, fan and hat girls among all this. The groups of milliners and washerwomen were especially delightful. Agriculture around Vienna formed the final part of the pageant with harvest and grape gathering dances.

The whole population of Vienna, those who weren't taking part in the pageant, turned out in full as spectators, starting from Bundespresident Miklas and Mayor Seitz. The round dances by the children stirred even the local dignitaries into movement. Countless pictures in the local papers on Monday showed the Mayor embracing children in the dance milling around him. A joyful wave of participation went through the public, rising to loud ovations when Laban drove along the procession, regulating and encouraging.

Film and sound crews were busily at work, so that one can hope to see something of the pageant everywhere. The whole undertaking can be regarded as a triumph of modern dance art. Many talked of a 'conquest of the Ringstrasse by the dance'. In any case it showed a broad-minded beginning of change in the attitude towards dance in our festival processions.

EVERYDAY LIFE AND FESTIVAL[9]

Once, in a large city, I was asked to organise a pageant for the crafts and trades. It so happened that it had long been a dream of mine to arrange a dancing procession and I had made a number of sketches for it years ago, so now I was able to produce firm proposals straight away.

'Of course you will have to teach the people yourself! We certainly want this pageant, but for the people to dance in it. . . .' With these words and a gesture of doubt the great man entrusted me with the organisation of the procession, and then dismissed me. I had to start from scratch. There was a list of a few guild officials, an empty office in the former imperial riding school and the comforting reassurance of the tourist bureau that it would all come right in time. But we had no time! In a few weeks, the giant snake, seven kilometres long with about ten thousand participants, countless decorated floats, costumes, and bands, was to move through the town, and so far nobody yet had shown any desire to come forward and join the crazy professor from Berlin whose mind was made up to lead the whole procession dancing through the city.

It was easy to win the hearts of the young, and to this day I think with gratitude and feeling of the battalion of laundry-girls and milliners who helped my ideas on to victory. It was more difficult to win over the young gentlemen, who at first declined with dignity to do any vigorous movement, though in the end they were very good at it. But it was really bad with the old gentlemen, who were worn out by political and economic struggles and who in endless meetings arrived at decisions which they painstakingly recorded and then abandoned after all. I ran from guild to guild. Invariably, I was received by a distrustful, grave-faced assembly of as many as a hundred or more grey-haired masters who pronounced my attempt at establishing a connection between their crafts and dance to be wicked nonsense. Only when they understood that I did not intend to organise a kind of public hop but a representation of the working movements used in their crafts did they begin to grow more amenable.

I had the most interesting experience in connection with this. There is hardly a trade which in its manual operations does not have a tradition of working movements and also a festive application of them. The metal crafts provided no problem. Forging and hammering have a natural rhythm. I myself had to swing a hammer and learn to forge a horseshoe in a Styrian, Scottish or Italian way. I learnt that furriers beat pelts in the spring with Spanish canes, heard what a wealth of forgotten songs and sayings the shoemakers, tailors, tanners, bakers and hundreds of other craftsmen have, witnessed strange ways of handling and stepping, and out of all this, with perseverance and imagination, wove the dance fabric of the pageant. The most important thing was to enlighten the guilds, from the masters down to the apprentices about their own traditions and to arouse their enthusiasm for them. In most cases this was completely successful and, even after many years, I had the satisfaction of hearing from one or the other that I had given them more than just a festival and a momentary advertisement. Young men, who have since become masters, have told me that because of the pageant they turned to their trades with far more understanding and love, and that for them the revival of old traditions especially helped to make their work pleasanter and lighter. On the other hand I had glimpsed the bottomless misery caused by loss of loyalty to work, and at first I sometimes felt so discouraged and disillusioned that I often wished the whole pageant would go to the devil.

Gradually, the conviction grew in me that it was not entirely pointless to awaken in working people a feeling for their work rhythm. As a certain easing of their difficulties and relaxation of their rigidity became increasingly apparent, I ignored all resistance and pressed on undaunted with my work. For this gigantic task would only succeed if I went straight for my target and ignored all the antagonism, derision, even, and malice.

In my mind was the simple but disdained idea of dancing, which was regarded so askance, and I had not only to revive feeling gone rusty but also steer through the high tides of passion which were nourished by the political and economic confusion these poor people had to suffer. Until then, as an artist, I had hardly concerned myself with politics and even less with economic questions, which were not within my professional sphere.

All at once I found myself confronted with the intrigues and animosities which were the order of the day between trade and industry and between retailer and manufacturer. Quite apart from narrow-minded disputes over competence, which frequently interfered with my arrangements, professional jealousy and class hatred between representatives of the various trades made agreement almost impossible. According to their social standing and material circumstance they made all sorts of impossible requests, usually with the aim of somehow humiliating their professional rivals. All this was not conducive to producing a festive atmosphere.

To many people I soon became a confidant and adviser on these matters, and sometimes even arbitrator when controversies were too strong – all for the sake of the festival. What

I got to know at that time about individual fates, filled me with both compassion and horror. When one had established a more or less personal contact with ten thousand strangers, almost as if by magic, and had to share their joys and sorrows, it was impossible to remain unmoved. As always the magic wand which opened their hearts to me was my art. When at least we were able to absorb ourselves in play and movement I witnessed over and over again their tired eyes lighting up and their distress disappearing, at least temporarily. Worst of all, however, and far more serious than the economic differences, was the raging national chaos which occupied their hearts and minds. I had been to many countries and wherever German was spoken I felt at home.[10] In all these struggles factiousness played a great part. Even if a Bavarian grumbled about a Prussian, or if in the north, east or west strange views were circulating about the opposite point of the compass, nowhere had one so much the feeling of a complete uprooting or the impression of a branch dying away on a huge tree as in this large city. People were un-German, and would have liked to be different.

The tradesmen and artisans belonged to the most diverse political camps. One guild was right-wing, another left-wing, and even within the guilds themselves there were factions which abused and denigrated each other with all their might and main. When it was all overcome, it seemed a fantastic miracle that I had succeeded in bringing these contrary fellows to an understanding at all. There was no trace of this awful jumble of convictions when they followed one another dancing happily and peacefully, united in the celebration of craftsmanship.

But we were not there for a long time yet. Already at the time of our endless consultations I and my small staff of assistants[11] had completed the designs for the floats, cars and costumes. When judging the designs, the hideous errors in taste that had infiltrated the once so exemplary craftsmanship in this city became very conspicuous. Again there were endless disputes, and every conceivable kind of stupid trash was proposed to me. A helpless, mawkish pathetic love of kitsch was the order of the day. There was hardly ever an original idea of style in which a creative capacity could be sensed. It was pitiful to see the stubbornness and lack of imagination with which the dullest travesty of a faded philistine splendour was defended. Yet another educational task! But in the end the allusion to work rhythm, work attire and work atmosphere was understood. After a few wild attempts to persuade me to accept a cheap strolling theatre of the Middle Ages as traditional, forms were at last found which also corresponded with my fundamental ideas.

The worst offenders were the painters, sculptors and architects who were called in as consultants by the guilds. If they were not out to flatter the inartistic taste of their employers, they proposed their own home brew which would have made even the hair of a lunatic stand on end. Expressionism was fashionable and there was no distortion and destruction in representation that was not used to replace a lost and healthy sense of form. The fundamental idea – dance and its possibilities – was fiercely opposed. Never before and nowhere else did I meet such ignorance concerning my ideas as with these disciples of art. To break their resistance with brusque rejection would have injudiciously drawn down on my head the animosity of a large group of people with whom I had after all to work. I therefore took great pains to convince them and finally managed to win over most of these quarrelsome artists to my plans.

Meanwhile my staff had grown considerably in size. To my two small office rooms were added quite a number of halls and workshops on all floors of the huge baroque building. They were essential, as each of the four hundred different trades which wanted to take part needed one or more decorated floats, and a fair number of the participants had to be suitably dressed. The large riding arenas were turned into rehearsal halls and two thousand five hundred young people came every evening after work to prepare for the dancing pageant. They marched, walked, solemnly processed, practised swings and dance steps, and above all did the dance which has its home in that city – the waltz. The waltz in all its variations and forms, many newly created for the occasion, was a kind of red thread running through the whole festival procession. People who were stiff and out of training were taken out and made more flexible with simple gymnastic exercises. Unmusical ones – not many in that city – were 'rhythmicised' until they could keep in time with the others. As far as possible I tried not to turn down anyone who wanted to have an active share in our festivity. In one of the halls a hundred girl umbrella-makers rehearsed with their little round sun defences. Charming parasol plays were created and the girls, who were mostly pretty and graceful, were thrilled with them. The milliners and dressmakers paraded in another hall; they were one of the largest groups, several hundred strong. When I wanted to encourage them with praise and said – most rashly – 'Excellent, beautiful, made for kissing!', they took me at my word and a few hundred of them lined up for a kiss. It was lovely but rather exhausting.

Every day was full of amusing or serious episodes, liveliness, gaiety and enthusiasm and also of heavy responsibility. By the time the festival came, we had all become such bosom friends that I forgot the earlier ill-feeling and happily got down to the last-minute preparations. I shall never forget that night when I conducted the dress rehearsal in the huge quadrangle of the old royal stables in moonlight and under a brilliant starlit sky. In addition to the two thousand five hundred dancers, a number of amusing special groups were present, consisting mostly of professional dancers and actors. Then there were also the craft groups with their occupational dances. A giant loudspeaker was placed high up in the background. Some three thousand participants assembled in procession order, and their costumes were scrutinised for the last time. Then the loudspeaker bellowed out its songs and dances.[12] The leaders took their places and we were off. All around me – for I stood alone in the middle of the quadrangle – began such stepping, gliding, jumping and turning by these thousands as I never beheld before or since. In those hours the dream of a dancing master became a reality. These groups of happy young people dancing round me in the light of the full moon moved me more than the numerous ovations which I had received on the stage over the years. The complex structure of this festive procession had been exacting work. But the marvellous devotion to dance which my young friends showed was worth all the toil of a lifetime. Their enthusiasm was boundless. It was as if everyone was under the spell of the unifying, inspiring power of the dance. Countless people shook my hand, their eyes shining, and my favourite battalion, the little milliner-girls, almost drowned me with a rain of flowers, which they had arranged for the end. It was an unusual experience being buried neck-deep in flowers with the dark blue, starry sky above and thousands of ghost-like faces radiant with happiness. The best part of all was that we had no spectators – it was our own festival before the festival. Then as morning drew on it became quite cool. For the last time I refreshed my troupe with coffee and cakes in one of the halls. Another two days and the great event would start. . . .

At last, towards morning, I am alone in my office. There, the telephone is already rattling away. Everything is as grey as grey outside, and rain is quietly enjoying itself drizzling down the window-panes. It's the radio station asking: 'Is the festival going to take place or not?' A difficult half-minute of reflection and then I say down the telephone 'We shall dance whatever happens.' What a responsibility, setting a million spectators into motion, turning a whole bustling city upside down and all for a leap in the dark! But there is no choice. Feverish activity begins in the courtyard; some of the floats which were delivered only during the night, are knocked and hammered into shape. I go off to inspect the routes and main stands. It has stopped raining. Organized by two old generals, a district has filled up with cars and people. The sun is coming out, it's getting warm, hot, wonderful! At last, the giant snake begins to move and its march-past lasts for hours. From my central stand I direct operations with powerful steam sirens, telephones, messengers on bicycles, radio and flag-signals. Several times I had to dash along the seven-kilometre route by car to where the procession would disband and back again, as incidents were reported over the telephone. Each time, it was more difficult for my car to get through. The spectators became aware of me through the cheers of my dancers, and when I was recognised, the cordons in some places were quite useless. The hundreds of thousands of people lining the route got into motion and I was feted in a way which I had never dreamed of. A victorious general might have been used to such things, but a dancing master . . .

ABOUT MOVEMENT CHOIRS

I have already mentioned that a large movement choir took part in this festival procession. When, more than a dozen years ago, a number of young people from all walks of life had come to our courses and lectures to refresh themselves through physical exercise and to study the basic elements of the dance-form developed in Germany nobody had ever heard of a movement choir, and even the concept of it did not exist either here or anywhere else. Gradually, out of our exercises, grew at first modest, and later more extensive plays which not only appealed greatly to the participants but also to the occasional visitor. These plays differed in many ways from the new dances which originated in the circle of our professional dancers. They were really quite different from what had so far been called dance. The movements were simpler and the basic ideas of the plays were not show or stage biased. We conquered space in common swinging and leaping, in measured, slow stepping or sprightly walking and running. It was soon evident that the interweaving paths as well as the bodily attitudes and kinds of movement accompanying them had an import whose significance is rooted in the human psyche. Audiences were excluded for the time being, except for the occasional chance visitor. The sensitivity and spontaneity of expression of the participants were greatly heightened and clarified through moving together in common rhythm. It was a time when the world was filled with vague unrest on the one hand and a forced desire for unlimited amusement on the other. In both these mental attitudes there was a lack of dignity and innocent enjoyment, of healthy delight in physical ability and of natural poise which is implicit in the human form and its simplest movements. The discovery and practice of this ideal bearing in states of collectedness and in vital dynamic movement became the basis of our first movement choir plays.

We soon got the impression, which was reinforced by our occasional audiences, that we should show our compositions to the public, for nearly everyone who watched us was stimulated into joining in. Meanwhile, our plays had developed into small choir-works. One of the first was Dawning Light[13] in which we experienced the change from stepping in subdued sadness to the awakening of the revitalising capacity which is dormant in the body. I emphasise 'experienced' and not 'presented' because at this stage we had no wish to show or convince an audience – although later on, a presentation-style emerged effortlessly and without our doing. We were solely concerned with experiencing in ourselves and in togetherness the increased vigour of the spiritual-emotional-physical forces which are united in dance. Why? Because we were drawn to it, we benefited from it, and we were inspired by it.

Once during one of our social gatherings the question arose of what name we should give our activities. There was no school, and there were no courses at which anything was taught or drummed in. It was decidedly community dance but not professional dance or social dance in the traditional sense. People who came to join us had no wish to become professional dancers. They liked stage dance – as spectators – and had learnt to appreciate it better since they had come to move themselves. Then from somewhere a voice said: 'Really, we are a movement choir.' This designation met with unanimous approval, though we had no idea that this newly-coined word would spread so widely in such a short time. In the lightning speed with which the movement choir idea travelled through Germany and soon abroad as well, it had quite a chequered career. Though the original pure concept was preserved by us and others, movement choirs got used for all kinds of other purposes, and were even abused. Well-trained groups of people were ideal for walking-on parts in the theatre, for dance groups and other similar things. They could also be used for representing communal experiences and in no time at all movement choirs were founded for ideological, political, and even scientific purposes, in which the movement experience retreated into the background and gave way to the conscious representation of some ideology or other. Many groups were formed hurriedly and without adequate preliminary training, and they soon brought the original idea of dance-experience into discredit.

By now it has been proved that a movement choir festival can hold its own before a dance-critical audience. Such a festival, however, should concentrate not so much on the audience's desire for entertainment as on manifesting the joy of moving together. All things have their evolution. It is indisputable that the movement choir work preceded the art form of choric dance, and it can be assumed that individual choirs will develop further in the direction of festival productions in the future.

Notes

1 *ER*, p. 218.
2 *LD*, pp. 11–13.
3 Preston-Dunlop (1998: 21–26).
4 Ibid., p. 33.
5 Ibid., p. 39.
6 Ibid., pp. 145–147.
7 Harry Prinz in *Der Tanz*, 1929 (in JHA, Folder 39, Item 40).
8 *Singchor und Tanz*, 1 July 1929, vols 13/14, no. 46. p. 182 (in JHA, Box 27, Folder 30, Item 2).
9 *LD*, pp. 142–150.
10 Laban's mother tongue was Hungarian, and French was his second language. But since his work had developed mainly in German-speaking parts of Europe, the German language provided an immediate link with people. [Note by Lisa Ullmann.]
11 Laban's main assistant was Fritz Klingenbeck, who later became a well-known theatre director, dramaturge and playwright in Austria. Also assisting was Lotte Krause, later a leading choreographer and dance teacher in Israel. [Note by Lisa Ullmann.]

12 Sound amplification was in those days still very crude and a great hazard. [Note by Lisa Ullmann.]
13 An attempt at translating the German title *Lichtwende*, meaning 'solstice', the turning-point of the light, and in this movement choir work the turn is towards the increase of light. *Lichtwende* was performed by the first movement choir of 80 lay-dancers in Hamburg in 1923, and it contained a section for percussion only, without any dance, which was executed on the stage by the dancers – an entirely new experience for an audience in those days. [Note by Lisa Ullmann.]

Chapter nine

Laban and Movement Notation

Selection and translated by Roderyk Lange

Introduction

Roderyk Lange

The area of dance is a latecomer to literacy. The problem of devising a system of notation, which incorporates the three-dimensional aspect of movement, concurrently with the progression of time, seemed to be insurmountable over centuries. The most common way was to describe dances verbally. However, any verbal description cannot convey the content of movement. It is a very different idiom from the spoken language.

With the codification of the European court dance, from the Renaissance on, arose the need to register the various dance progressions so as to keep them unified for instruction. One started to use the letters of the alphabet to denote the particular *pas*. These letters were recorded alongside the relevant music notation (Figure 9.1):[1]

R   reverence
r   reprise
b   branle

s simple
d double
c congé

Figure 9.1 Dance instruction in the work by M. Toulouze, *L'Art et Instruction de bien Danser*, Paris, 1488

During the reign of Louis XIV, the court dance was further developed under the royal dance master Pierre Beauchamp. A special dance notation was then devised, which was published in 1700 by Raoul Auger Feuillet (Figure 9.2).[2] Again, this system concerns only the one convention of the codified court dance, and cannot be applied to any other dance tradition. Additionally, one has to point out that the 765 signs of the Feuillet dance notation are only mnemonic signs for the particular *pas*, which were well established and commonly known within the European court dance culture. Only the time aspect was universally denoted, with bar strokes introduced along the line of the progression.

Figure 9.2 The minuet recorded in the Feuillet system
Source: K. Tomlinson, about 1730.

This court dance notation, however, lasted only until the French Revolution, as the dance convention of the following period changed fundamentally. During the nineteenth century many attempts were made to introduce a workable solution (Figure 9.3).

All these endeavours failed, as they were not based on the relevant movement factors. Instead, successions of static stick figures and some other graphic signs were used, which could not convey the full progression of movement (Figure 9.4).[3]

The very much-needed solution in establishing a full graphic movement notation was found by Rudolf Laban only in 1928. For the first time a universal system of movement notation was devised. Laban called it Kinetography. This system allows one to notate concurrently the three dimensions in space and the time element. With this it became possible to notate the progression of movement, involving the continuous changes in space and in time.

Rudolf Laban was the prominent practitioner of modem dance in the twentieth century, but he was also an outstanding movement theoretician. Very early he recognised the desperate need for a universal system of movement notation. He also devised some other solutions in movement analysis (Effort, Choreutics). Generally, Laban established dance technology, as opposed to dance technique.

In his seminal book *Choreography* of 1926, he deals with his concept of the 'Art of Movement' and he introduces a system of notating specific regularities in movement manifestations. For this purpose he devised sets of particular signs. This, however, was not yet a full graphic notation.

Then, suddenly, in 1928, Laban published a brief introduction entitled '*Grundprinzipien der Bewegungsschrift*'[4] (The Basic Rules of a Movement Script). In this article Laban states:

> Kinetography, or the movement script, has clearly two differing aims. The first is the task to register movement sequences and dances. The advantage of such a possibility is clearly discernible. It was sought after over centuries and many more or less effective attempts were continuously undertaken.

LABAN AND MOVEMENT NOTATION

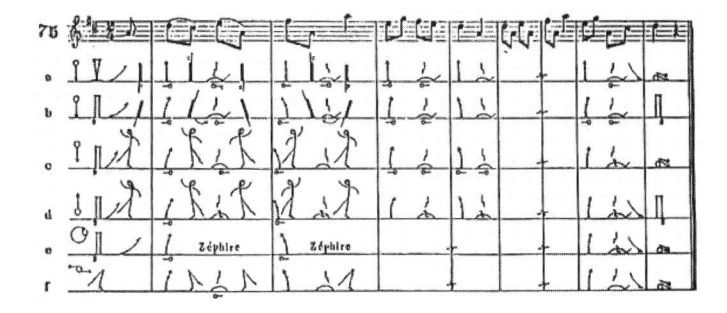

Figure 9.3 'Pas de Zéphire', recorded by A. Zorn, 1887

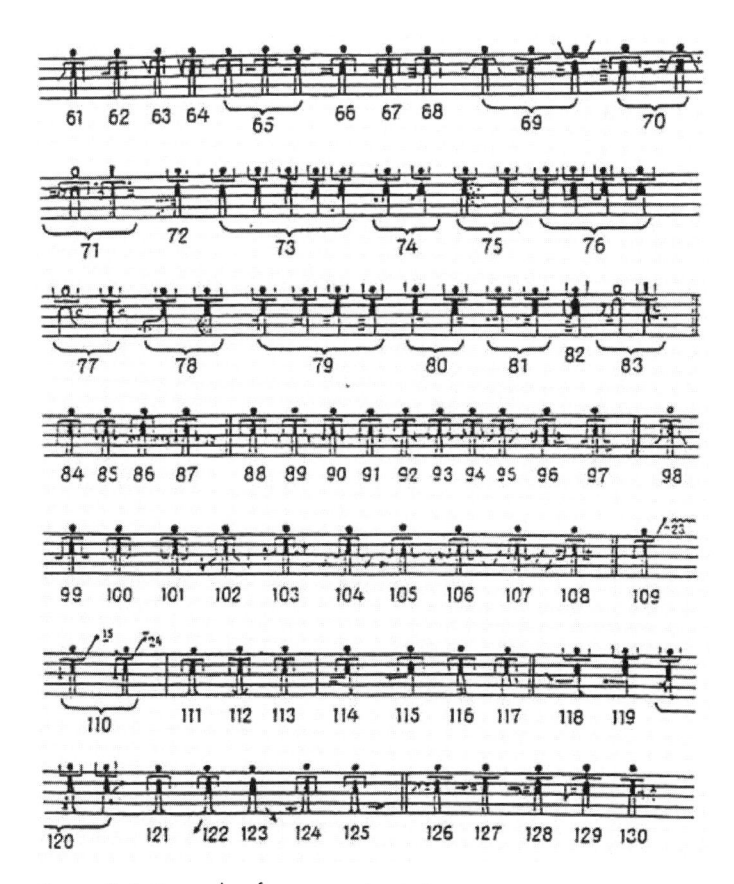

Figure 9.4 Example of movement notation
Source: Desmond, *Rhythmographik*, Leipzig (1919).

> The other task concerning the mental aspect is far more important. It deals with the aim to make the analysis of a movement progression more precise and to relieve it of any indistinctness, which makes the dance idiom unclear and additionally monotonous.
>
> The first clear difference to be made, in viewing a movement progression, is the divided examination of the movement flow (the time rhythm) on the one hand, and of the movement shapes (space rhythm) on the other.
>
> The time rhythm will be recorded linearly by longer and shorter lines, which represent proportionally the duration of the movement.

In this article of 1928, he concludes: 'The final aim of kinetography is, however, not a dance script, but a dance arising from notation.' This became the name for the whole movement he instigated.

The well-known publisher Universal Edition, in Vienna and Leipzig, in 1928 started the journal entitled *Schrifttanz*, being the organ of the then established German Association for *Schrifttanz*. This publication was headed by Alfred Schlee, and it contains Laban's seminal articles and some other contributions of that period. *Schrifttanz* appeared between 1928 and 1931. Eleven issues of the journal were published, together with two separate booklets. These two separate publications contain in detail the outline of the new notation system and its application:

1   1928/29 Methodik – Orthographic – Erläuterungen *(Methods – Orthography – Commentaries)*
2   1930 Kleine Tänze mit Vorübungen *(Short Dances with preliminary exercises)*
3   Four group and solo dances by Laban and Dussia Bereska.

In the introduction to the first of these issues, Laban states:

> This publication contains a full and complete presentation of all movement recording possibilities within Kinetography Laban. The introduction to this notation

system is divided into two sections or parts: the Method and the Orthography.

The first part, concerning the method, contains a straightforward explanation of the signs applied. This was presented in this form, so as to allow the dancer to gain a clear overview of all the signs used.

The Orthography explains the application of various signs for particular movements. (Here we already have some notated movement sequences which have been recorded and which can be physically performed.)

With this publication, the first-ever universal, full graphic, movement notation was established. Laban applied his notation widely and had his own choreographies recorded and reconstructed from scores. His big movement choir composition, entitled *Titan* (see Chapter 6), was recreated from notation in 1927 in Magdeburg, and in 1928 in Hamburg. In 1929, his recorded choreography *Wandlung* (Transformation) was performed by the movement choir in Mannheim. In 1930, Laban's notated choreography to Wagner's *Tannhäuser* (Bacchanals) was recreated in Bayreuth.

> Besides scoring numerous opera ballets, my colleagues and I transcribed into this notation several large communal dance-plays which were then produced directly from it. In conjunction with my friend Knust, I wrote the movement score of a festival play for a thousand performers, and sent the notation to sixty towns from which the performers at the festival meeting were drawn. As our scores had been studied by the sixty local groups, the whole thousand people were able to dance together at the first rehearsal, performing not only the main motives, but the whole rather elaborate choreography, lasting two hours, with very few mistakes or interruptions.[5]

In 1926, Laban established his Choreographisches Institut Laban in Würzburg (see Chapter 7). In 1927, it was transferred to Berlin-Grünewald. Gertrud Snell was the assistant for notation there. She was directly involved in the development of Kinetography. Many choreographies were then recorded and notation courses conducted.

Laban in his endeavours in establishing the system of Kinetography was helped by many of his pupils and co-workers, like Dussia Bereska, Kurt Jooss, and at a later period by Valerie Preston-Dunlop. The most prominent contributor was Albrecht Knust. Laban acknowledges his input to the system in the Preface to Knust's *Handbook of Kinetography Laban*[6] of 1956 (the English version appeared in 1958):

> When I said before that Knust has used my kinetographic alphabet, I have to add that the development to a full-fledged language of movement with its own logic and orthography is due to a very large extent to his own relentless work. He has especially developed a fundamental categorisation of group formations, without which the practical use of the script would have remained very much restricted.

By 1930, Knust had, together with Laban's daughter, Azra von Laban, already established the *Tanz-Schreib-Stube* (the first Dance Notation Bureau) in Hamburg and transferred to Berlin in 1935. He eventually became the first-ever full-time kinetographer-movement notator.

During 1946–1950, Knust wrote his major work *Das Handbuch der Kinetographie*. It comprises eight volumes, 2,400 pages and 20,000 kinetographic examples. This work, however, remains in typewritten copies and a few microfilms. No publisher was ever ready to take on this work for printing. Knust's final work, *A Dictionary of Kinetography Laban* (*Labanotation*),[7] appeared posthumously in 1979. The second edition of this basic reference book was published in 1997.

Kinetography Laban spread gradually all over Europe. It was used in Germany, Poland, Hungary, Bohemia, Croatia, Austria, France, Italy and England. This was accomplished to a large extent thanks to Albrecht Knust's teaching activities. In 1936, Laban's whole dance work was condemned in Nazi Germany as 'politically unbearable'. Kinetography was then also forbidden. With great difficulty Laban left for Paris in

1937 at the invitation of Rolf de Maré. The period of his life in England, between 1938 and 1958, was devoted to concluding his work on movement manifestations with a series of publications in English. Among these, he issued in 1956 his *Principles of Dance and Movement Notation* (*PDN*). This was to recapitulate the system as his invention. In the 'first part' of the book, Laban states:

> The motion characters of the script are compounded according to simple orthographical considerations which we have learned to appreciate in the long exercise of our experimental notation activity. Knust has collected in his great standard work some 20,000 basic movement graphs. This should not frighten anyone, for a modern dictionary contains some 40,000 to 50,000 words with explanations.[8]

> A notation based on the combination of motion characters makes it possible to write down all styles of dance, including classical ballet. Ballets of every style use movements built up from the same motor elements. The variety of movement which can be built up from them is almost infinite, and any style with a limited number of variations, whether self-imposed or traditional, must of necessity build its movement forms out of these basic constituents of movement. Just as poetry, in every language, can be written down phonetically, so every stylised movement can be written down 'motorically'. The motor movement notation is the equivalent of the alphabet.[9]

Laban acknowledged the spreading of his Kinetography:

> In England, Lisa Ullmann and Sigurd Leeder, together with an appreciable circle of fellow movement notators, are spreading the use of the script in general and theatrical education. They emphasise the value of notating movement exercises and educational dance studies. All active notators are used to stressing the importance of notation

as a means of keeping choreographic invention free from distortion by busy imitators. Besides the practical issues connected with the copyright of dance works, the use of notation has the effect of preserving the integrity of original works.[10]

Laban's system of movement notation was well established in the USA by Ann Hutchinson. She studied Kinetography at the Jooss–Leeder School in Dartington between 1936 and 1939. She coined the system 'Labanotation',[11] and energetically developed the Dance Notation Bureau in New York. Her Handbook entitled *Labanotation* appeared in 1954, and many further editions followed. Laban also acknowledged this development:

> Ann Hutchinson, and her staff of the Dance Notation Bureau in New York, have the great advantage of witnessing in that cauldron of all races a large number of dances in every style. The most active American stage dancers have taken up our notation as an instrument urgently needed in the profession, and this is largely due to the work of Ann Hutchinson.[12]

Over the years huge collections of notated dances and dance scores came into existence. Kinetography (Figure 9.5) is widely used in theatre work, as well as in scholarly dance research.[13]

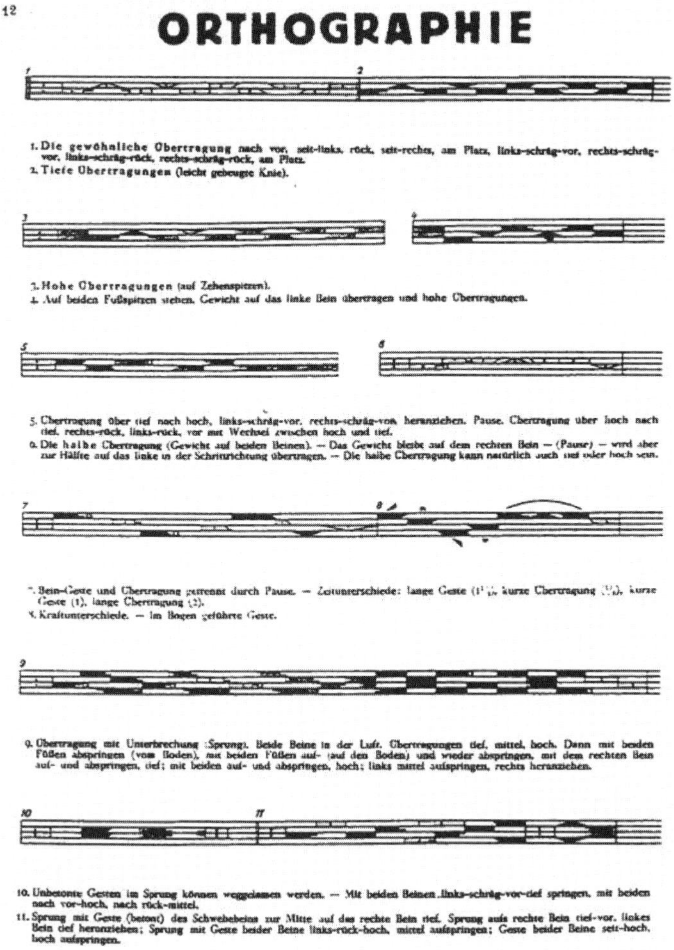

Figure 9.5 Example of Kinetography

Source: Rudolf Laban, *Schrifttanz, Methodik-Orthographie-Erläuterungen*, Universal Edition, 1928, p. 18.

Notes

1. As, for example, in the *Livre de basses danses* of Margaret of Austria, ca. 1450, or in *L 'Art et Instruction de bien Danser* by M. Toulouze (Paris, 1488).
2. Raoul Auger Feuillet, *Chorégraphie* (Paris, 1700).
3. Friedrich Albert Zorn, *Grammatik der Tanzkunst* (Leipzig: J.J. Weber, 1887); Olga Desmond, *Rhythmographik* (Leipzig: Breitkopfu, Hartel, 1919).
4. Rudolf von Laban, '*Grundprinzipien der Bewegungsschrift*', *Schrifttanz*, Leipzig: Universal-Edition, no. 1, July 1928, pp. 4–5.
5. *PDN*, p. 11.
6. Albrecht Knust, *Abriss der Kinetographie Laban* (Hamburg: Das Tanzarchiv, 1956. English version, 1958).
7. Albrecht Knust, *A Dictionary of Kinetography Laban (Labanotation)* (Plymouth: Macdonald & Evans, 1979). Second edition, *Institut Choreologii* (Poznan, 1997).
8. *PDN*, p. 20.
9. Ibid., p. 15.
10. Ibid., pp. 18–19.
11. Ann Hutchinson, *Labanotation* (London: Phoenix House, 1954).
12. *PDN*, p. 18.
13. Mary Jane Warner and Frederick E. Warner, *Laban Notation Scores: An International Bibliography* (New York: ICKL, Vol. I, 1984, Vol. II, 1988, Vol. III. 1995).

Chapter ten

Rudolf Laban's dance films

Translated by Stefanie Sachsenmaier and Dick McCaw

Introduction

Evelyn Dörr

During his first working period the choreographer Rudolf Laban was fascinated by film. Early on at his school in Zurich in 1915 he had introduced cinematography as a mandatory subject in the curriculum and had developed film-pantomimes.[1] In the 1920s he resumed his efforts and acquired further practical film experience. Together with Wilhelm Prager, the director of the 1925 cult film *Wege zu Kraft und Schönheit* (Ways to Strength and Beauty), Laban staged the pantomime for the film *Drachentöterei* (The Killing of Dragons), and participated in the direction of this successful danced fairytale. With film, Laban had found a gap in the market for himself that presented both a financial opportunity and an artistic challenge. Moreover, Laban saw the medium of film as a vehicle for mass art and therefore an extremely efficient opportunity for the dissemination of his choreosophic ideas. He wanted to write educational dance films as sound film treatments that would be an appropriate pedagogical means for modern education to systematically teach Laban's choreographic methods. Laban's educational dance film scripts, *Das lebende Bild* (The Living Image)[2] and *Gruppenform-Lehrfilm* (Group Form–Educational Film), created in 1929, had a strictly didactic character. With such dance pedagogical films Laban wanted to propagate the basics of his dance notation and his teaching of movement and spatial harmony. *The Living Image* was to be produced by Propagandafilm Company, and, as Laban wrote in 1929, 'my method' will be taught as a kind of 'correspondence course' (*Unterrichtsbriefe*).[3] The film, consisting of both image and text, represented 50 typical movements, 'which could be the model for students',[4] who could then teach themselves his choreography. In this way, the dance pupils learned the elements of dance notation and Laban's teachings of movement and spatial harmony. During this period Laban was also occupied with writing screenplays and immersing himself in his film ambitions. Laban's screenplays written at the end of the 1920s – *Tanz ist Leben* (Dance is Life), *Tanz der Menschheit* (Dance of Humanity), or *Die Befreiung des Körpers* (The Liberation of the Body) – were aimed, as dance documentary and/or dance cultural films, at presenting dance in an artistic and cultural dimension. Here his ideas were given expression in film.

Laban was excited by the technical and dramaturgical possibilities of film: the combination of cross-fades, close-ups, time-lapses or cuts. Laban was fascinated not only by the scope of 'film-dance' designs and their enormous combinations but above all by how perfectly his choreosophic ideas of the 'dance in all things' could be artistically realised.

As Laban wrote in the manuscript *Tanz im Film* (Dance in Film) in 1929 he was planning 'to enliven the feature films so common today through dance-rhythmic movement'.[5] Hence, for him, the directing of the dance film *Ein Spiel Karten* (A Game of Cards), first shown under the title *Spuk im Spielklub* (Ghost in the Casino), produced with the members of the Berliner Staatsoper in 1934, was probably the high point of Laban's creative work in film.

DANCE IS LIFE[6]

(A film by W. Prager and Rudolf von Laban)
Brief overview of content

Dance is life, stillness is death!

In the *prelude* of the film the round-dance opens with fluttering blossoms, waves, clouds and a flurry of snow – nature's dance through the seasons. The crystal clearness of winter leads on to blossoming people who unfold their limbs from the bondage of the laws of movement into a free, lively play of dance. (The law of dance movement is represented by an icosahedron – a crystal structure which is a schematic emblem of the movement scales of the dancing body (Figure 10.1).)

Next, in the first part of the film, there are examples of male dance – a war dance, martial arts and the art of fencing – which for a long time, before dance became the prerogative of women, constituted a high level of culture in terms of physical discipline which resulted in a restrained form of dance. From the beginning of time, battles were followed by dance. In ancient

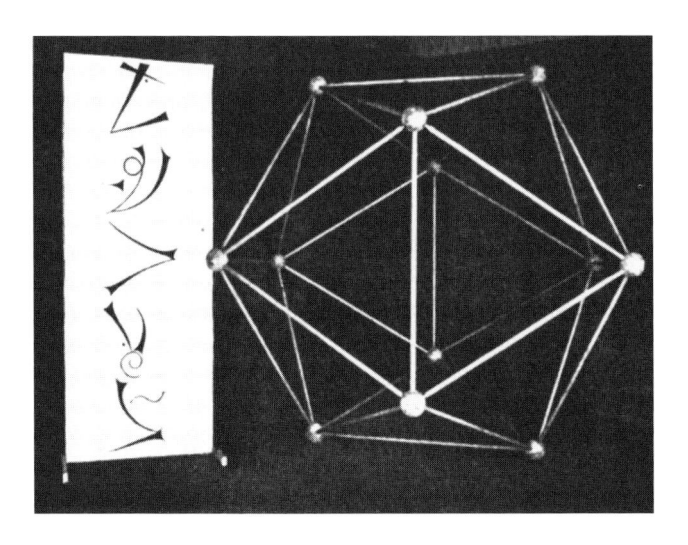

Figure 10.1 Photograph of the icosahedron (1928)
Source: From *Tanz Fur Alle*, Martin Gleisner, Leipzig 1928.

times celebrations of victory were linked with dance: from antiquity when already Homer in the *Iliad* sings about these dances, via the wild *Lansquenet*[7] dances of the Middle Ages through to the passionate Waltz in the era of Biedermeier.[8]

Part II. After battle, victory and dance which daintily-clad women bring into the lives of men. It is interesting to experience what dance tells us, how dance expression forms itself. In billowing veils, made from natural materials, dancing girls perform the primordial concept of dance – rhythm, Pavanes, negro-dances, *Schuhplattler*,[9] spinning dances, Cossack dances, rhythms of machines and instruments – swirl around in their various forms of rhythmic play. The world of dance in terms of its form becomes more and more distinct until through clearly marked footprints, perhaps left in the snow, the archetype of all dance script emerges. Laban's modern dance script and its pictorial correlations with the movements of swinging, jumping dancers, male and female, end the second part.

The third part portrays the content and meaning of dance. Pure form dances (i.e. Tiller girls) lead to a portrayal of emotional impulses in dance. Following the Dying Swan of Pavlova there are mimes, dance dramas and bizarre grotesques of our times. In between there are recurring parallels from different times and countries, hunting negroes dressed up as ostriches, imitating the behaviour of this big bird through dance. All important races and nations join in the round-dance with their most typical dances.

In the fourth part dance is portrayed as the liberator. Emotional and physical hardship is remedied or at least alleviated through the free swinging rhythm of dance. After unhealthy work that is carried out in a sitting position, which brings so many physical disadvantages to humankind, it is the free movement of the limbs which the female factory workers experience as redemption when dancing on the roof of the factory to tunes from a gramophone. In the times when there were severe epidemics, people danced in order to keep up their spirits in order to face life. In this way the *Schläffertanz* came into being in Munich, which to this day is performed every year in the streets of Bavaria to commemorate an epidemic of the plague. The Orient has numerous cultic dances: India, Arabia, Japan foster dance not only as performance or social dance, but as a means of religious elevation and liberation from the battles of everyday life.

The fifth part shows dance as a stage art. The old and the new school of our cultural circle, ballet and modern dance, compete with exotic theatre dances, in order to move the spectator with their lively stage patterns. Dance also contributes to an intensification of stage expression in opera and drama. Who wants to do without dance in Shakespeare's *A Midsummer Night's Dream* as well as in many other works for the stage? Is not all acted gesture – dance? Here the experts of stage dance appear in their own works. A show which presents a persisting document of our dance artists! The sense of beauty in our aspirations to work creatively with our bodies comes closer to dance – is dance.

The theme of the fourth part consists of the beauty of physical exercise and how it becomes dance. A military manoeuvre and pyramids in gymnastic and mass demonstrations of movement choirs, which elevate physical education again to a status of cultic celebration, form the finale. The great style of this cultural film demands a rhythmic interweaving of seriousness and joviality. Countless strangely enlivening ideas and unsettling images of our time, which are connected to the history and the nature of dance, could not even be touched upon here. The tragic change from Rococo minuet to revolutionary Carmagnole,[10] toys and acrobatics, animal dances and, last but not least, the dance of world literature and in the fine arts are woven into the manuscript.

Associated film images:

Prelude:

Image 1: A bird-house for starlings hangs underneath a branch in blossom, two starlings merrily jumping to and fro on the bar in front of the hole of the house. In slow-motion capture May beetles fly around the couple in the natural rhythm of their flying motion. Scattered white petals dance through the image, let loose by the wind. [*Cross-fade*]

Image 2: Blossoming reeds sway in the wind above the happily dancing waves of a little meadow stream. A rhythmic sinking and lifting. White butterflies and opalescent dragonflies perform a summer round dance. [*Cross-fade*]

Image 3: Between scattered beeches at the edge of a forest gusts of the autumn wind scatter the withered leaves on the ground. The slow-motion capture of leaves, which fall from the top downwards through the image, is montage over this image. [*Cross-fade*]

Image 4: In the cross-fade the falling leaves transform first into slow and then fast falling snowflakes. In the end they whirl so tightly onto the ground that the landscape is fully covered by the whirl-dance of these snowflakes. One sees only the merry snow flurry. [*Cross-fade*]

Image 5: [*Cross-fade*] The falling of the flakes slows down. The flakes are only falling sporadically. The last ones merge into crystals. Five or six of these transformed flakes show the manifold symmetric structures of ice crystals. [*Cross-fade*]

Image 6: [*Cross-fade*] The crystals from image 5 fade downwards out of the image, apart from a star-like structure, which remains in the centre. The remaining crystal slowly transforms into an icosahedron. It grows until it almost fills the whole frame of the image. [*Cross-fade*]

Image 7: The icosahedron, which is made up of sparkling and glowing areas, shows gradually an arrangement of poles which are tied together by strings at their ends. The whole structure rests on a cloud-like surface. In the background, towards the top, stars are shining and inside the icosahedron a human skeleton appears, which fills it entirely. While the stars are beginning to run their course, the skeleton begins to twitch, moving like a marionette. Finally it jumps like a jack-in-the-box. [*Cross-fade*]

Image 8: With increasing musical chords the moving stars slow down their journey. At the same time the skeleton transforms into a human being of flesh and blood, namely into a woman. Once the transformation from skeleton into human being is completed, the female creature begins to swing the basic scales of dance movement. She increases the rhythmic-gymnastic play and ends with a large pose. During this play the image becomes brighter and transfigures more and more. With the final chords of a maestoso, shining rays pass in the background from a concentrated point, like in a rising sun, from the bottom of the image over the whole area. During the performance of the swinging, the icosahedron slowly fades out of the image until the female figure stands freely in the landscape, in the background the moving surface of the rhythmically billowing sea. [*Slow fade-out*]

DANCE IN FILM

It is certainly tempting to relate the purest art of movement, which is dance, to film, whose nature it is to draw its artistic and affective impact from human movement. But it is not possible to transfer dances that have been made for the stage onto the screen, it is rather necessary to transform the movement action, which does justice to the special expressive character of film. But it seems to me that not only a filmic processing of dance and dance performances will have an artistic future, but also the integration of film play in conventional film drama can strongly gain certain impulses from dance movement. Because in film the impact of the image is merely an expressive form of second degree. The main impact of a film is always in its rhythm, and it is this that dance and film both have in common.

This fact has a special significance for sound films, where a unified expression is created through the simultaneous recording of music and movement. Already today we have a kind of film music, which adapts to the essence of this art form and the successful interplay of film music and film dance can without doubt produce very precious results.

From this consideration I have worked several times on sound film experiments. The added images are excerpts from a dance piece of a small jovial mime called *The Killing of Dragons* [*Drachentöterei*], choreographed by Dussia Bereska, and which I have adapted to film, together with Willi Prager.

In my opinion, this piece proves that dances accompanied by music can be effectively transformed for sound film.

The other task, which is to enliven today's humdrum movies through dance-rhythmic movement, shall also be tackled soon and will be able to provide the European film production with a special stamp, for which it has strived for a long time. It is worth noting that a piece such as *The Killing of Dragons* was already fixed beforehand in dance script (Kinetography Laban) which resulted in a particularly easy adaptation for film. In this sense I also believe that dance script will be of significance for the future of film.

Notes

1. There are further references to the dance films by Laban mentioned in this introduction in my two books: *The Dancer of the Crystal* (2008), p. 146ff., p. 234ff. and *Rudolf Laban – Das choreographische Theater* (2004), pp. 503–538.
2. The German original can be found at the Dance Archive Leipzig, Rep. 028 III. 3. No. 3. It is reproduced in full in the author's dissertation: *Rudolf Laban – Leben und Werk des Künstlers (1879–1936)* (Berlin, 1999, vol. 2, pp. 409–442).
3. First draft, *The Living Image* (*Das lebende Bild*), October 4, 1929, p. 1.
4. Ibid.
5. *Rudolf von Laban: Dance in Film*, in Dance Archive, Leipzig, Rep. 028 IV. b. 1. No. 30.
6. A copy of this proposal can be found in JHA, Box 11, Folder 18. The text is by Laban, even though he refers to himself in the third person.
7. German country dances. [Note by Dick McCaw.]
8. Between 1815–1848. [Note by Dick McCaw.]
9. A folk dance from Bavaria. [Note by Dick McCaw.]
10. *Carmagnola* is the title of both a song and its accompanying wild dance that was popular during the French Revolution. [Note by Dick McCaw.]

Chapter eleven

Choreutics, written in 1938, published 1966

Introduction

Valerie Preston-Dunlop

The first part of this book was written by Laban on his arrival in Great Britain as a non-English-speaking refugee in 1939. It was designed to introduce his principles of the dynamic space of movement to his host country, somewhat desperately since having to leave behind all his archives and writings when he fled Germany. The text lay in safe keeping until his death.[1] At that point a second part was compiled and added by his close collaborator Lisa Ullmann in order to make a comprehensive publication, based on notes by Gertrud Snell, Laban's assistant at his *Choreographisches Institut* in the 1920s and 1930s.

Choreutics presents the grammar and syntax of spatial form in movement and the nature of movement's harmonic content. The first chapters of the book are accessible but it is not an easy read on the more complex ideas without accompanying the read with practice. But it is a profound book. Laban discusses three-dimensional geometric form, notoriously difficult to describe, let alone illustrate, on a two-dimensional page. While the harmonics of spatial movement manifest themselves in practice within the 3D map of space of an icosahedron,[2] Laban starts his discourse illustrating it with diagrams of a cube to ease a reader into the material. He only introduces the icosahedron after presenting the basic choreutic principles, and that is not until Chapter 10. While this will assist the newcomer to choreutics, it may confuse the practitioner expecting icosahedral maps.

In the second part of the book Ullmann uses the icosahedral map. As she says, to comprehend the material, you need studio practice of them with a teacher. Ullmann's part is useful for people with considerable practice to draw on. For a newcomer to the subject it becomes formidable because she uses a code to identify three-dimensional lines in space. To understand it the reader must know the grammar of the standard transversal scale, or A scale, on which it is based. While that might have been expected knowledge in 1966, many of today's readers are disadvantaged by not having that background.[3]

Notwithstanding those difficulties, *Choreutics* has been in print continuously since 1966 and contains some of Laban's most quoted statements.

To whom was the book addressed? Initially, to anyone interested in dance and movement with the curiosity to look below the surface. Now its strongest impact is in professional development where the text, Part One in particular, enables people to look afresh at their own dance and movement heritage, ballet in particular, and see it not as a fixed lexicon of steps and positions but as 'living architecture', that is, dynamic spatial forms with the potential for change.[4]

Laban entitled his text 'A New Aspect of Space and Movement'. It is much more than a textbook of the scales and rings that have today become the stuff of space harmony practice. He includes connections between the geometry of space and of human motion, and of the human person as a whole. He shows the wider connections of choreutic principles with the geometry of the cosmos and of daily mundane actions. The text is peppered with references to his sources, to Plato's *Timaeus* and to Pythagoras' mathematics, to his own experience as an expert fencer, equestrian, dancer and observer of his fellow men.

Less direct are references to the *Weltanschauung* of his time. The emergence of psychology through Freud and Jung parallels his look for a correlation between the outer form of an action with its psychic functioning. Early writings on phenomenology and flux, Bergson and Husserl particularly, parallel his validation of subjective experience in movement knowledge. His earlier books cite writings on crystallography and the geometry of all organic and inorganic matter that science was revealing, here embedded in the text of *Choreutics*. Since his student days the spiritual aspect of human life was a cultural concern and embodying it in arts practice, along with his fellow artists, was a shared endeavour.[5]

His training at the École des Beaux Arts led him to bring the grammars of architecture to his study of movement as his term 'living architecture' shows. He was well on in his diligent researches for a notation of movement and dance as his choreutic theory was first evolving. The analysis of movement which that required is ever present in the objective side of this discourse.

To express his ideas, he introduces new terminology: the kinesphere, the dynamosphere, trace-forms, scaffolding, scales, choreological order are a few. He puts before the public his vision of choreology as the practical theory of dance and movement, giving it a parity with the '-ologies' of the sister arts, musicology in particular, and, of choreosophy, the deeper wisdom that has been found in movement forms from prehistory to the present day.[6]

In choosing the excerpts to present here I have prioritised, first, writings directly related to the range of choreutic practice that a reader might encounter currently in the studio, and, second, topics that are known to have assisted professionals in the movement arts to look at their practice anew. With the brief introduction to each chapter I hope to direct the reader to the spread and depth of topics that Laban deals with in *Choreutics*.

In the Preface, Laban introduces the broad layers of his discourse. In the Introduction, he explains the perspectives he proposes for discussing choreutics. In Chapter 1, 'Principles of Orientation in Space', he places orientation in space and its graphic description as a starting point for choreutic study.

In Chapters 2–6, he deals with the following topics: 'The Body and Kinesphere' introduces circuits in the kinesphere and their 'mirroring of the ever-circling motions in the universe'. 'Exploration of the Dynamosphere' presents the interdependence of the spatial form and dynamism of movement. 'Natural Sequences and Scales in Space' shows that circuits (scales) exist in mundane human activity. 'The Body and Trace-Forms' discusses drawing trace-forms and the wider impact they have on the performer's experience and expressivity. 'Natural Sequences in the Dynamosphere' penetrates further into the inseparability of space from time, force and expression.

In Chapter 7, 'The Standard Scale', he deals with the more technical aspects of space harmony practice using terminology, such as 'scales', to connect with music and 'chains' to connect with ballet's *enchaînement*. The terms 'cluster' and 'girdle' name sequences that are more widely referred to today as 'an axis scale' and 'an equator scale'. Laban is at pains to show the connection between one scale and another in a coherent harmonic system. The 'standard scale' is more widely termed 'the primary scale' of 12 parts around the edge of the kinesphere.[7]

Laban goes on to demonstrate why it is 'standard' (and by inference why he later termed it 'primary'), showing that the scale systematically passes through the girdle and cluster on every second location, through the three basic planes on every third location and basic triangular forms on every fourth location.[8]

We pick up the discourse where the transversal standard scale is illustrated. More widely known as 'the A scale', this is the trademark scale of Laban's space harmony practice. The mirror image he describes is now known as 'the B scale'. All these scales are explained in Ullmann's section of the book, using the newer terminology (see Section 11, *Sequential Laws*) and oriented, as they are in practice, in an icosahedral map.

In Chapter 8, 'Bodily Perspective', he focuses on the mover's view of experiencing form and the extra 'shadow-forms' that occur as you move.

Chapter 9, 'Stabilising and Mobilising of Trace-Forms', deals with the innate dynamism of form in practice and demonstrates his masterly understanding of the interconnectedness of all aspects of human movement in practice. He ends the chapter by describing the lemniscate form that normal human movement creates unconsciously because of the propensity of shifting between gathering in and scattering out in expressive gestures.

Chapter 10, 'Cubic and Spheric Forms of the Scaffolding', is where Laban finally comes to the icosahedron, showing how it is the crystal form compatible not only with the skeletal frame of the body but also with the angles of movement of the joints.[9]

In Chapter 11, 'Choreutic Shapes Performed by the Body', he sums up with the integration of mind and body in space harmony practice.

In his final chapter, 'Free Inclinations', he opens up the infinite nature of the space–time configurations of human movement and their significance.

Ullmann's textbook Part Two, 'Rudiments of Space-Movement', follows and the reader may use it to understand further the technicalities of choreutic theory that Laban has introduced philosophically in Part One.

PREFACE

'Choreosophia' – an ancient Greek word, from choros, meaning circle, and sophia, meaning knowledge or wisdom – is the nearest term I have discovered with which to express the essential ideas of this book. These ideas concern the wisdom to be found through the study of all the phenomena of circles existing in nature and in life. The term was used in Plato's time by the disciples and followers of Pythagoras. Although there is little real knowledge of the work of Pythagoras, we do know that about 540 BC he founded a philosophical and religious colony in Sicily, in which the cult of the Muses, the divine protectorates of the arts, seems to have played an important part. We do not know much about the fate of this Pythagorean community except that the surrounding population turned against the persistently grave demeanour of Pythagoras and his pupils. It is said that they were burnt alive together and that the colony's writings and works of art also perished in the flames, but the memory of Pythagoras is perpetuated by his discoveries in mathematics. One of these was the mathematics underlying musical scales, but best known is his theorem dealing with the harmonic relations of the different sides of a rectangular triangle.

Plato, in his *Timaeus*, and other contemporaries and disciples of the great philosopher give us a more exhaustive picture of the knowledge accumulated in the Pythagorean community, but this knowledge derives from even more remote times. The wisdom of circles is as old as the hills. It is founded on a conception of life and the becoming aware of it which has its roots in magic and which was shared by peoples in early stages of civilisation. Later religious, mystical and scientific epochs continued the tradition. The original conviction of the extraordinary role which the circle plays in harmony, life, and even in the whole of existence, survived the many changes in mentality, mood and feeling which abound in history.

Choreosophy seems to have been a complex discipline in the time of the highest Hellenic culture. Branches of the knowledge of circles came into being and were named 'choreography', 'choreology' and 'choreutics'. The first, choreography, means literally the designing or writing of circles. The word is still in use today: we call the planning and composition of a ballet or a dance 'choreography'. For centuries, the word has been employed to designate the drawings of figures and symbols of movements which dance composers, or choreographers, jotted down as an aid to memory. There exist many systems, old and new, of dance notation and notation of movement in general, but most of them are restricted to a particular style of movement with which the writer and reader are familiar. Today we need a system of recording which can be universally used, and I have attempted to forge a way in this direction. My study of some hundred different forms of graphic presentation of characters of the different alphabets and other symbols, including those of music and dance, has helped me with the development of a new form of choreography which I called 'kinetography'. The system itself was inspired by that of Beauchamp and Feuillet (around 1700) and was mainly evolved alongside my investigations of the various branches of *choreosophia*.

The two other subjects of the knowledge of circles, choreology and choreutics, are not as well known as the first. Choreology is the logic or science of circles, which could be understood as a purely geometrical study, but in reality was much more than that. It was a kind of grammar and syntax of the language of movement, dealing not only with the outer form of movement but also with its mental and emotional content. This was based on the belief that motion and emotion, form and content, body and mind, are inseparably united. Finally, the third subject, choreutics, may be explained as the practical study of the various forms of (more or less) harmonised movement.

Movement is one of man's languages and as such it must be consciously mastered. We must try to find its real structure and the choreological order within it through which movement becomes penetrable, meaningful and understandable. In an attempt to do this, it has been found necessary to use various graphic signs, because words can never be entirely adequate in dealing with the changing nature of the subject before us. They are abstractions and, as it were, short cuts in the flow of life. Therefore, in order to gain a new aspect of movement and space, some elementary knowledge of choreography is needed, as through this the various choreutic elements can be identified.

In this book I have endeavoured to give a general survey of the central idea of choreutics, as well as a particular account of it. Because of an almost complete lack of knowledge about these things in the present day, it will be necessary for the reader to become quite clear about the first preliminaries, and this will demand a certain effort on his part. However, the choreographic, choreologic and choreutic matter through which I should like to lead the reader will, I hope, be more than a preparation, for when these aspects are both experienced and clearly understood, they are the real substance of the wisdom of circles.

INTRODUCTION

Empty space does not exist. On the contrary, space is a superabundance of simultaneous movements. The illusion of empty space stems from the snapshot-like perception received by the mind. What the mind perceives is, however, more than an isolated detail; it is a momentary standstill of the whole universe. Such a momentary view is always a concentration on an infinitesimal phase of the great and universal flux.

The conception of space as a locality in which changes take place can be helpful here. However, we must not look at the locality simply as an empty room, separated from movement, nor at movement as an occasional happening only, for movement is a continuous flux within the locality itself, this being the fundamental aspect of space. Space is a hidden feature of movement and movement is a visible aspect of space.

When we wish to describe a single unit of space-movement we can adopt a method similar to that of an architect when drafting a building. He cannot show all the inner and outer views in one draft only. He is obliged to make a ground-plan, and at least two elevations, thus conveying to the mind a plastic image of the three-dimensional whole.

Movement is, so to speak, living architecture — living in the sense of changing emplacements as well as changing cohesion. This architecture is created by human movements and is made up of pathways tracing shapes in space, and these we may call 'trace-forms'. A building can hold together only if its parts have definite proportions which provide a certain balance in the midst of the continual vibrations and movements taking place in the material of which it is constructed. The structure of a building must endure shocks from alien sources, for instance, by the passing traffic, or by the jumping of lively inhabitants. The living architecture composed of the trace-forms of human movements has to endure other disequilibrating influences as they come from within the structure itself and not from without.

The living building of trace-forms which a moving body creates is bound to certain spatial relationships. Such relationships exist between the single parts of the sequence. Without a natural order within the sequence, movement becomes unreal and dream-like. Dream-architectures can neglect the laws of balance. So can dream-movements, yet a fundamental sense of balance will always remain with us even in the most fantastic aberrations from reality.

The above viewpoints represent degrees on a scale of temperaments of observers who unavoidably are in the same stream of existence but look at it from different angles. Such a scale obviously has more degrees than those described, but for our purpose, which is to find characteristic views offering a foundation for a multilateral description of movement, we may find it useful to select the following three aspects:

1. That of a mentality plunged into the intangible world of emotions and ideas.
2. That of the objective observer, from outside.
3. That of the person enjoying movement as bodily experience, and observing and explaining it from this angle.

These three aspects can be taken as the three views – the ground-plan and the two views of elevation – on which we project the image of the object of our investigations: the unit, movement and space.

A synthesis of these three aspects operates constantly in each one of us. We are all emotional dreamers, and scheming mechanics, and biological innocents, simultaneously: sometimes we waver between these three mentalities, and sometimes we compress them in a synthesised act of perception and function.

To experience trace-forms from several viewpoints, integrating the bodily perspective, the dynamic feeling and the controlling faculties, necessitates a certain spiritual emphasis; this is unavoidable when penetrating into the real structure of human movement and motion in nature. The approach from different sides is, however, aimed at the discovery of a unity of movement. It is, without doubt, a fact that such a unity existed in ancient times in the paths of gestures which we have called trace-forms. Because it could not be explained, it assumed a magic significance and it is curious that even now it remains magical, in spite of being analysed.

Principles of orientation in space[10]

Man's movement arises from an inner volition which results in a transference of the body or one of its limbs from one spatial position to another. The outer shape of each movement can be defined by changes of position in space. Everyday terms of language suffice to describe, with precision, the position from which a movement starts, or the place to which it intends to go, and at which it finally arrives. The link between two positions is the 'path' which the movement follows.

Wherever the body stays or moves, it occupies space and is surrounded by it. We must distinguish between space in general and the space within the reach of the body. In order to distinguish the latter from general space, we shall call it personal space or the 'kinesphere'. The kinesphere is the sphere around the body whose periphery can be reached by easily extended limbs without stepping away from that place which is the point of support when standing on one foot, which we shall call the 'stance'.[11] We are able to outline the boundary of this imaginary sphere with our feet as well as with our hands. In this way any part of the kinesphere can be reached. Outside the kinesphere lies the rest of space, which can be approached only by stepping away from the stance. When we move out of the limits of our original kinesphere, we create a new stance, and transport the kinesphere to a new place. We never, of course, leave our movement sphere but carry it always with us, like an aura.

When we take a step forward, we carry our kinesphere the length of a step forward through space. The stance is always beneath the point of equilibrium of the body, never at the side or in front, or behind it. We feel each stance as a part of ourself, and each new movement grows from it.

The basic elements of orientation in space are the three dimensions: length, breadth and depth. Each 'dimension' has two directions. With reference to the human body, length, or height, has the two directions up and down; breadth has the two directions left and right; depth has the two directions forward and backward. The centre of gravity of the upright body is approximately the dividing point between the two directions of each dimension. Thus this point becomes, as well, the centre of our kinesphere.

The three-dimensional form composed of height, breadth and depth, which is the easiest to visualise, is the cube. Oblique lines, which may be called 'diagonals' of space, lead from each corner of the cube to the opposite corner, and each is a kind of axis, which is surrounded by three dimensions. There are four such space diagonals in the cube, and they intersect at a point in the body which coincides approximately with its centre of gravity, which is also the centre of our kinesphere as has been mentioned above.

These four diagonals do not have such clearly denned names as the dimensions. In general, they are named by the three surrounding dimensions, for instance, a diagonal may lead towards high, right, forward, and in the opposite direction, deep, left, backward.

We also distinguish axes which lie between two diagonals and two dimensions. We may call them 'diameters' and consider them to be 'deflected' from the dimensions or from the diagonals. There are six such diameters in the cube and they also intersect roughly at the centre of gravity.

The six diameters, again, have no clearly defined names in everyday language. They can be described, however, by the two dimensions between which they lie.

For instance, a diameter lying between high and right side leads towards high-right, and in the opposite direction, deep-left. It is only in the art of movement, and particularly in dance, that these spatial relations need to be precisely defined, and as a first step towards the understanding of the new aspect of movement we employ the terminology of the dancer to describe relations of positions in space.

In the well-known five positions in dance, the dancer places his feet and his body either in the directions of the three dimensions, or in the diagonal directions between them. In the first position the feet are placed with the heels together and toes apart. It is this position which creates the stance.

Movements directed towards the stance lead downward. In the second position the feet are placed apart sideways, on a line extending between the left and right dimensional directions. In the third position the feet are placed at an angle, with the heel of one foot by the instep of the other. The feet indicate an oblique line lying between the two spatial extensions of depth and breadth; for instance, between forward and right, and backward and left. In the fourth position the feet are placed apart one behind the other, on a line extending between the forward and backward directions. In the fifth position the feet are placed closely one behind the other. In this position no special direction is accentuated except perhaps that of upward because of a tendency to stretch the whole body in this situation. We employ the fifth position, therefore, as the position which is symbolic of height.

With regard to the positions of the legs and arms, when in the air, there is no uniform tradition. In the movement notation which the author has developed, and which has been used for some time in the fields of dance, work and education, the directions of the positions of the legs and arms, when in the air, correspond to the general directions of the aforesaid five classical positions of the feet.

Three different spatial levels may be distinguished: one on the floor, another at the mid-height of the body, and the third at the height of the hands, when raised above the head. The following names and symbols can be used, in order to make the directions clear (Figure 11.1).

THE STANDARD SCALE[12]

It now becomes necessary to give further attention to the structure of the kinespheric 'scaffolding'. This is characterised by two main types of tensions:

1. Between the surface-lines or edges.

The symbols for directions directly in front of or behind the body are as follows:

at medium level:	at high level:	at low level:
forward:	high forward:	deep forward:
backward:	high backward:	deep backward:

The symbols for the four oblique directions are:

at medium level:	at high level:	at low level:
right forward:	high right forward:	deep right forward:
right backward:	high right backward:	deep right backward:
left forward:	high left forward:	deep left forward:
left backward:	high left backward:	deep left backward:

Figure 11.1 Notation of symbols

2. Between the lines traversing the scaffolding – the dimensions, the diagonals, the diameters and the 'transversals'. The latter distinguish themselves by not intersecting at the centre of the kinesphere, while all the others do (see Chapter I). They lie between three diagonals or three dimensionals, or more precisely athwart them and, therefore, do not form a plane with any two. We consider them to be 'secondary deflections' from the diagonals and dimensionals. They always connect two endpoints of two different diameters. They never link endpoints of dimensionals or diagonals, or form a surface-line of the scaffolding.

The scaffolding of the kinesphere built up so far has 24 surface-lines which are parallel to the six primary deflected inclinations, which we call diameters. Each diameter has four parallel surface-lines. For instance:

Each diagonal is surrounded by a chain of six transversals (a 'cluster'), a chain of six surface-lines (a 'girdle') and two 'polar triangles', each of which joins by surface-lines the extremities of the transversals forming the cluster.

As an example we may take the diagonal dfl–hbr. This is associated with the cluster which is illustrated in Figure 11.2a and Figure 11.2b. The same diagonal is surrounded as

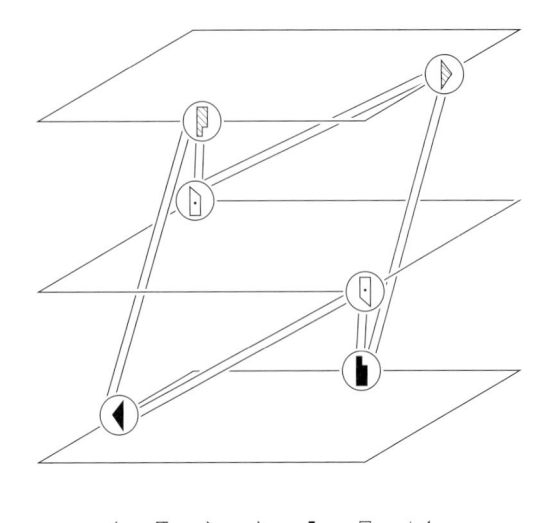

Figure 11.2a The cluster

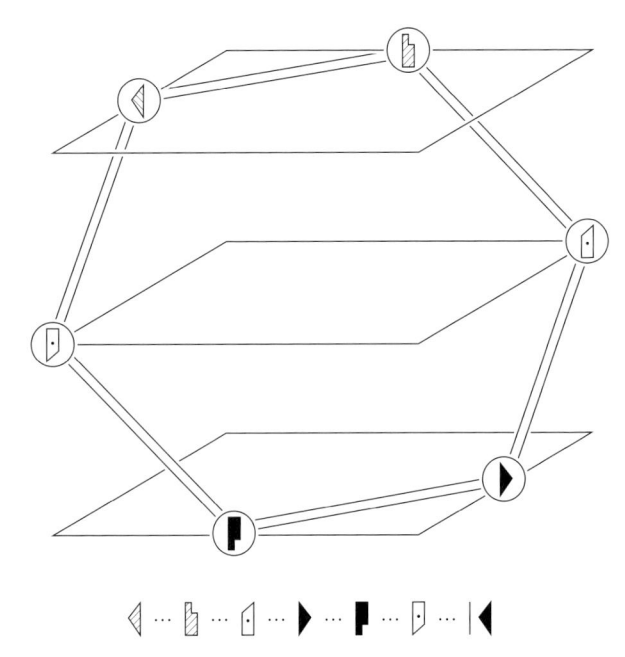

Figure 11.2b The girdle

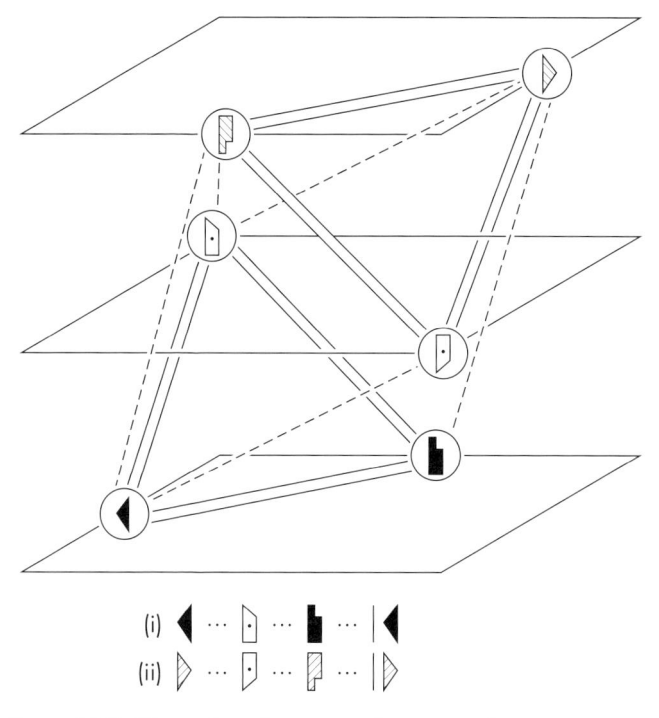

Figure 11.3 [Illustration of transversal movement]

illustrated in Figure 11.3, where the broken lines represent the transversals of the cluster which connect the two triangles.

A diagonal which is the axis of a cluster of six transversals is comparable to the axis of the earth, while the girdle of six surface-lines corresponds to the equator.

(NOTE: it should be mentioned that as the earth rotates on its axis, this tilted axis moves around in a circle forming a double conical trace-line. We can understand the two polar triangles mentioned above as the line along which the axis of the cluster makes similar revolving movements.)

We can follow both the cluster and the girdle with our movements. Movements which follow the chain of the cluster are seen in nature among animals in captivity, or, in the swaying of a drunken man, or one who is tired or falling asleep. It is, in general, an unconscious and involuntary movement.

Movements which follow the chain of the girdle are seen in nature in emphatic gestures and actions. They are, in general, voluntary movements. The emphasis contains, however, a certain state of unconscious excitement, but this excitement is a kind of day-dream. Man is awake in the equatorial, and not asleep as in the axial cluster movements.

The hybrid offspring of these two contrasting kinds of movement, the automatic, sleep-like one, and the inspired wakeful one, is a third mode of movement which is more difficult to describe in a single word than the two others. In this mode, man follows a series of intermediary chains of trace-forms which, like an electrical discharge, strike from the cluster to the girdle, and vice versa. In our ordinary everyday working movements and general locomotion, we employ these intermediary chains of trace-forms, sometimes falling into automatic movement, and at others into emphatic movement. In dancing and fighting, man has a tendency mainly to use emphatic movement. This is also the case in emotional outbursts which are often characterised by uncontrolled jumps from the emphatic to the automatic, leaving out that mode of movement which is apparent in ordinary everyday working actions and general locomotion. In other words, in cases of emotional outburst, we use cluster and girdle trace-forms in turn without intermediary links.

These links form the third mode of movement which becomes evident in a simple surface-line connecting the cluster with the girdle. It starts from one point on the girdle and travels to the next on the cluster, and so on alternately, until the circuit is completed. The circuit touches twelve points. Figure 11.4 is an example in which the chain revolves around the diagonal axis.

The first sequence (a) represents the complete chain. The second sequence (b) indicates the points of the cluster extracted from the chain, and the third sequence (c) shows the points of the girdle also extracted from the chain. It can therefore be seen that beginning, for instance, with deep left which is a point of the cluster, each second step is again a point of the cluster, alternating with one of the girdle.

All this has a deeper meaning. The unconscious automation associated with the cluster is counterbalanced by the

Chain of twelve surface-lines—peripheral standard scale—revolving around axis:

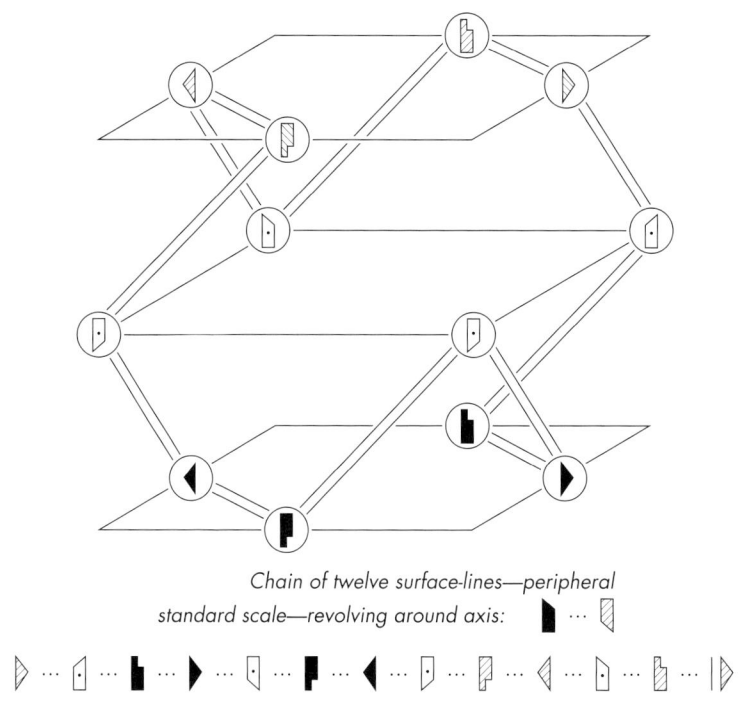

Figure 11.4a [Peripheral standard scale]

When we examine the chain the following picture arises:

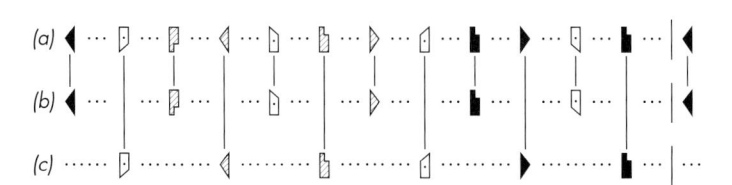

Figure 11.4b [Peripheral standard scale]

wakeful emphasis associated with the girdle. Therefore, movements which are neither automatic nor emphatic will follow trace-forms of a chain within the twelve-link chain, which is the prototype of all ordinary movement chains, and thus it may be considered as the 'standard' scale. This standard scale can revolve around various axes with different orientations, but its form remains the same. The inner cause of a change of axis is a change of mood or feeling, or of practical intention. For instance, the need or decision of attack or defence causes either an increase of mobility or an increase in stability. It may be recalled that series of other mental and emotional nuances are reflected in the particular orientation of the axis (see Chapters III and IV).

The standard scale is especially useful as it can be shown to contain a series of shapes which are the basic elements of almost all trace-forms employed in movement. Each chain of twelve links can be divided into six, four, three or two parts. The points of these divisions when joined together form regular polygons, that is, hexagons, quadrangles, and triangles, and in the case of two parts, a straight line. An uneven division of the chain would produce a series of irregular polygons.

STABILISING AND MOBILISING OF TRACE-FORMS[13]

Dance is the transition into a world in which the illusory, static appearances of life are transformed into clear spatial dynamism. Awareness of this spatial world and its exploration open up a horizon of unexpected breadth. From the simplest motion to the artistic creation of dancing, the flowing stream of movement expresses dynamic space, the basis of all existence. All movement emerges from this infinite abyss and disappears into it again.

Dynamic space, with its terrific dance of tensions and discharges is the fertile ground in which movement flourishes. Movement is the life of space. Dead space does not exist, for there is neither space without movement nor movement without space. All movement is an eternal change between binding and loosening, between the creation of knots with the concentrating and uniting power of binding, and the creation of twisted lines in the process of untying and untwisting. Stability and mobility alternate endlessly.

Stability in dance does not mean either complete rest or absolute stillness. Stability has the tendency to facilitate temporary and relative quietude which is equilibrium. Mobility on the contrary means a tendency towards vivid, flowing movement, leading to a temporary loss of equilibrium. For instance, in a flying turning leap (grand jeté en tournant), the whole body is in a mobile state. When the jump is terminated and the feet touch the floor again, there is a tendency towards quietude and equilibrium. Stability follows the former state of mobility.

Stability is not always guaranteed, however, by the act of standing on the feet. An exaggerated, wide circle, performed with the upper part of the body can provoke a temporary imbalance, or mobility, which is afterwards retransformed into stability. All our steps and gestures of the arms are rhythmical changes between stability and mobility.

Movements with axial counter-tensions are generally stable. Surface movements which affect the whole body promote mobility if they are not counteracted by polar tendencies. However, surface movements are generally executed by gestures of the limbs only when the axis of a trace-form does not play a prominent role in the tension of the body. The axial counter-tension is almost always hidden in an inner shadow-form, which provokes the characteristic tensing of the muscles, which we call strength, or, in a wider sense, dynamism. The shadow-forms are composed of the elements of the dynamosphere, as we have already seen. Their relationships are so infinitely manifold that they cannot be enumerated, but each of them can be understood as a characteristic stage of a harmonic development.

There is a veritable chain of inclinations which could be called a standard scale of the dynamosphere and which has two different forms. One of these is a knot and the other is a twisted circle.

A standard scale of the dynamosphere evolves around a diagonal but it is clearly orientated towards one of the two directions of the diagonal. An image which can facilitate our understanding is that a standard scale of the dynamosphere does not form either a cluster or a girdle, like a standard scale of the kinesphere, but a kind of basket, the bottom of which is orientated towards one direction of a diagonal, while its opening is orientated towards the other direction of the same diagonal. The three transversals of the basket occupy half the scaffolding, so to speak, and do not transgress to the other side which is divided off by the girdle around the diagonal. The other parts are symmetric forms all of the same structure, but they are differently orientated. Yet this basket is not regular or symmetric, but has a spiral form like that of a snail shell. This can be seen in Figure 11.5.

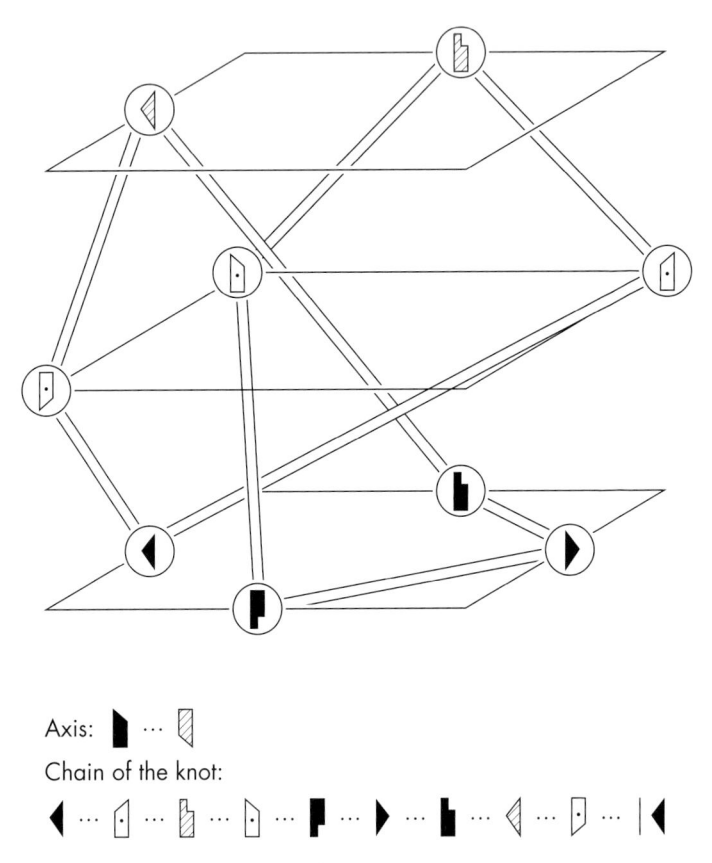

Axis: ▌ ⋯ ◪
Chain of the knot:

◀ ⋯ ◁ ⋯ ◱ ⋯ ◳ ⋯ ▐ ⋯ ▶ ⋯ ▌ ⋯ ◩ ⋯ ◰ ⋯ |◀

Figure 11.5 [Knot-form around an axis]

Notes

1 The document was given to Dorothy Elmhirst of Dartington Hall for safe keeping during the war while Laban moved on to write *Effort*, *Modern Educational Dance* and *Mastery of Movement*.
2 A 20-sided spherical form with 12 corners.
3 Most contemporary space harmony practice bypasses the code and uses the numerical system for the 12 locations of the icosahedron. Understandably Ullmann is attempting, as did Laban, to identify motion rather than position but, just as he had, in 1928, to complete his notation system, he succumbed to the need to take account of the limitations of human perception, so here, as there, he decided to describe motion as positions passed through.
4 See Heidi Gilpin and Patricia Baudoin's *Proliferation and Perfect Disorder* that discusses the questions *Choreutics* has inspired for the innovative choreographer William Forsythe.
5 See Wassily Kandinsky's *Concerning the Spiritual in Art*, and Rudolf Steiner's *Eurythmie*.
6 His earliest writings on choreosophy are in the deeply esoteric book *The World of the Dancer* and his struggles to find a notation are in his 1926 book, *Choreography*.
7 Laban does not say here that all these scales have four versions, one to each 3D diagonal of the kinesphere. That can be found in Ullmann's section. He has chosen to illustrate this with the hrb–dlf diagonal while in practice the primary scale regarded as standard today is on hrf–dlf, being more compatible with the movement range of a right-handed dancer.
8 It is for this reason that he eventually numbered from 1–12 the locations on the hrf–dlb primary scale at the time that he presented the mixed seven rings (published for this 70th birthday in 1949) and these are the ones preferred by practitioners.
9 See J. Longstaff, doctoral thesis, interrogating Laban's choreutic theory as a whole and body compatibility in particular.

10 Chapter 1, pp. 10–13.
11 Sometimes called 'place' [Laban's note].
12 Chapter 7, pp. 68–73.
13 Chapter 9, pp. 93–95.

Chapter twelve

Laban's concept of Effort and his work in the 1940s and 1950s

Introduction

Dick McCaw

Effort was at the centre of Laban's thinking about movement behaviour in this period. However, we have already seen that he was writing about movement qualities in the 1920s when the four motion factors were: Force, Space, Time, Flight. He called this aspect of movement analysis Eukinetics: the Greek prefix *eu-* has the senses of 'good', 'well' and 'easily', while *kinetics* comes from the Greek verb *kinetikos*, moving. Dancer and choreographer Aurel von Milloss remembers working with Laban in 1929: 'We experimented, improved and throughout it all we concerned ourselves with Eukinetics.'[1]

'Effort' eludes easy definition. The sketches for Laban's Introduction to *Effort and Recovery* include the following definitions:

Effort

1. Exertion of Power, physical or mental

2. A production as of art or oratory

Synonyms: Exertion, endeavour, attempt, essay, trial, application; struggle, strain, pains; labour, toil, trouble.

Exertion is in general the active (often vigorous, but not always!) or laborious exercise of any power of faculty.

Effort commonly suggests a single action often with a definite object in view (consciously approached) rather than (but not always) a continued activity; for example, as to be wearied by *exertion*; to make a supreme *effort*.

Application is assiduous exertion; for example, as intense *application*.

Pains is toilsome or solicitous effort.

Trouble implies exertion that inconveniences or incommodes; ex, as, the dumb may, sufficient pains, be taught to speak; it is so no trouble to do so.

Derivation: Latin; *exfortiare*, *ex* + *fortis* (strong).

From the first line we can see that [Effort can be both physical and mental – in this sense, Effort is the deployment of human energy in the pursuit of a particular task.] But we shall see how Laban refuses to limit the analysis purely to external movement: to understand the outer movement, one has to grasp the inner intention behind it. One way of describing Laban's work on Effort is that it deals with different qualities of movement.]

Below I shall summarise the basic concepts of Effort since Laban's own definitions are not always that succinct. Indeed, Laban's terminology was always on the move, and as his ideas about Effort developed, so he coined new terms and concepts to explore the correlation between mental activity and movement expression. His 'Glossary of terms as used in Movement

Psychology' of 1954 has therefore been included on p. 351 of this volume to help guide the reader through these later texts.

In *Effort*, Laban writes about every movement consisting of four Motion Factors, each of which has two opposite poles, indulging and contending (also 'Fighting against').

	Indulging	Contending
Space	Flexible	Direct
Weight	Light	Strong
Time	Sustained	Quick
Flow	Free	Bound

The first three **Motion Factors** combine to create eight **Effort Actions.** Each of these actions can be performed with either Free or Bound Flow. Table 12.1 (on pp. 200–201) draws on descriptions of actions in *Effort* and demonstrates the incredible subtlety that this analysis can achieve.

Table 12.1 Effort

Strong Efforts

FREE FLOW	BOUND FLOW
Punching (direct, strong, quick) –	**Fighting against Weight, Space and Time**
'forcing a shovel into dry sand or a spade into clay'	stress on weight
'to thrust a fork into hay or a chisel under the lid of a box'	stress on direction (space)
'to poke a coal fire or to pierce leather with an awl'	stress on time
Pressing (direct, strong, sustained) –	**Fighting with Weight and Space, Indulging in Time**
crushing 'fruit with a crusher or granules with a mortar'	stress on weight
cutting 'leather with a sharp knife or wood with a carver's knife'	stress on direction (space)
squeezing 'a bulb or squirt with the hand or suitings with shears'	stress on time
Slashing (flexible, strong, quick) –	**Fighting with Weight and Time, Indulging in Space**
beating 'a carpet with a beater or a nail with a hammer'	stress on weight
throwing 'coal with a shovel or a package from hand to hand'	stress on direction (space)
whipping 'an egg with a whisk or the branches of a hedge with a billhook'	stress on time
Wringing (flexible, strong, sustained) –	**Fighting with Weight, Indulging in Space and Time**
pulling 'a trolley with shafts or a cork with a corkscrew'	stress on weight
plucking 'feathers by hand or thinning out seedlings by hand'	stress on direction (space)
stretching 'elastic or cloth by hand'	stress on time

Light Efforts

FREE FLOW	BOUND FLOW
Dabbing (direct, light, quick) –	**Fighting with Space and Time, Indulging in Weight**
patting 'dough with hand or level index cards by hand'	stress on weight
tapping 'typewriter key or morse key with hand', shaking 'sand in a sieve or water sprinkler by hand'	stress on direction (space)
	stress on time
Gliding (direct, light, sustained) –	**Fighting with Space, Indulging in Weight and Time**
smoothing 'cloth by hand or lace with iron'	stress on weight
smearing 'whitewash with brush or mortar with trowel'	stress on direction (space)
smudging 'putty with thumb or oil paint with palette knife	stress on time
Flicking (flexible, light, quick) –	**Fighting with Time, Indulging in Weight and Space**
flipping 'dry towel or wet towel with hand'	stress on weight
flapping 'coins counting them or counting notes in a similar way'	stress on direction (space)
jerking 'bottle rinsing it or breaking string with hand'	stress on time
Floating (flexible, light, sustained) –	**Indulging in Weight, Time and Space**
strewing 'seed by hand or powder on a surface'	stress on weight
stirring 'water by hand or oil paint with stick'	stress on direction (space)
stroking 'vessel, polishing it or brushing clothes'	stress on time[2]

Source: From *Effort*, 2nd edn, 1973.

The notation of Effort is very different to that of the notation of dance. It takes the form of what he calls the Effort Cross (Figure 12.1).

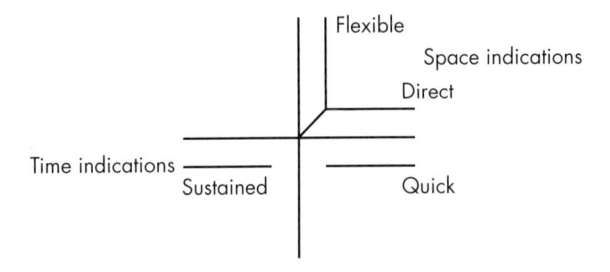

Figure 12.1 The Effort Cross
Source: From *Effort*, 2nd edn, 1973.

Thus, the eight Effort actions can be represented as follows (Figure 12.2).

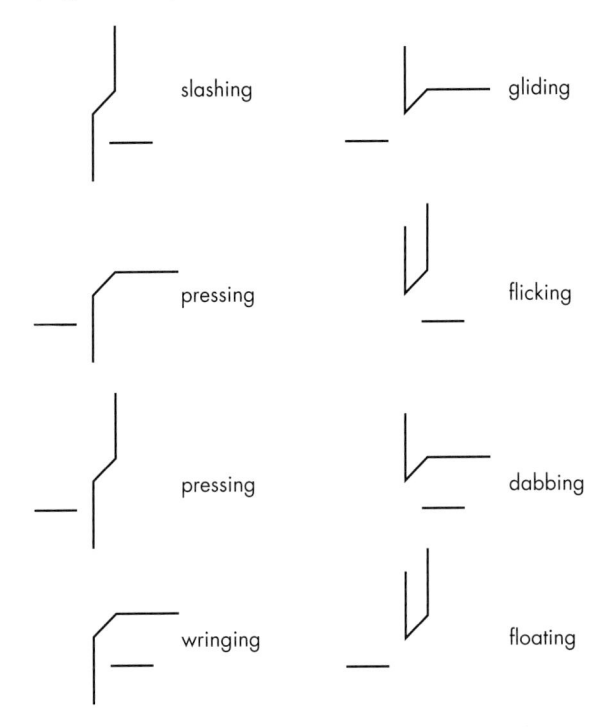

- slashing
- gliding
- pressing
- flicking
- pressing
- dabbing
- wringing
- floating

Figure 12.2 The eight Effort actions
Source: From *Effort*, 2nd edn, 1973.

Broken or incomplete efforts

In *The Mastery of Movement* Laban explored what happens when one of the four elements is missing, creating a broken or incomplete effort:

> Without flow there is *action drive*
> Without weight there is *vision drive*
> Without time there is *spell drive*
> Without space there is *passion drive*[3]

Bartenieff calls these 'Transformation Drives' and offers a helpful gloss:

> However, even an untrained observer can see the principal moods and qualities of a Transformation Drive, describing them metaphorically: 'He has a hypnotic (Timeless) quality', or 'She was so passionately involved in her diatribe that she didn't even hear me enter' (Spaceless), or 'He was drawn out of himself into the vision of the many possibilities before him' (Weightless).[4]

When only two elements are present in an action, Laban described these as Inner Attitudes or States. Combinations of two effort elements are sometimes called Incomplete (Basic Effort Actions) or Inner Attitudes or, preferably, Inner States. Instead of drives, they produce mood-like qualities in movement that can be metaphorically described as Awake, Dreamlike; Remote, Near; Stable, Mobile.[5]

To summarise in tabular form (Table 12.2, p. 204).

Bartenieff writes about the difference between the effects of Efforts and Drives and Inner Attitudes:

> It is a dramatic experience to observe either three-element or two-element combinations – Transformations and Inner States – after working with only Basic Effort Action drives. Another color tone takes over and changes the quality. This can often be seen when a Basic Effort action is performed inadequately by accident or choice during

the process of change, and its function – to Punch, for example – is not fulfilled. It has veered off into a Transformation drive or an Inner State. The movement has a less literal or tangible quality, not so much associated with action as with affect, or mood.[6]

At bottom, Laban and Bartenieff are proposing that Effort Actions are to do with functional movement while movements with two or three motion factors tend progressively towards psychological states. Laban used the term 'Shadow Move' to describe barely perceptible movements, often facial expressions, which are entirely affective or psychological and these are described in a brief section of their own.

Table 12.2 Drives and attitudes

Drives Consist of <u>Three</u> Motion Factors

Drive	Motion Factors			
Doing	Weight	Space	Time	*no Flow*
Passionate	Weight	Time	Flow	*no Space*
Influencing	Weight	Space	Flow	*no Time*
Visionary	Space	Time	Flow	*no Weight*

Inner Attitudes Consist of <u>Two</u> Movement Factors

Movement Attitude	Motion Factors		
Stable	Weight	Space	*no Time, no Flow*
Mobile	Flow	Time	*no Weight, no Space*
Near	Weight	Time	*no Space, no Flow*
Remote	Flow	Space	*no Weight, no Time*
Awake	Space	Time	*no Weight, no Flow*
Adream (Dreamlike)	Flow	Weight	*no Space, no Time*

Source: From *Effort*, 2nd edn, 1973.

Overview of later chapters

In a letter of 23rd March 1951 to André and Bibi Perrottet, Laban offers an overview of his work of the 1940s and 1950s in England:

> After my professional views of movement in industry, education and in theatre (these three have already been published) there is therapy, particularly in nervous disorders. I have also done a lot of practical work in mental hospitals and have finally found there a few normal people. It is quite probable that I shall concentrate in this field for the rest of my days, firstly because my assistance is much in demand and secondly because there I do not have to leap around with large groups which is something my doctor has forbidden me to do for some time.[7]

The texts in this section of the book follow the order indicated above: *Effort* (1947) (Chapter 14) where he deals with movement in industry, *Modern Educational Dance* (1948) (Chapter 16), in education, and *The Mastery of Movement on the Stage* (1950) (Chapter 18), in theatre. As to therapy, Laban noted in a letter to Albrecht Knust that his activities had been enlarged in 1949 by 'movement therapy', which at that time had 'been decreed to remain only a part-time occupation'. His final, unpublished work, *Effort and Recovery* (written 1951–1953) (Chapter 19) dwells on the therapeutic dimension of movement. One could call this his fourth 'Effort' book. To these are added printed notes from a visit he made in 1949 to the Withymead Centre – a therapeutic community operating a form of Jungian psychoanalysis (Chapter 20).

In between the extracts from these four 'Effort' books are shorter texts and extracts which help amplify and explain key terms and concepts. The section begins with an article that provides an overview to his thinking across the whole period (Chapter 13). After excerpts from *Effort* (Chapter 14) is a short text from a pamphlet on industrial rhythm, which gives a flavour of Laban's industrial work, as well as further explaining his concept of rhythm (Chapter 15). *Modern*

Educational Dance (Chapter 16) is followed by passages on shadow moves (Chapter 17), and after *Mastery of Movement on the Stage* (Chapter 18) is Laban's own 'Glossary of terms as used in Movement Psychology' on p. 351, which explains terms used in the excerpts from *Effort and Recovery*.

Notes

1. Transcript of an interview with JH (in JHA, Box 30, Folder 41, Item 10f.).
2. *E*, pp. 35–39.
3. *MM* (1960: 84–85).
4. Bartenieff (1980: 63).
5. Ibid., p. 58.
6. Ibid., p. 59.
7. In JHA, Box 26, Folder 24, Item 3.

Chapter thirteen

The Art of Movement in Education, Work and Recreation (mid-1940s)[1]

Introduction

Dick McCaw

This extraordinary article demonstrates the breadth of Laban's interest in movement. We have seen that in the 1910s and 1920s Laban engaged in a similar breadth of activity, all of which centred upon dance. In *Effort and Recovery*, he argues that it was the theatre (and I think he means performance on stage, be it dance or theatre) that led to his interest in other forms of movement:

> The growing realism of the theatre of those days led me to a thorough investigation of working movement in agriculture and industry.... My interest in the theatre has never entirely faded, but my movement observation became more acute during all these years and also gained a broader significance.[2]

In *Mastery of Movement*, he argues that the two are inextricably tied: 'all through history, movement on the stage drew its inspiration from the occupational motions of the now most numerous part of the population, the workers'.[3] Later he builds on this relation:

> Now in our time the industrial revolution has given new concepts of aesthetical beauty to all the arts, for the newly acquired knowledge of the workers' movements has led to a fresh mastery of movement on the stage. The procedures in training for skill and efficiency in industry show many parallels with the new training methods of the modern stage artist.[4]

However, let us not assume from this that Laban made a shift from dance to theatre – his conception of both was movement orientated. He sees theatre in terms of movement, and his idea of dance was quite theatrical, and it also focused on working movement (as we saw in the Vienna parade of 1929, in Chapter 8).

Laban's article begins with his ideas on education, where he argues that teachers need to understand their own effort profile before they try to address that of their pupils (which echoes his ideas in *Gymnastics and Dance for Children*). His section on industry gives two vivid examples of his approach to problems of movement in work and an example of how swinging (so central to his early conception of dance training) has now been applied to everyday work. An important theme in the final section on therapy is that students try to avoid a 'lopsided' development of their efforts and instead find a balance between the different qualities of movement. One-sided development was mentioned in *The World of the Dancer*, and, like swinging, returns here in a different key.

THE ART OF MOVEMENT IN EDUCATION, WORK AND RECREATION

Inasmuch as movement is fundamental to life, so must the study of movement and the activities of human beings be of paramount interest to everybody, and more especially to those responsible for the movement and action of others in the spheres of education, work and recreation.

Everybody realises that the actor and the dancer use movement to present their works of art, but distressingly few people are aware of the important role which the principles of the art of movement play in everyday life. For those who are engaged professionally in dealing with people whose activities require mastery of movement, the art of movement is indispensable. Noticeable deficiencies in the mastery of movement are widespread in the world today as revealed by lack or loss of equilibrium within certain physical and psychological components of a personality. The re-establishment of this inner balance is an urgent need and calls for teachers and leaders who can recognise in people such signs of serious movement inhibitions and through the technique of the art of movement enable them to recapture something of the instinctive mastery of rhythm of their early childhood days.

The solution to this problem through the art of movement implies no mere mobilisation of joints and strengthening of muscle groups, but an adjustment through an understanding of the effort capacities of each individual. In nurseries, schools, factories and clubs, and in fact in all walks of life, people at play or at work are making a continual series of efforts. A trained observer of movement will see exaggerations and discords which are due to a one-sided development or an impoverished use of effort by the individual. A clear example can be seen in the case of people who appear to proceed in their tasks in an unnecessarily jerky, hasty manner, continually fighting against time. They have lost the ability to indulge in time even when opportunity presents itself. Others may reveal a markedly cramped attitude, and no longer enjoy the natural full extensions of the body into space.

In the art of movement we find the common denominator of all human expression. It is movement which is the basis of poetry, drama, music, dance and the other arts. Through dance, which is the natural flowering of the study of movement, the child is given opportunity for a refreshing swim in the 'flow of movement'. The flow of movement permeates all our functions and actions, releasing us from damaging inner tensions; it is a means of communication between people, since all our forms of expression, speaking, writing, singing, are carried by the flow of movement.

Today, after years of suffering resulting from regimentation of the people, the call for the means to restore individuality sounds clear. Teachers of many nationalities who have studied the art of movement confirm both the need and hope that future improvement in human relationships might and could be promoted by introducing its study into schools. We do not aim in the school at artistic perfection or the creation and performance of sensational dances, but the beneficial effect of the creative activity of dancing upon the personality of the pupil. But this is not all.

The art of movement in education

The art of movement in education provides a simple and efficacious means of assessment, in education both of the children's capacities and progress, as well as of the teacher's activities. The teacher can learn to use a nice balance of efforts, giving the class opportunities to experiment with and increase their effort experiences. The teacher who has acquired a working knowledge of the study of movement and has applied it to himself, is then in a position to understand more fully the spirit of the class he teaches. In the past his adjustments have often been intuitive or at the most the result of a vague and haphazard method of observation. For example, many teachers attempt to stimulate an apathetic class by assuming a cheerful voice and superficially brisk manner. The student of the art of movement will realise that this is not sufficient to help the children. They must learn to adopt a more active attitude towards movement and effort. In the case of an excitable class the reverse procedure is needed. The same principle applies to the individual child who may unjustly be termed lazy by the teacher unschooled in effort assessment. Because the child tends to indulge in time, he must be helped to take up an active approach to it by experiencing such efforts as slashing, thrusting, dabbing and flicking, which develop quickness. This will prove much more expedient than continual nagging, reproaches and injunctions to hurry, or not to waste time. . . .

Only a teacher who is able to observe his own efforts, and modify and develop them where necessary, will be able to use movement tuition to ensure a healthy development of the efforts of his pupils. It should also be realised that this increased power of movement observation will be of untold value in all manual activities in the school such as handwork, gardening, carpentry, games, cookery, etc. The teacher who assists in dramatic productions will be able to use the full range of efforts to increase the significance of the gestures and actions of the players, and thus contribute not only to a better and more sensible dramatic performance, but also to the natural growth of the personality of the children in question.

The art of movement in industry

Most successful foremen, supervisors and managers think involuntarily in terms of effort, but many of them are blinded by the ordinary conception of the task which must be accomplished, and they fail to study how it is done. Clumsy methods may be continued because work has been done in this way or that for years, and those responsible unconsciously shirk the fight against difficult conditions and circumstances. Someone who is able to visualise the rhythm of the efforts used in a job is often confronted by a spectacle which is, to him, grotesque.

During experimental investigations in a sawmill, the loading of a van with small staves was once witnessed. The workers employed in this job were a dozen heavily clad, strong men, whose ordinary job was the transport of heavy trees from the forest to the gantry, where they discharged their lorries, piling up the tree trunks in gigantic heaps and balancing on them with remarkable acrobatic skill. Delegated to the loading of the small staves which were piled up for drying under a shed, they formed a solid row from the piles to the van and passed on, one to another, a voluminous bundle of staves during which process a considerable number of staves fell to the ground. The two men in the van had great trouble in heaping the irregular bundles of staves inside the vehicle, with the result that many of them were broken and the loading space could not be used to its full capacity. Replacing the twelve men by five girls, three of whom were standing equally spaced between the stacks and the van, while one collected the staves one at a time from the piles and another arranged them in the vehicle, the task was performed in half the time by less than half the number of workers and the van was filled to its complete capacity without breakages. The men disliked the work and grumbled when asked to do it, while the girls enjoyed the large swinging movements by which the staves were picked up, passed from hand to hand, and restacked in the van.

In this example attention is drawn to the simple swinging movements in contrast to the complicated and cramped efforts of gathering and transmitting haphazardly formed bundles. The sight of the overcrowded row of men working with bound flow immediately generated in the mind of the trained observer the contrasting desirable vision of a light and simple free flow of material. The employment of a lesser number of more flexible operators was the natural outcome of this vision.

To emphasise still further the application of the vision of flow in work a second example out of a vast number of experiences may be quoted. In this case it concerned workers in an orchard. Complaints of customers called attention to the fact that the lower layers of cherries collected in the baskets were ripe while the upper layers were unripe. Carelessness on the part of the Land Army girls, who did the job, was assumed to be the cause. Observation of the flow of their operational movements showed, however, that those movements, which were at first quite determined and relatively regular, afterwards became erratic and undecided. It turned out that after a time they could no longer discern the red colour of the ripe cherries from the yellow unripe ones. The cause of the disturbing irregularity was detected by the observation of the changes of efforts which resulted finally in movements characteristic of blind people. This increasing hesitation and restless way of working was obviously due to eye-strain. In staring at the small spots of colour among the green foliage fluttering in the wind, the operators soon lost the power to discern the colour of the cherries. Red and green are complementary colours which are confused naturally by colour-blind people. The remedy for the temporary colour-blindness consisted in short relaxations of the eye-muscles by looking at a spot of neutral colour or shutting the eye for a moment. The result was not only baskets full of ripe cherries but a much quicker filling of the baskets.

The rhythm of man in his work and in his whole life should achieve the adaptation of the flow of material to the dance of life, benefiting the producer and worker as well as the consumer, and avoiding many disturbances of an industrial civilisation. The rediscovery of the meaning of rhythm can contribute towards a solution of the purely human problems arising where many people work for long hours together in a common task. . . .

The therapeutic use of the art of movement

The principles governing the use of the art of movement for therapeutic purposes are similar to those used in education, but are applied with a bias in various directions to suit people who show a personality imbalance.

Among these people symptoms such as these are to be found: inability to concentrate; exaggerated fear without a known cause; acute depression; anxiety; uncontrollable excitement or aggression; obsessional ideas; feelings of unreality; or inability to express overwhelming emotion. Many of these people find it very difficult to live in harmony with the group of people at their work or in their homes, and many are out of harmony with themselves. These symptoms show themselves in movements which have, perhaps, an exaggerated attitude towards one or other of the elements of effort, and which frequently lack flow. These abnormalities become apparent in dance movements, working actions and shadow movements. Experience in the observation of movement, the analysis of movement in working actions, and movement as a creative art is thus a great help to anyone dealing with people suffering from psychological difficulties.

Any creative and expressive activity demands the sustained effort of the whole personality, imposes its own discipline, and in turn re-creates the artist. It is not an easy task to apply the rehabilitating power of creative activity for remedial purposes, but attempts have been made, with promising results. Teaching must be adapted to the special needs of the participants. Use can be made of pure dance, or of dance-mime which supply a training in emotional control and self-discipline, and the opportunity to experience changes in mood. A sense of responsibility to the work of the group helps to develop the social sense, and teaches the patient to appreciate his own values in relation to other people.

Individually, a patient's attitude to the elements of movement, and so to life, can be retrained. Everyone has a tendency to select certain ways of moving which permeate his whole behaviour. This unconscious choice of often quite a limited range of movements indicates an inner attitude. If certain qualities are exaggerated while others are limited, a harmonious balance can be restored by using dance exercises involving transitions between the overdeveloped faculty and the neglected one. Such movement sequences or dances may be created by patient help from the teacher, who should encourage the individual's inherent capacity for finding his own effort balance, and help him to recover some of the instinctive and spontaneous flow of movement of his youth.

The knowledge that movement has power to influence mood, and even ways of thinking and behaviour, has been used consciously and unconsciously at all times, and still today people can go to a recreational dance class weary and dispirited, and feel refreshed and invigorated afterwards. Awareness of this two-way interplay and relationship between movement and inner attitude and feelings is the basis of the remedial trainer's work. He must observe all the external signs objectively and without prejudice, and adapt his teaching to each patient's needs.

Knowledge of the patient's history and the reasons for his lack of psychological balance is not essential to the movement teacher. His particular contribution is to assess the patient as he sees him, and to help him to find an inner balance through developing his latent capacities.

The art of movement offers a wide field of research to the psychotherapist, psychologist, and psychiatrist in the discovery of personal problems through effort assessment, and in the observation of symptomatic behaviour. The occupational therapist will find a knowledge of the art of movement a valuable help in the rehabilitation of skills.

The art of movement applied in education, recreation work, stage-craft and rehabilitation follows similar principles since the efforts underlying all movements are actually the same, no matter for which practical purpose they are used. The knowledge of man's effort life not only throws a new light upon the actions and characteristics of human beings but is a valuable means of training and selection. There is a large field of exploration and practical application extending beyond the domains here discussed.

Notes

1 Published by the Laban Guild. In the catalogue of the British Library the publication date is given as 1953, but this is indicated nowhere on the 19-page document itself.
2 ER, NRCD, File 10, p.37.
3 MM (1950), p. 104.
4 Ibid., p. 105.

Chapter fourteen

Effort (1947)

Introduction

Warren Lamb

I arrived at the Art of Movement Studio a year before publication of the first edition of *Effort* (1947). Rudolf Laban and Frederick Lawrence were looking for someone to train in succession to their main wartime collaborators in applying 'Industrial Rhythm' or 'Lilt in Labour', as they called it, in British factories. The collaborators were primarily Lisa Ullmann, who had started to concentrate on introducing movement into education, and Jean Newlove, who had become fully engaged in teaching movement to Theatre Workshop actors. My reason for being there was solely because I had become inspired after three months' research about Laban's work in Germany between the two world wars.

My inspiration arose primarily from learning about Laban's concept of Effort. It had also inspired the choreographer Kurt Jooss, whose group was then performing in England, and I was powerfully influenced by his ballet, *The Green Table*. There is no mention of ballet in the book but there is reference to rhythm and the authors' belief that everyone is a dancer is present on almost every page. To have invented a notation in which efforts could be described in terms of movement and rhythm seemed to me so desirable and useful that I left my job and started out on a whole new career.

Of course, we all talk about a task being an 'effort' or that something has been a 'waste of effort' or, say, things like 'It was such an effort getting out of bed this morning'. Laban's concept of Effort, in terms of movement, and the terminology given in the book, enable us to have a definitive understanding of whatever effort we make, in any situation and not only at work. It may be that we are using wrong efforts, lopsided efforts, do not know how to handle effort fatigue, or are applying much more effort to a task than is needed. The book *Effort* helps us to 'make an effort' very much better than we might otherwise do.

The book does not come in the self-help category, however. The authors advance a compelling psychology of movement, which tends more towards a philosophy than a list of tips.

Fundamental to the whole concept is rhythm. The book emphasises proportions, balance, ease, bound or fluent control, the richness of Effort. It is remarkable that British production managers, struggling to get maximum output, were prepared to employ two consultants who offered to teach their workers rhythm. It was opposite to the Work Study principles which prevailed at the time. And it was successful.

While Effort lives on in the vocabulary of teachers of movement what the term means is still under discussion. For example, Weight is currently under debate. Laban originally used the term Force. That such debate is still going on shows the permanence of Laban's work and the scope for continuing development. The concept of Effort in terms of movement was a stroke of genius but none of the terms used in the book has to be cast in stone.

One of the routes for further development is to seek links between Effort (which Laban also referred to as *Eukinetics*) and Shape (alternatively *Choreutics*) and a framework which combines both. Laban seemed to associate Effort with Industry and the Shaping of movement with Dance. Nevertheless, there are many references to Shape in the book *Effort* and, as mentioned above, his introduction of Effort into the dance scene in Germany between the two wars had an immense influence. Laban's genius has such wide-ranging implication that it may be a good thing to research it first under one heading, such as this book offers, then bring it together with writings under other headings in seeking to understand its overall impact.

Some of the writing in *Effort* is attributable to Lawrence and some to Laban. It is remarkable that Lawrence, a former army officer in World War I, a qualified engineer and accountant, respected member of professional institutes, the first person to set up a management consultancy business in Britain in 1923 and living conventionally with his wife and two children, could possibly team up with such a charismatic, unorthodox, unpredictable man as Laban. I was first apprentice, then collaborator with them both for more than ten years. They worked together harmoniously and highly effectively. Both took a lot of initiative in their very different ways. Their common feature was 'vision'. Their book *Effort*, which they truly wrote together, is forward-looking and their vision is still in the process of being realized.

THE APPROPRIATE USE OF MOVEMENT[1]

Any inappropriate use of movement is just a waste of effort. The only advantage is that the intelligent person using the inappropriate movement will, in time, learn by trial and error more or less accurately the movements appropriate to the job.

Skill through economy of effort

This, in fact, is the case in all learning. An occasional chance success will be noticed, and the learner will try to repeat the advantageous combination of motion factors. The inappropriate forms of effort will be discarded by degrees until the most appropriate form is almost automatically employed. This final stage of perfection is called skill.

Skill is acquired through the gradual refinement of the feel of the movement, and any training must promote this feel, which is basically the awakening of the sense for the proportions of motion factors. Some people will learn more quickly than others. The self-teacher, being restricted to the trial and error method, will acquire skill in a longer or shorter time according to his natural ability. The methodically trained learner has the chance to advance more quickly, even if he is less gifted. The best practical method consists of a combination of exercise and the awakening of the understanding of the rules of the proportionality between motion factors.

It is obvious that a learner, who has been made aware of the fact that he exerts too much or too little effort in his operation, will have the advantage of another learner who must detect the cause of failure by prolonged trial. Few people realise in the beginning of their learning period that they may lack the necessary capacity for exertion, and the finer distinctions in its display.

The trainer who is able to develop the lacking or latent capacity will implicitly convey the finer shades of exertion to his pupil. A shortening of the learning period will result in all cases, regardless of whether the pupil is gifted or not.

Mental understanding, which contributes to the awakening of the sense for the proportionality between the elements of effort, is closely connected with the capacity for control. This understanding can be developed in a similar way to the capacity for exertion. The learner will not know in the beginning whether he lacks control or if his efforts are too meticulously controlled. The capacity for control increases with the awareness of the degrees of control which represent the finer shades between the contrasts of fluent flow and bound flow in movement. Movements performed with a high degree of bound flow reveal the readiness of the moving person to stop at any moment in order to readjust the effort if it proves to be wrong, or endangers success. . . .

In movements done with fluent flow, a total lack of control or abandon becomes visible, in which the ability to stop is considered inessential. . . .

The exertion dealing with weight is, however, not the only

one. Any skilled movement is led along a definite path in space. Deviations from this path hinder efficiency and make the effort to a greater or lesser degree inappropriate to the task. . . .

The swinging of an object will describe a definite curved path in space. Exaggeration of the curve constitutes a waste of effort and will diminish the effectiveness of performance. The same is the case when the curve of the path is too near to a straight line. In the example of putting an object cautiously down, where an almost straight line movement might be required, the action will become ineffective when the straightness is too accentuated or the curve too round.

The appropriate exertion dealing with space will have to be learned together and in connection with the exertion dealing with weight in each new operation which an apprentice tries to perform. The insecurity of the movements in space is very obvious with almost all learners. The cause of failure to do a job properly is very often the use of a wrong path in space. In order to record such failures, space indications can be added to the cross or to the effort graphs introduced above. . . .

The exertion in Time contains a further danger for the appropriateness of the effort. A movement can be too quick or too slow for the efficient proportionality of all motion factors, and therefore for the economic and efficient performance of the action.

The capacity to discern and to use shades of time durations rationally is well developed in people having a rhythmical sense. This is a rather widespread gift. The greatest obstacle for its practical application is the prejudice that high speed in work is valuable in itself. Exaggerated quickness developing into haste can be as detrimental to efficiency as the exaggerated use of any other motion factor. Many operations require sustained movements, and even slight accelerations of the effort might prove to be wasteful and detrimental to success. The learner will waste much time in discovering the right speed of his movements needed for the skilled performance of his task. Exercise and the awakening of the sense of proportion are as much needed in the exertions dealing with time as in the two other forms of exertion. The capacity of controlling speed goes with the control of the whole effort. . . .

EFFORT TRAINING[2]

People can be best trained to the performance of specific tasks in the most appropriate manner for the work and their personal capacities, when they understand the relationship and proportionality of motion factors. Skill is gained with less waste of effort and in shorter time than by the slow discovery through the usual trial and error method.

The understanding of the material technicalities of a task will be eased when the instruction, say, of handling a machine goes hand-in-hand with the understanding of the efforts needed in the operation.

Training in coordination of efforts

People trained in the performance of the eight basic actions combined with bound and fluent flow, will be more able to choose the appropriate movements for any tasks they face than those who rely entirely upon their natural gifts or intuition. Gifts are mostly lopsided and appropriate to a few tasks only. Moreover, complicated tasks contain combined efforts, and the person facing such tasks must be able to connect various movements and actions in unexpected ways. The gift for the combination of efforts is still rarer than that for performing short single actions skilfully.

Effort-training must therefore comprehend exercises for such combinations and for the understanding and practice of the rhythm contained in them.

In general effort-training stress is laid on the awakening of the bodily feel of the coordination of motion factors in complex efforts, and in sequences of them. . . .

In the following diagram [Figure 14.1], each corner represents one basic effort. Those connected by lines have two elements in common and differ, therefore in one element only. The letters W for Weight, S for Space and T for Time, inserted on the connecting lines, indicate which exertion has to be altered between two efforts.

The feel of incomplete efforts containing either one or two

EFFORT

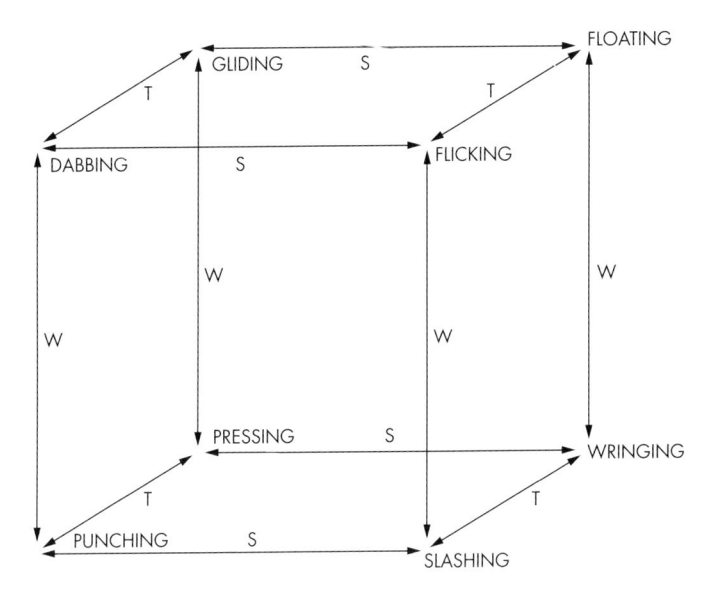

Figure 14.1 The Efforts

elements must be as a carefully trained as basic efforts and their connections.

It can happen that several intermediary movements of basic or incomplete effort character are inserted between the two subsequent efforts of an action, and it might be advantageous to make the trainee aware of the subtle structure of such combination because intermediary movements remain frequently unobserved and are not felt as having a definite effort character.

This is the case when the movements are very quick, or very small in extension.

Without exaggerating the importance of the analysis of the subtle shades of intermediary efforts in practical effort-training, it can be said that the study of incomplete efforts will be most useful for the economy of the Weight effort in the static exertions of gripping, holding and supporting, and in free locomotion when no tools are handled or objects worked on.

Many free locomotions are interspersed between actions, as in walking, turning and reaching for things. Their appropriate performance plays a substantial part in the economy of effort.

SELECTION AND EFFORT-BALANCE[3]

Man's body engine is constructed in a manner that in principle all imaginable effort-combinations can be performed with relative ease and balance. Balance and ease can be lost through long-lasting and therefore habitually lopsided use of a few of all the possible effort-combinations while others are neglected. Such loss is always regrettable but need not disqualify a person for all jobs. If in a job just those efforts are required which an aspirant habitually masters, and if his general effort make-up does not impede their efficient and constant use, he can be considered as eligible for the job. The converse is self-evident.

The restoration of a slightly unbalanced effort make-up can be achieved by relatively simple instruction. The restoration of the full effort-capacity of a person with extremely lopsided effort-habits requires a long effort-training, and this should comprehend the conscious assimilation of the essential rules of balanced effort display.

PSYCHOLOGICAL ASPECTS OF EFFORT CONTROL[4]

The contemporary inclusion of industrial psychology as a part of work study arose from the recognition of the immense importance of the human factor and the unaccountable behaviour of individuals and groups within industrial concerns. Mechanical planning has been spoiled by the uncoordinated efforts of people who have had to perform the various tasks. Both the work study specialist and the industrial psychologist are able to profit from modern effort research.

Our arguments dealing with the economy and control of effort have made this clear so far as manual operations are concerned. An additional new light has, however, to be shed upon the psychological aspect of efforts appearing in work which is not manual or muscular. If we observe closely the distribution or economy of effort used by others, we get the following picture.

Time

People moving with easy effort seem to be freer than those moving with obviously stressed effort. The latter seem to struggle against something. We can learn more about what they are struggling against if we observe subjective movement – that is, those which do not deal with objects and have therefore no outer cause for struggle. But there is an obvious struggle visible in the sometimes painful deportment of a person.

It becomes gradually apparent that one of the main characteristics of effort is the presence or absence of rapidity. With this we have a clue concerning the nature of the struggle. Is it perhaps a fight against time? Time, or speed, is one of the factors of which the compound of effort is built up. This enables us to speak about an effort attitude towards time, in which either the struggling against or the indulging in time is prevailing.

Weight

We may also distinguish another main characteristic of effort, and this is the presence or lack of bodily force. Force is another of the factors of which efforts are built up. It is the degree of energy spent in overcoming one's own body weight, or that of an object, which expresses itself in the effort attitude towards the weight factor.

Someone's exaggerated effort may therefore be a struggle against time or weight, or both, while an easy effort may have its course in an almost complete neglect of any consideration of rapidity or of bodily force. Easy effort will show no struggle either against time or against weight, but rather indulgence in one or both of these factors. A person with an entire neglect of speed takes a lot of time. He or she is, so to speak, bathing, swimming or even submerging in a sea of time. The person whose bodily energy is lacking seems to enjoy his weightiness and to relax happily in being immersed in the general gravity of nature.

Now the strugglers against weight and the racers against time are surely different characters; and so also do those differ who are continuously immersed in a lot of time from those indulging in the experience of their own weight and in the weight of their surroundings.

Space

This is, however, not all that we can detect about the different attitude towards effort-elements. There are people who, without necessarily belonging to the groups of either time-racers or weight-forcers or their contrasts, appear, nevertheless, to move with stressed or easy effort. Since they do not appear either to swim in an ocean of time or to race against time, and as their attitude towards weight is also rather indifferent, what other kind of movement element are they stressing in their efforts? Easy movers might be observed to use a great deal of flexibility and twists in their efforts. That means, they apparently swim, circulate and twist most thoroughly through any possible region of space. Enjoying the space surrounding them makes them happy dwellers of a kingdom of which they know every corner.

But there are others who deal very sparingly with their moving space. Such people seem to take careful account of the extension and expansion of their movements, which appear to be as direct as possible.

It is as if they had an aversion against the manifold extensions of space. This aversion does not manifest itself so much in a tumultuous struggle, but rather in a kind of restriction in the use of many space directions. The need of an occasional excursion into space causes them a clearly visible and highly-stressed effort. These facts make it necessary to distinguish a special effort attitude towards space.

Flow

The three effort-attitudes towards the time factor, weight factor and space factor do not, however, cover all the basic phenomena observable. Persons do not move either suddenly or deliberately, weakly or forcefully, flexibly or directly only. There exists another factor, flow, which can be observed in people's movements, which together with the three factors mentioned above might give us a basis for a full account of effort phenomena. We can distinguish the flow of movement of a person, which can be free or bound, whatever velocity, space expansion or force the movements might have. With this observation we have discovered a fourth attitude towards the factors of movement, which, if prevailing in an effort, gives it the character of either a struggle against, or an indulgence in, the flow effort.

Some people seem to enjoy letting their movements flow whilst others show an obvious reluctance to do so. One can see how the latter endeavour to withhold and almost to stop the flow or progress of their movement at any moment of their action. This may cause them to make very large and perhaps roundabout movements. The reluctance is not directed against space, but they carefully abstain from letting movements flow freely. Their complicated movement-patterns are drawn in the air with a meticulous guidance which need not, however, be explicitly either slow or quick. Sometimes the shapes are traced with such withholding reticence that they are like a child's first attempts in writing and drawing. A real bound flow of this kind need not, however, be accompanied by any weight-accent – that is, a cramped use of force; it can be weak or entirely indifferent so far as weight is concerned.

People who indulge in flow find pleasure in the unrestricted freedom of fluency, without necessarily giving much attention to the various shades of the time, the weight and the space development of the movement. Movements with free flow cannot be easily interrupted or suddenly stopped; it takes time until the moving person gains the necessary control over the flow in order to stop. Those persons who tend to bind their flow will be able to stop their movements at any instant.

Having now distinguished the typical kinds of effort attitudes towards time, weight, space and flow, we can say that each of these may be either 'struggled against' or 'indulged in'. We have gained a vocabulary for the basic impressions we can receive from the observation of efforts.

Before penetrating into further investigations of the more complicated regions of effort manifestations, it should be remembered that the relative largeness of a movement has nothing to do with its effort-character. The tiniest, shortest movement of a muscle can show any of the differentiations of effort – that is, it can be the expression of a struggling against or an indulgence in any of the four motion factors, as we might from now on call time, weight, space and flow.

Combination of motion factors

Even the tiniest jerks of muscles can show multiple combinations of the use of motion factors. It has already been said that efforts are less easily observed in small and single movements than in large and repeated movements. This is not caused by the absence of effort-characteristics, but by the restricted capacity of the unskilled observer to see them.

Another thing can be mentioned in connection with the fact that personal efforts and personal character-qualities might be related. The existence of four motion factors might suggest that there could be a connection between them and the four fundamental types of human temperaments, which are usually distinguished in the oldest as well as in the most recent psychological treatises.

There is, however, no cause to search for the possible kinship between effort types and types of temperament. Such search would rather restrict than help the extension of effort investigation. There exist a few – as we submit, four – clearly distinguishable motion factors in which effort evolves, but it is not possible that any one person could be addicted to one motion factor exclusively. On the other hand, any one of the motion factors may be predominant.

In observing children, adults, workers and dancers, one will hardly find a normal individual who exclusively submerges or indulges in time or in any other of the four motion factors.

Neither will we find a person, healthy in body and mind, carrying out throughout the whole of his life a quixotic fight against space or flow or weight.

The richness of people's efforts consists just in the fact that their effort characteristics are an incredibly subtle mixture of many degrees of attitudes towards several motion factors. They may indulge in several elements simultaneously, one balancing the other as well as possible. They often fight against the whole bunch of motion factors which nature has placed at their disposal. That both this great and unified struggle and its opposite, total surrender, are stimulated by experiences and circumstances, is a secondary consideration with which effort research has to deal.

The first point of immediate interest in effort study is the theory that movements are bound to evolve in space as well as in time – if one prefers to say so, in Space-Time – and that in this evolution of movement the weight of the body is brought into flow.

It has been found practical to use in the description of efforts appearing in human motion the previously introduced diagrammatic signs, in which, roughly speaking, the 'fighting against' and the 'indulgence in' single motion factors are shown by easily understandable symbols. Two such compound signs are of paramount importance, namely – 'indulgence in' and 'fighting against' all motion factors.

More as an example than as preliminary explanation, it might be considered what kind of worker, and what kind of personality, an individual would be, for one of these compound symbols to be characteristic.

As a worker – and one should include here all the people in any activities from, say, labouring to dancing – a person indulging in all motion factors will be able to deal with all tasks demanding free flow of motion, fine touch, flexibility and sustainment, such as delicate repair or assembly work.

Such a worker will find difficulty in dealing with tasks of the opposite kind. The person habitually fighting against all the four motion factors will best deal with work exacting controlled or bound flow of motion, great strength, use of the shortest and most direct way in all his movements and an ability to function with quick impulses, such as in lumbering, hand forging and heavy repetitive work; but the examples are legion.

If the efforts are not observed in working movements but in the small movements of everyday behaviour, as in the way a person sits, stands, or the odd movements a person might show in his or her facial expression during idleness or conversation, one will find the same contrasts. One individual may fight against and the other indulge in all the motion factors. The personality expressed will be quite different in the two cases. The person with free flowing, light, sustained and flexible muscle movements will be quite different from the other who shows controlled flow of motion together with strong, quick and direct movements. To call one gentle and the other energetic is a very poor rendering of the real facts.

It seems that the only thing one can do is to renounce all psychological terms, especially as there exist an almost infinite number of combinations of every degree and shade. This makes clear the advantage of using the compound signs with the great variety they can show, rather than verbal descriptions. Words cannot express the precise degree to which an individual neglects or prefers the different motion factors.

The personality value of the characteristics shown in everyday behaviour has, however, very real significance if we want to assess the ability for intellectual work, work which consists of mental exertion, as for instance in administrative activities in business or artistic occupations. The 'indulger in' all the motion factors will have a greater ability for delicate mental operations, while the 'fighter against' all the motion factors will be able to deal with mental work in which quick decision and accuracy are demanded. Yet one must never forget that these absolutely fundamental types do not exist; they are illustrations only of the two basic compound symbols.

Notes

1   *E*, Chapter 3, pp. 14–24.
2   Ibid., Chapter 4, pp. 25–42.
3   Ibid., Chapter 5, pp. 43–50.
4   Ibid., Chapter 7, pp. 62–75.

Chapter fifteen

Answers to Ten Questions on Industrial Rhythm (early 1950s)[1]

1. WHAT IS THE MAIN PURPOSE OF INDUSTRIAL RHYTHM?

To introduce Rhythm Study into industry, as a simple and efficient instrument of control and production and of welfare during work.

2. BY WHAT PRACTICAL STEPS DOES INDUSTRIAL RHYTHM HOPE TO ACHIEVE THIS AIM?

Through a special method of movement observation yielding exact characteristic of the capacities needed for each job or activity occurring in an enterprise.

The same method of movement observation serves also as a testing method without instruments for selection and assessment of effort.

The method of movement observation makes it further possible to determine the best cure for personal deficiencies as well as to detect inadequacies in the material rhythm of any working procedure.

Instruction and training of newcomers and apprentices can be shortened and intensified by taking the results of the job movement observation into account.

Where rehabilitation services are introduced, the study of job rhythm can be of great help in several respects.

Specific ways of occupational therapy through movement training can be detected and the progression from job to job according to the improvement of the functions can be rationally regulated.

3. IN WHAT WAY DOES THE MOVEMENT OBSERVATION OF INDUSTRIAL RHYTHM DIFFER FROM THE USUAL FORMS OF MOTION STUDY?

In emphasising the study of rhythm.

Utilising an original form of recording, the analysis of the observation is simpler and less expensive than the usual forms of Motion Study because it requires no instruments, laboratory tests, films, etcetera, and because it can be effectuated without disturbing the observed persons at their job.

Industrial Rhythm records the full activity of the operator when handling specific objects and using specific tools.

If it is possible to record with the same notation the efforts of persons engaged in non-operational activities, for example, activities of office personnel.

4. WHAT ARE THE ADVANTAGES OF RHYTHM OBSERVATION?

In *Rhythm Study* much more than only series of single movements is observed. The investigator endeavours also to trace the relationship between the movements, because a harmonious coordination of movements is the first condition of skill and efficiency and for the decreasing of unnecessary and harmful exertion.

While *Motion Study* is usually only concerned with average skilled performance and does not allow for above average potentialities, *Rhythm Study* can and must take into consideration all such potentialities. It aims at increasing the skill of the below average worker as well as that of the average work to a higher level.

5. HOW IS INDUSTRIAL RHYTHM INVESTIGATION CARRIED OUT IN A FACTORY?

An observer visits the factory in order to assess the characteristics of the capacities needed in each job or operation in a given department. This is done by comparing the individual effort-rhythm of the present personnel.

The time needed for this investigation depends upon the kind of work, the number of jobs and the number of persons engaged.

The observation is unobtrusive and does not in any way interfere with the normal flow of work.

The progress of the investigation is discussed at regular intervals with the leading executives. Finally, a definite list of job characteristics, together with recommendations for measures of ensuring the rational expending of efforts, is handed over to the management.

6. HOW CAN PEOPLE BE INSTRUCTED IN THE RATIONAL EXPENDING OF EFFORT?

By making them aware by discussion of operational details and, if necessary, by movement training of the importance of harmony and rhythm as a means of achieving better and easier performance and of avoiding strain and fatigue.

Standard methods elicited through movement observation are not rigidly imposed. The individual optimum of performance will be best decided by mutual discussion and trial.

7. IN WHAT CASES IS MOVEMENT TRAINING NECESSARY?

Movement training is used mainly for female workers and boy apprentices, as an instruction for newcomers, as a compensation for one-sided strain, as a remedial measure in rehabilitation, and in other cases where physical capacities, for example, lifting power, are not equal to the task.

8. ARE INSTRUCTIONS AND MOVEMENT TRAINING CARRIED OUT IN WORKING HOURS AND, IF SO, HOW MUCH TIME IS NEEDED?

Instruction and training must definitely form a part of the working day. Time needed depends on the individual cases.

As an example, one could say that apprentices should receive daily training. Compensatory training time will vary according to the degree of strain, while as a remedial measure training should take place in slight cases twice or three times a week, in more serious cases daily.

The average training time per session will vary between thirty and forty-five minutes.

9. WHAT WILL BE THE REACTION OF THE PERSONNEL TO THE INTRODUCTION OF RHYTHM AND HARMONY INTO THEIR WORK?

It will be necessary for everybody to understand that even in highly mechanised enterprises the real basis of industrial efficiency is well-balanced human effort and collaboration.

It must be further understood that any action has a definite rhythm. In skilful performance the single parts of the action are harmoniously connected and follow each other in easy flow.

True automation, an important feature of skill, is only possible where the rhythmical qualities of the action are perfectly assimilated.

Work requiring free decision will also be best done by people who are able to coordinate rhythm and harmony in their efforts.

This refers to handwork and brainwork equally.

In giving to everyone concerned the opportunity of experiencing the physical and mental benefits of effort regulation in work, a favourable reaction can be expected, provided sufficient support of the management is given to the scheme.

10. COULD INDUSTRIAL RHYTHM BE CALLED A BRANCH OF WELFARE?

Yes and no, because if the striving for rhythmical perfection is fostered, both the enterprise and the individual collaborating in it draw equal benefit.

Rhythm in industry is an essential element of welfare as well as an essential implement of production control.

Note

1 In JHA, Box 24, Folder 18, Item 11f [photocopy of a four-page typescript].

Chapter sixteen

Modern Educational Dance (1948)

Introduction

Anna Carlisle

1.

The genesis of Modern Educational Dance and Rudolf Laban's role as founding father of dance in the English state education system are little known today. The story is embedded in extraordinary circumstances; its recognition as a school subject established during the turbulence of the Second World War. In 1940, Laban was evacuated to the isolation of Newtown in rural Wales. With 'alien' status, no work permit and a negligible command of the English language, the situation appeared bleak. Several aspects of fortune rapidly converged, however, to effect major changes and to reignite Laban's international reputation as the prime mover in the evolution and development of Central European Modern Dance and to offer up an opportunity to realise his dream of dance for all children in the general education system.

The prevailing pre-war Progressive Education philosophy, arts-oriented and child-centred, had presented problems for the world of Physical Education. A directive to introduce more freedom and creativity into curriculum activities and a recommendation in the 1933 Syllabus that one period of the physical education timetable be given over to dance, had precipitated a flirtation with a variety of dance forms. Swedish gymnastics, the revived Greek Dance, Madge Atkinson's Natural Movement and Dalcroze's system of Eurythmics had all created imprints and traces in the Physical Education field.

In 1941, in the knowledge that a number of important aspects of Laban's work were closely attuned to the Progressive perspective, a small group of enthusiastic practitioners of Central European Modern Dance organised a landmark conference under the auspices of the Physical Education Association.[1] Attended by an influential group of educationalists and members of Her Majesty's Inspectorate, it was designed to present the concepts of Laban's 'free dance' form and to investigate its educational potential. The success of the symposium, attributed mainly to the contribution made by Laban and Ullmann, effected a move which was to influence the course of dance education for the next thirty years. The Association made an official request to the Board of Education to promote 'Modern' Dance in schools. The event marked the beginning of an era in which dance was to gain a stronger hold in education: a period in which Laban's ideas formed the basis of what came to be known as 'Modern Educational Dance'.

As Laban gained strength, recognition and momentum, his characteristics as a polymath in the field of Movement were reinvigorated. Between 1941 and 1945, he was invited to apply his work to aspects of industry, psychotherapy and theatre. His interest in education went undiminished but Laban had moved on. It fell to Lisa Ullmann to become the major activating force for the translation and development of his ideas into education. By the end of the war, Ullmann's inspirational teaching had engendered a groundswell of enthusiasm for Modern Dance in schools and colleges. During the post-war years, in a political climate of radical social change, Modern Educational Dance began to spread and take root in the Primary Sector. It was enthusiastically pioneered in the South by two of the major women's Physical Education

Colleges, Bedford and Chelsea. In the North East, Sir Alec Clegg, Chief Education Officer for the West Riding of Yorkshire, inaugurated dance programmes which were to become models of good practice. In 1948, Laban responded to urgent calls for a textbook, *Modern Educational Dance* (*MED*).

2.

In the Preface to *Modern Educational Dance*, Laban describes the text as 'a guide to educationists and parents interested in the subject'. The slim volume is divided into five chapters. The Introduction, printed below, presents Laban's seminal ideas on the educative powers of movement and dance – a medium he described as 'living architecture', a primary art which could enliven, enrich and develop personal and social harmony. The introductory material is both general and specific. General in the sense that it provides explication of the concepts which impelled him to create and develop a revolutionary new dance form – and specific in its application to dance education in the school curriculum.

Chapter 1, 'Dancing Throughout the Age Groups', charts the processes of child development in a schema which is close to a Piagetian model. Chapter 2, 'Sixteen Basic Movement Themes' – together with theoretical explications of aspects of Eukinetics and Choreutics in Chapters 3 and 4 – present an outline syllabus for practitioners. This material is not for the novice. The translation, application and realisation of the content here presuppose a dance teacher with considerable knowledge and expertise in the concepts and practice of Laban's work, together with a high degree of creative and organisational ability. (The task of amplifying and clarifying Laban's outline syllabus later fell to Valerie Preston-Dunlop in her publication, *A Handbook for Modern Educational Dance*.[2])

The final chapter, 'The Observation of Movement', extends aspects of the introductory rationale. Here, Laban places strong emphasis on a profound understanding of his theories of Effort and Dynamics, taught as a means of encouraging experience of the rich and complex range of human expression. He states:

> When we realise that movement is the essence of life, and that all expression, whether it be speaking, writing, singing, painting or dancing, uses movement as a vehicle, we cannot help seeing the importance of understanding this outward expression of the living energy within, and this we can do through Effort study.[3]

He believed that the study of Effort, coexistent with creative practice, facilitated harmonisation and integration of the whole personality.

3.

The Introduction to *Modern Educational Dance* presents ideas and material which may be new and challenging for the contemporary reader. My introduction, therefore, places Laban's seminal proposals in a wider educational context. It aims to illustrate their relevance and urgency for dance education today. At the heart of Laban's work was a drive to generate a new movement consciousness, to secure a wider recognition of the central role of movement as an activating force in the life of the individual and consequently for the life of society. His formulation of Modern Dance addressed contemporary man in an industrial society.

Aligned to earlier dance revolutionaries, Jean George Noverre and Isadora Duncan, he eschewed forms of traditional dance, prescribed stylistics, themes and conventions. He states: 'One of the most obvious differences between the traditional European dances and Modern Dance is that the former are almost exclusively step dances, while the latter uses the flow of movement pervading all articulations of the body.'[4]

He considered specific dance forms, and in particular, dance forms which aspired to the training of dancers for the stage, to be inappropriate for the child at school. Educational

Dance, he proposed, should be based on experience and understanding of the principles of movement, on universal forms, on archetypal or prototypical rhythms and spatial configurations. It should foster expression of the inner life of the child, facilitate the preservation of spontaneity and offer a rich and harmonious range of movement possibilities in the service of nurturing and developing creative and expressive agency. Exploration and improvisation were to be balanced by the fostering of artistic expression and discrimination through dance composition and through the participation in dance works created by the teacher. Musical accompaniment, he suggested, was not a prerequisite. The demands of a set score worked against the discovery of the unique rhythmic flux emergent in individual dance sequences. Looking back to his earliest experiments in 1912, he proposed silence, voice and live percussion as alternatives to the dictates of melody and metric pulse.

There was an emphasis on direct experience, on intention and embodiment, on corporeal imagination, on engagement and absorption in process, on dance which was charged with meaning and alight with the confidence of ownership. The educative nature of the free dance form was holistic, engaging the intellect, the life of feeling and the spirit in creative dance activity. The role of the teacher was cast as the activator of the imagination, guardian of individuality and agent of the development of intelligent action. Participation in dance, he believed, was efficacious, celebratory and life-enhancing.

The teaching of Modern Educational Dance, he insisted, should engage in a sustained interweaving of theory and practice. Already in place were the fruits of long years of research to investigate the lineaments of human movement, to formulate a comprehensive analysis which could be applied to all forms of dance and fields of movement. Here, then, for dance educationalists, was a theoretical body of knowledge, subject-specific, which aimed to parallel the study of music and thus offer credibility and parity with all other art forms. Here too was an exposition of the grammar and semantics of movement which made available an articulate and common language for teachers and students.

4.

From a wider perspective, although Laban's references to the *expressive* nature of movement and dance were dominant in his writing and teaching, his research had led to an interesting conclusion. He believed that movement – and in particular, repetitive movement and the crystallisation of a limited variety of movement habits – had powerful and often detrimental, *impressive* effects. He saw dance as a significant counterbalance to the restricted nature of the mechanical movements necessitated by work tasks in an industrial society (and here, we could add, of a technological society).

Resonances with the tenets of Progressive Education reveal strong reasons why Modern Educational Dance was supported and promoted by the Educational Establishment. For the next three decades, with Ministry backing for teacher training and sustained political support for the arts in general, dance in education began to spread on a wider scale.

By the end of the 1960s, it was the subject of fierce and divisive debate. A number of influential dance educators had begun to voice concern over the ways in which a refusal to expand the parameters of dance education to encompass dance as a performance art had effectively led Laban's work into a cul-de-sac. The boundaries between dance and physical education, they proposed, had become blurred and philosophy and practice confused.[5]

Such critiques were sharply highlighted in the early 1970s with the advent of new B.Ed. courses, proposals for a BA in Dance and the Certificate in Secondary Education (CSE). Validating bodies called for a clarification in aims and objectives and for the first time, academics from other disciplines were consulted to assist in defining the nature of dance in education. Out of the ensuing debates, a new perspective emerged to connect dance education to a world outside the gymnasium. It pressed for an alignment of dance in the province of the expressive arts, for a formal concern with the development of three major strands: choreography, performance and appreciation, and for the inclusion of such theoretical aspects as analysis, anatomy, history, criticism, aesthetics and notation.[6]

Although *Modern Educational Dance* was skilfully updated to encompass a directive to teach dance as art form, the influence of Laban's work gradually diminished as dance educators turned somewhat uncritically towards the pool of expertise presented by the London Contemporary Dance School and the work of Martha Graham.[7]

5.

A retrospective sweep of the changes and transformations that have shaped the current dance education scene in England indicates that references to Laban's work are superficial, fragmented and often inaccurate.[8] The place of dance in primary schools today is minimal and somewhat *ad hoc*. At secondary level, there has been an exciting explosion in GCSE and A-level courses. What is lacking is a coherent body of theoretical knowledge which informs the study of movement; that is, the dynamics of expression within the plastic domain of space.

That Laban's conception of Modern Dance, formulated between 1913 and 1919, was avant-garde is yet to be recognised. It is interesting to note that those aspects of Modern Educational Dance which were criticised by the professional world in the early 1960s – improvisation, the dancer as creator, the dancer as collaborator in choreographic works – seen then as messy and unstructured, are common practices today.[9] In addition, the current resistance to prescribed training techniques, the interest in somatic studies, the blurring of boundaries between amateur and professional dance, the rise in the popularity of site-specific works and the enormous growth in what is currently termed 'Community Dance', all point back to Laban's genius and call for a serious reconsideration and recognition of the uniqueness of his role in the making of European Modern Dance and his seminal contribution to dance education in the UK.

PREFACE

This book is devised as a guide for teachers and parents. The ideas incorporated in it deal with that branch of the art of movement which in English-speaking countries has been called 'Modern Dance'. The original name used for the new kind of dancing was *la danse libre* or 'free dance'. Why this name was chosen will be manifest from the context. The spreading of the work in many countries of the European continent led to the name 'Central-European dance', though the same dance-forms were initiated simultaneously in America. Europe was, however, the cradle of a comprehensive theory. The prominent representatives of the new dance-form on the stage, in recreation and education, and of the application of the newly discovered movement principles in industry, were recruited from many nations all over the globe.

INTRODUCTION

It is more widely realised today that school education must take the subject of dance-tuition into consideration. The question which arises is, how shall we proceed? Do the remnants of the historical art of dancing offer a sufficient foundation on which to build up the new dance-tuition in school, or do we need, in our highly differentiated civilisation, a new approach to the problem? The answer is, I think, that we must look around us and compare the conditions of life in our time with those of the days in which the traditional dance-forms originated.

We should also investigate what connection exists between the dance-forms and the general behaviour, especially the working habits, of an epoch.

Compared with what is known in this respect concerning the other arts, our knowledge in the field of the art of movement is very scanty.

The history of architecture, sculpture, painting, music and poetry describes the changes which these arts have undergone in the various epochs and periods of civilisation. The differences between Greek temples, Gothic cathedrals and the skyscrapers of our time are so obvious that everybody can see them clearly. It is easy to awaken an interest in the changes in the social order and life conditions during history and explain how the typical forms of, say, an architectural period are connected with the general trend and character of the public life of that age. Similar connections between social life-forms and the products of all the other arts except that of dance can be easily demonstrated. It is even so that few people think in this connection of dance, the fundamental art of man. Whereas all the other arts have left witnesses in the form of buildings, pictures, manuscripts of poetry and music, the art of movement of past epochs has faded away, leaving no traces other than incidental descriptions either in words, which are inadequate to give a picture of movement, or in choreographies which nobody can really decipher.

The tradition of dance-practice has kept a few of the dances of more recent periods of civilisation alive. We know some of the medieval folk-dances and the dances of the period of absolute monarchies which preceded the recent political and industrial revolution. Yet the whole inheritance of the art of movement throughout history is so meagre that it has hardly occurred to the great public that there is a connection between the changes of social life and dance. The methodical study of the movement-forms contained in dances and of their repercussion upon the various fields of public life has hardly started. The role of the art of movement in education has only lately been rediscovered. All we know is that in ancient times dance played a much greater role in public life, yet the primitive forms of communal dancing, as still seen today with natives of other continents, are as strange to us as their whole civilisation. They cannot serve either as a model or as a sufficient source of inspiration.

It thus seems that modern man has to build up his own art of movement, and a beginning to this can be seen in those dance-forms of our time which the Americans and, with them, other English-speaking countries, call 'Modern Dance'.[10]

Compared with the relics of medieval folk-dances and with the movement-forms of the times of absolutistic kingdoms,

'Modern Dance' is richer and freer in gestures and steps. A second outstanding characteristic of the contemporary art of movement is the congruity of the new forms of dance-expression with the movement-habits of modern man. Our time has not inappropriately been called the epoch of industrial revolution, and it might be permissible to call 'Modern Dance' the movement-expression of industrial man.

Dances have had at all times a profound connection with the working habits of the periods in which they arose or were created. About the middle of the 18th century (1760) a remarkable man, Jean George Noverre, a French ballet-master, turned intuitively away from the Court dances of his time. We can surmise that it was the French Revolution which opened his eyes, though he never tells us whether this was really the case. It might also be that he foresaw the coming development of industrial civilisation, and out of the vision of new, hitherto unseen forms of human working actions he endeavoured to create a new movement-expression on the stage. However this may be, Noverre was in any case the first to find both the old peasant dances and the King's amusements unsuitable for the man of the rising industrial centres.

What he did in practice was to abolish the old stage costumes, head-dresses and decorations which impeded the free flow of movement. He created the *ballet d'action*, in which, instead of ceremonious bows and niceties, the full scale of human passions found their expression. But, in my opinion, his greatest deed was that he sent his pupils into the streets, market-places and workshops in order that they should study the movements of their contemporaries instead of copying the polite behaviour of princes and courtiers. The movements of the latter were without doubt charming and showed great aesthetical perfection. The crux was, however, that they lacked life, or rather that connection with the buzzing life of the cities filled with the representatives of a new race, the first forebears of industrialism.

Noverre was an artist, and he worked exclusively for the stage. The description of his ballets and his own writings show, however, that he was a visionary who foretold the spiritual trends of our present time. The curious thing is that he expressed these predictions not in words, but in movements.

Since his time many dancers and producers of ballets have followed his new trend of movement-expression, although the dream world of fairies and princes, with their stylised evolutions in space, have continued to attract the public for more than a century.

It was in industry that the new movement research was inaugurated. Since it became obvious that the working processes of a mechanised age are so profoundly different from those of the pre-revolutionary periods of European civilisation, several attempts have been made to adapt the workman's movements to the new needs.

A man who must be mentioned in this connection is Frederick W. Taylor, the initiator of the so-called 'scientific management'. He was one of the first people who tried to penetrate the riddle of human movement from an entirely new point of view. His aim was, of course, to increase the efficiency of workmen operating machines, without ever thinking of the aesthetical values which their movements might have. But he had an inkling of the educational value of movements, especially so far as the education of industrial apprentices was concerned.

A contemporary of Taylor, though without any connection with him, and probably even without knowledge of his industrial endeavours, was Isadora Duncan. She was convinced that the liberation of movement from the fetters of traditional habits could be achieved only by returning to the dance-forms of earlier periods of dance history, and especially to the movement-forms of Ancient Greece. Taking Greek sculptures and vase-pictures as models, she tried to reconstruct the dance-forms of two thousand years ago. Pictures can never give reliable indications of the rhythms and shapes of dance, because they are static images of such stages of the movement as are pictorially interesting. I think Isadora Duncan's valuable dances were for the most part the expression of our time, and that they had no other than external resemblance to the movement-forms of Ancient Greece.

In freeing the dancer's body from excessive clothing, which hinders the flow of movement, she contributed very much to the tendency of contemporary man to overcome his self-consciousness expressed in the hiding of his body. The main achievement of Duncan was, however, that she reawakened a form of dance-expression which could be called dance-lyrics, in contrast to the mainly dramatic dance-forms of the ballet. There was the story behind her dances, which were, as she herself termed it, the expression of the life of her 'soul'.

She reawakened the sense of the poetry of movement in modern man. At a time when science, and especially psychology, endeavoured to abolish radically any notion of a 'soul', this dancer had the courage to demonstrate successfully that there exists in the flow of man's movement some ordering principle which cannot be explained in the usual rationalistic manner. It was especially the influence which the repeated performance of similar movements has on man's internal and external attitude to life which interested Duncan as an educationist.

Movement considered hitherto – at least in our civilisation – as the servant of man employed to achieve an extraneous practical purpose was brought to light as an independent power creating states of mind frequently stronger than man's will. This was quite a disconcerting discovery at a time when extraneous achievements through will-power seemed to be the paramount objective of human striving.

Industrial movement research has confirmed that this intuitive discovery of the artist is true. We know today that modern working habits frequently create detrimental states of mind from which our whole civilisation is bound to suffer if no compensation can be found. The most obvious compensations are, of course, those movements which are able to counterbalance the disastrous influence of the lopsided movement-habits arising in contemporary working methods.

In the pre-industrial epoch of our civilisation, craftsmen and peasants had a rich movement-life. In all their occupations the whole body was engaged at various times in the widely different activities which each man had to perform. They had to think, because every man was the organiser of his own business. Procuring raw material, buying, transporting, the productive process itself, and selling, were done by one and the same man. Today's industrial worker is specialised not only in one of these jobs, but in a particular function of a job, frequently in one relatively simple movement-sequence which he has to perform from morning till evening throughout his lifetime. He has to think, but within a very restricted sphere of interests. His leisure time is inadequately filled with pleasures lacking that integration of bodily and mental enhancement which in former times arose from pride in work and organisatory independence. The pride in work incidentally found its expression in festive dances. During their school-time children of our day have not learnt to appreciate movement. They hardly know how much their future happiness depends on a rich movement-life.

Education today endeavours to supply a counter-balance to this state of affairs by paying more attention to the arts in general, including the art of movement since it is realised that dance is the basic art of man.

Dance has today re-entered the realm of the arts, and even the historical forms have regained a new lease of life through the intuitively felt need of almost everybody to obtain, if not inspiration, at least information concerning one of the most powerful features of man's bodily and mental make-up, movement.

In modern educational dance, consideration is given to all that has been discovered and felt concerning this art by its most prominent pioneers, including those who have studied movement from the more prosaic aspect of working efficiency. This consideration finds its expression in the richness of liberated movement-forms, gestures and steps, as well as in the use of movements which contemporary man uses in his everyday life.

A new conception of the elements of movement based on modern work research has been introduced into dance tuition. The basic idea of the new dance training is that actions in all kinds of human activities, and therefore also in dance, consist of movement-sequences in which a definite effort of the moving person underlies each movement.

The distinction of a specific effort becomes possible because each action consists of a combination of effort elements.[11] The effort elements are attitudes of the moving person towards the motion factors Weight, Space, Time and Flow. The new dance-training fosters the development of a clear and precise feel of man's attitude towards his efforts and the movements resulting from them guaranteeing the appreciation and enjoyment of any, even the simplest, action movements.

The knowledge concerning human effort, and especially the efforts used by industrial man, is the basis of the dance tuition applied by many pupils of the author who, becoming teachers or artists, have played a prominent role in the building up of this contemporary art of movement.

It becomes necessary at this point to clear up a few fundamental conceptions concerning the art of movement, which comprises more than dance in its narrower sense.

The art of movement is used on the stage in ballet, pantomime, drama, and in any other kind of performance, including films. All forms of social dancing, country or ballroom dancing and so on, constitute part of the art of movement, as well as a great number of party games; masquerades and many other social plays and entertainments.

The art of movement is implicated in all ceremonies and rituals and forms part of the speaker's outfit in all kinds of oratory and meetings. Our everyday behaviour is ruled by certain aspects of the art of movement, and so is a great part of the behaviour and activity of children in schools. Games imply the knowledge and experience of the movements used in them, which requires a technique of moving. This technique, like that used in the skilled performance of industrial operations, is a part of the art of movement.

The technique of moving has several aspects, one of which is that cultivated in dance tuition.

Traditional dance technique deals with the master of individual movements required in particular style of dancing. The performance of dances is not restricted to the stage. Apart from the theatrical dance compositions of the ballet, each of the social forms of the art of dance, such as national, folk and ballroom dances, has its own forms of movement and technique.

The new dance technique promoting the mastery of movement in all its bodily and mental aspects is applied in Modern Dance as a new form of stage dancing and of social dancing.

The educational value of the new dance technique can be ascribed to a great extent to the universality of the movement-forms which are studied and mastered in the contemporary aspect of this art.

The methodical approach to the universal forms of movement is bound to be different from that needed for the mastery of a particular stylisation of movement embracing only a relatively small section of human movement-expression.

One of the most obvious differences between the traditional European dances and Modern Dance is that the former are almost exclusively step dances, while the latter uses the flow of movements pervading all articulations of the body.

The richness of movement in Modern Dance demands a different approach for its mastery. It is, indeed, impossible, taking the flow of human movement as a whole, to study the almost infinite variations of body carriages in the same manner as can be done with the restricted number of steps used in the stylised dance-forms. Instead of studying each particular movement, the principle of moving must be understood and practised. This new approach to movement, the material of dancing, involves a change of the inner attitude towards the flow of movement and its elements.

It is, as we think, mainly the inner attitude mirrored in the new dance technique which makes its application to education desirable and successful.

In olden times dance technique was adapted to the practical needs of performances of dancing, and it is in our time only that certain parts of dance technique have been applied to other fields of human activity.

The importance of a new form and spirit of movement-education in our time is evident in several respects.

First, the great variety of operations in the over eighteen thousand occupations of modern man demands the study and mastery of the common denominator of the technical exertions involved in all his working actions. The common denominator is the flow of movement.

Secondly, the unsurpassed amount of intellectual knowledge required for the mastery of modern life needs a balancing factor in which the spontaneous faculties of man can find exercise and outlet. The study and mastery of the spontaneous functions of man which have to be fostered point to the same common denominator, the flow of movement.

The new dance technique offers the possibility of systematically training the new movement-forms by propounding at the same time their conscious mastery. The industrialists and educationists, who have seized the opportunity given by the present-day movement research which the pioneers of Modern Dance have evolved, have tried to apply the new methods of movement-training in factories and schools.

It is to be noticed that it is not dancing proper which has been applied for these purposes, but the technique used for the movement-education of the dancer. Modern Dance as an art has its place on the stage and in recreation. The performance of Modern Dance compositions, even in the modest form of simple recreational dances, shows a perfection which demands the inspiration of creative and reproducing artists who will not be always available in schools and factories.

In schools, where art education is fostered, it is not artistic perfection or the creation and performance of sensational dances which is aimed at, but the beneficial effect of the creative activity of dancing upon the personality of the pupil.

The question of producing dances in schools must therefore be treated with extreme delicacy, and will have to follow definite outlines and procedures which must be discussed in detail.

The essential tool which can be offered to the educationist in Modern Dance is the universal outlook upon the principles of human movement.

The practical use of the new dance technique in education is manifold. The innate urge of children to perform dance-like movements is an unconscious form of outlet and exercise introducing them to the world of the flow of movement, and strengthening their spontaneous faculties of expression.

The first task of the school is to foster and to concentrate this urge, and to make the children of the higher age-groups conscious of some of the principles governing movement.

The second and no less important task of education is to preserve the spontaneity of movement and, with it, to keep this spontaneity alive up to school-leaving age, and beyond it into adult life.

A third task is the fostering of artistic expression in the medium of the primary art of movement. Here two quite distinct aims will have to be pursued. One is to aid the creative expression of children by producing dances adequate to their gifts and to the stage of their development. The other is to foster the capacity for taking part in the higher unit of communal dances produced by the teacher.

A further task can be seen in the awakening of a broad outlook on human activities through the observation of the flow of movement used in them.

The terminology, and the inner attitude gained through the assimilation of the new dance technique, can help towards the recognition of one's own and other people's movement deficiencies. The teacher might more easily find the appropriate measures for improving deficient movements, while the pupil will accept his advice more readily and with a better understanding.

Considering the central position of movement in all human activities, many more opportunities of applying the principles of the new dance technique can be imagined and will without doubt emerge from practice. It should be mentioned finally that the new dance technique endeavours to integrate intellectual knowledge with creative ability, an aim which is of paramount importance in any form of education.

A technique complying with all these requirements must submit the new outlook upon the child's attitude to dance to closer scrutiny, and this we proceed to do.

Notes

1 Leslie Burrows, Louise Solberg, Joan Goodrich and Diana Jordan founded a dance centre in Chelsea in 1939 to promote the techniques and philosophy of *Ausdruckstanz*.

Goodrich and Jordan had introduced Central European Modern Dance into a number of physical education teacher training colleges and in 1938, Jordan produced the first English textbook on dance education: D. Jordan, *The Dance as Education* (Oxford: Oxford University Press, 1938).
2 See Bibliography for full publication details.
3 *MED*, p. 98.
4 Ibid., p. 10.
5 G.F. Curl, 'Philosophical Foundations' (PF), II, *Laban Art of Movement Guild Magazine* (*LAMGM*), 1967b, 38: 7–17; PF, IV in *LAMGM*, 1968, 40: 27–38; PF, VI in *LAMGM,* 1969, 43: 37–44; G.F. Curl, 'Laban's Philosophical Foundations Revisited', in *Order or Chaos: Laban's Artistic and Philosophic Foundations . . . and Beyond* (Laban Notation Institute, University of Surrey, 2001), and H.B. Redfern, *Concepts in Modern Educational Dance* (London: Henry Kimpton, 1973).
6 J. Adshead, *The Study of Dance* (London: Dance Books Ltd, 1981).
7 It must be remembered, however, that *Modern Educational Dance* took shape in 1948 in a cultural climate which offered no references to any existing models of British Modern Dance. Please refer to A. Haynes (aka Carlisle), 'The Dynamic Image: Changing Perspectives in Dance Education', in P. Abbs (ed.) *Living Powers: The Arts in Education* (London: The Falmer Press, 1987).
8 A pilot research project in 2008 at the University of Bedfordshire, PGCE Dance Department, was designed to investigate both the level of knowledge and application of Laban's work to current dance education and through practical workshops, ascertain its relevance to the sample of GCSE and A-level teachers involved. This resulted in the creation of a new MA Module in Laban Studies at the University of Bedfordshire which is ongoing. A report on the research findings can be found in: M. Killingbeck, 'Laban: The Way Forward in Dance Education', in V. Preston Dunlop and L-A. Sayers (eds) *The Dynamic Body*

in Space: Developing Rudolf Laban's Ideas for the 21st Century (London: Dance Books Ltd, 2010), p. 118.
9. For Laban practitioners, this view of Modern Educational Dance, thrown into relief by Modern Dance Theatre works created by London Contemporary Dance Theatre and the Rambert Dance Company, became part of the oral culture.
10. This term, though occasionally used in the present publication, is ambiguous, because many people will think of modern ballroom dancing. [Laban's note.]
11. See R. Laban and F. C. Lawrence, *Effort* (London: Macdonald & Evans, 1947). [Laban's note.]

Chapter seventeen

Shadow Moves

Introduction

Marion North

In *The Mastery of Movement* Laban defined Shadow Movements as 'tiny muscular movements such as the raising of the brow, the jerking of the hand or the tapping of the foot, which have none other than expressive value. They are usually done unconsciously and often accompany movements of purposeful action like a shadow.'[1] I would add that shifts of the whole body can sometimes be considered in the same category as Shadow Movements. Later in the book he notes that: 'They are the key to the understanding of what could be called the alphabet of the language of movement: and it is possible to observe and analyse movement in terms of this language.'

He goes on to say that a person's 'mental attitude and inner participations are reflected in his deliberate bodily actions as well as in the accompanying shadow movements'.[2] Unlike Effort Actions which may involve all four motion factors, Shadow Movements are 'incomplete'.

> Shadow actions of all kinds are mostly incomplete actions, since not all their motion elements are equally stressed. It

is only under excessive excitement that a subjective motion will be performed as a full-scale thrust, slash, or other basic action.[3]

One can see the contrast by comparing what a person says with their non-verbal behaviour. For example, I can say, 'Yes, I will tell you everything I know about this', at the same time stepping backwards, closing my arms across my body while my head sinks down onto my chest. You would then know that I was not really intending to tell you anything. All people are to some degree observers of movement and it is usually these non-verbal communications which make us say of someone we've just met, 'I don't know why, but I just don't trust him.' Why do we say this, what have we observed about him? It is mainly by our Shadow Movements that we reveal what we really are, what we think and feel. The messages we convey in unconscious movement patterns tend to be subtle and occur in phrases or sentences which can be notated. An acute observation of Shadow Movement of a person in different situations and at different times will show the consistency of that individual's basic attitude and personality. The Shadow Movement and its meaning are part of the person's make-up, and the pattern, the rhythm, the phrasing of these movements will appear time and time again in their repertoire. Laban himself could observe accurately and swiftly the patterns and range of capacities in adults and children as is evident in a passage from *Effort and Recovery (ER)*:

> The struggle between shadow-moves and functional action is one of the most interesting subjects for the movement observer. On the whole one will find that efforts and functional activities derive from the earliest developed layers of a primeval movement capacity. Everybody has exercised them already as a baby, before he or she has learnt to walk. All the functional actions learnt and exercised later are variations and combinations of these first exertions of man.[4]

I worked with Laban for the last 10 years of his life. We developed the Youth Advisory Bureau for Young People where we observed their movements, both practical and Shadow Movements, some of which were active and other of which were latent.

One day, we were responding to a request from a man, to help him focus his life. Laban delegated the observations to me saying, 'Show them to me when you're finished.' I spent days and days trying to see the sense and patterning of the infinite number of movement qualities and rhythms he had revealed, but to no avail. When I said to Laban, 'I could not see any patterning there', he looked at the observations in their raw state and said, 'The one patterning that *you* could not see is that there is no patterning. The inner life of this man is a veritable maelstrom.'

In 1969, I started on a longitudinal study of babies from three days old which showed that at birth patterns of movement are distinguishable for individual babies, while other patterns – what one might call 'baby movements' – are common to all the babies of this age. How they develop their unconscious movement patterns is a record of their growing personality and their particular gifts and limitations. Some children have a wide range of movement capacities, effort qualities, and combinations of movement. Others have a much more limited range. Thirty years ago I predicted that the richer the variety and range of movement capacities of each child, the higher their intellect and emotional intelligence. Checking on two of the individuals in the study at the much later age of 30, similar patterns could be seen as were observed at birth, thus supporting my claim.[5]

Laban used to say: 'It is these enlarged Shadow Movements which form the material for dance.' The ability to consciously create seeming Shadow Movements is an inherent part of the actor's skill. Any good acting involves incorporating those Shadow Movements through an almost unconscious absorption of the characteristic of the role.

A quotation from a letter from Laban to me in 1956 reveals that he considered that the Dance Notation was of conscious movements, while Effort notation was of unconscious movements:

> . . . there is much demand for a notation in all camps. It is difficult to explain that my notation has two aspects, dealing either in the main with the unconscious, or, on the other hand, with the more conscious production of movement.[6]

There are two brief references to Shadow Movements in *Effort*: 'In office work, the observation of the subtle shadow moves accompanying action, or of a body tension within a rest, will become increasingly significant to the observer of effort.' He contrasts this index of mental activity with the functional movements of manual work and then concludes:

> Reflection and mental control, of course, make up part of any industrial activity. The question is simply whether the mental activity is connected with clearly discernible motoric efforts or whether the mental activity seems to be separated from motoric work – that is, whether it happens during a total or partial rest of the body.[7]

Later he discusses the different effect Shadow Moves have in the rhythm of effort and regeneration in manual as opposed to clerical work:

> Emotionality might have a greater influence on the performance of the office worker than on that of the bench worker, because with the former relief through muscular strain is lacking. When the office worker has become used to the burning up of nervous tissue without the relief offered by bigger movements, his performance will be less disturbed by the addition of emotional shadow moves. It is the same with a child who has become used to sitting quietly at a desk.
>
> Automatism can be achieved in mental work as well as in manual work. The rhythmic energy used is the same in both. Regeneration will take place along slightly different lines. Muscular strain is relieved, as already stated, by direct relaxation, mental strain is relieved through discharges of accumulated muscular energy in shadow moves.[8]

In other words, the muscular action of Shadow Moves allows office workers moments of relief from their mental effort.

I would like to clarify Laban's use of the word Tension. 'Tension' is not one isolated phenomenon and it is not solely related in Laban's work to the aspect of 'flow' or physical action. The way that Laban used the word when I was working with him signified that all movement has tension but it also has a flavour to that tension, and is not just a physical event.

A telling passage from *The Mastery of Movement* describes how Shadow Moves can reveal the inner tensions within a person:

> Efforts disguising egoism are visible in shadow moves. The warmth of a gesture might be contradicted by the cold stare of the eyes, or the twitching movements of the face-muscles. One part of our body may assent, another part deny. We might breathe heavily or excitedly while otherwise displaying an external calm. The struggle of efforts within ourselves is part of the drama. Almost all our decisions are the result of an inner struggle which can become visible even in an entirely motionless body-carriage. Bodily position is always the result of previous movements or the foreboding of future movements that leave or foreshadow their imprint on the body-carriage. It is astonishing that an inner struggle can be transmitted to the spectator without perceptible movement or sound, but effort-analysis can explain this with great exactitude.[9]

There are many references to Shadow Moves in *Effort and Recovery* where he is particularly interested in the tension between outward and inner behaviour:

> The monotonous tramp, tramp of heavy feet in the road, of an endless column of men wearing uniform and marching in rigid formations, is an example of mechanical action unmitigated by shadow-moves. The automaton-like gait, without an additional expression in face, hands or other parts of the body, is a kind of mixture between sleep-walking and fanaticism.[10]

Conventions of movements impress the observer often as man-made and prefabricated, no matter whether they are used in religious services, at nationally important ceremonies, or in traditional dances and social meetings. What alone makes these stereotyped actions interesting for the observer of efforts are the Shadow Moves accompanying them. Such Shadow Moves sometimes stand in obvious contrast to the conventional gesture. The inner revolt against the prescribed form of movement and the compulsion to perform it shows itself in Shadow Moves by which we clearly discern that the conventionally performed movement is insincere.[11]

Shadow Moves reveal a person's inner humanity even when it is disguised beneath the mask of socially imposed, stereotypical behaviour:

> What makes such stereotyped actions, however, interesting for the observer are the shadow-moves of the individual. . . . Civilised man, not only of our age, but of all ages, is expected to do certain things, to utter symbols of certain inner stirs, regardless of whether he really feels them or not. This expectation of our surroundings or of the community that we act and move in a definite way, of course, kills much of our personal expression. The latter is then reduced to appearing in shadow-moves, which are supposed to remain unnoticed.[12]

In the final excerpt, he argues very plausibly that Shadow Moves accompany our speech:

> Speech or any human sound utterance is coloured by audible shadow-moves which accompany the functional actions of voice-production. These shadow-moves make the voice quite different if a person speaks either with or without emotion. The sentence which our by now almost legendary baker addressed to his cousin were quite differently coloured than the words he spoke to the bus conductor. These shadow-moves of the voice-producing organs could have been similar in both cases, although the conductor would have been a bit astonished to be talked

to so sweetly, and the cousin would have been probably upset if the baker had addressed her in the same matter of fact tone he used with the conductor.[13]

Notes

1 *MM* (1950: 12).
2 *MM* (1960: 110).
3 *ER*, p. 120.
4 Ibid., p. 222.
5 Documented in Marion North's DVD, *Early Movement Profiling of Babies* (London: Trinity Laban, 2009).
6 Marion North's personal collection.
7 *E*, p. 69.
8 Ibid., pp. 72–73.
9 *MM* (1950: 124).
10 *ER*, p. 63.
11 Ibid., p. 125.
12 Ibid., p. 174.
13 Ibid., pp. 144–145.

Chapter eighteen

The Mastery of Movement on the Stage (1950)

Introduction

Dick McCaw

When Laban came to England, his artistic emphasis shifted from Dance Theatre to a Theatre of Movement. Once Lisa Ullmann and Sylvia Bodmer (another of Laban's former students from Hamburg in 1924) had established the Art of Movement Studio on Manchester's Oxford Road, he developed close relations with the Theatre Workshop of Joan Littlewood and Ewan McColl, whose base was almost opposite the Studio. From 1947, he started teaching in the Northern Theatre School in Bradford that was created by the Actor/Director Esmé Church whose pupils included actors Tom Bell and Bernard Hepton, educationalist Dorothy Heathcote and director David Giles. At the end of each year the school performed plays, two of which were taken to London and are described in a review from *The Times Educational Supplement* of 3 April 1948:

> In the hands of producers, Miss Esmé Church and Mr Rudolf Laban, this was more than an adaptation; it was

the re-creation of fairy-tale in terms of the theatre. The producers all captured the sense of pattern which belongs to all fairy stories. Dance was woven through the whole presentation: the gay dance of the people of Fandango, the sinister dance caused by the kettle, dances celebrating the first meeting and final betrothal of the soldier and the princess, all giving intricate form to the play. Movement was stylised, mime was used delightfully.[1]

We should note the emphasis on mime and movement which are central to the contents of his third 'effort' book *The Mastery of Movement on the Stage* (MM) and which link up with his earlier preoccupation with pantomime in Zurich in the 1910s. He puts his choice of stage movement into a historical context:

> It is not so long ago that the fashion in acting suddenly changed from pompous gesticulation to a naturalism devoid of any movement-expression at all. Playwrights, actors and producers became bored with the ballet-like over-acting of an epoch saturated by melodramatic sentimentality, and turned to the imitation of everyday life on the stage. But they were unable to appreciate the almost invisible finer movement-tensions between people conversing in everyday life, and the immobility which they cultivated gave birth to a dead style of acting. The stupid passivity of movement resulting from these attempts to behave in a natural manner failed to touch the public.[2]

In his Preface, he explains that this book requires a 'kind of mobile reading' – a brilliant expression to describe how we should read all his books. As in *The World of the Dancer* he notes that movement cannot be understood intellectually.

> Almost every sentence in this exposition is written as an incentive to personal mobility, so the reader should be prepared to avail himself or herself of these incentives. It is hoped that the perusal of the text itself will indicate how to accomplish what is really a kind of mobile reading.[3]

Later in the book he argues that only by learning how to 'think in terms of movement' can we achieve the 'mastery of movement'.[4] Even so, 'The actor or dancer, using movement as a means of expression, will rely more on the feel of the movement than on a conscious analysis of it.'[5] A feeling for movement is a central requirement for the actor:

> One of the leading ideas was that an actor would never achieve the display of personality required in acting without having previously experienced full abandonment to the passionate human urge for movement as manifested in mime and dance.[6]

More pithily he concludes that 'the theatre is dead' when mime is 'entirely forgotten or neglected'.[7]

The Mime artist of *The Mastery of Movement on the Stage* is equivalent to the Dancer of his writings of the 1920s. The Mime is more than just an interpretative figure, but an artist who, possessing a sensitivity to and awareness of movement, can reveal truths about people. As with his earlier books, he argues that although the general public has lost what might be called a sense of kinaesthetic empathy, at least actors – and more specifically the Mime – can still achieve this. Central to this kinaesthetic sense is a feeling for Effort. 'Mime based on mobile effort-thinking is the basic theatrical art. The conflict of effort in the struggle for value is most truly revealed in mime.'[8]

In this book, we see him explore both working Efforts, that is, external actions, and what he called 'inner efforts' – the psychological dimension of movement behaviour. Much of the argument about character and psychology is a development of Chapter 7 of *Effort*. Laban is interested in understanding 'that part of the inner life of man where movement and action originate'[9] rather than in 'the simple imitation of external movement peculiarities. Such imitation does not penetrate to the hidden recesses of man's inner effort.'[10] In Chapter 2, he notes that 'the change of habitual effort-make-up expressed in body-carriages and movement will be one of the essential means by which the actor builds up his characterisation' and later adds, 'We see in other people's movements what they feel, and even what they think, and can sympathetically identify ourselves with them.' My teacher Geraldine Stephenson related that Laban once asked a group of actors, 'How would your character not sit down on a chair?' Each character on the stage and each personality in everyday life has their own way of moving. Effort-analysis is not just about understanding *how* a person moves but *why*.

The second concept from *Effort* that he develops is how a character (or personality) can have a tendency either to *fight with* or *indulge in* one of the four motion factors:

> The variety of human character derives from the multitude of possible attitudes towards the elements of movement. Tendencies to *fight against*, or *indulge in* definite elements of movement can become habitual. It is of greatest importance for the actor-dancer to recognise that such habitual inner attitudes are the basic indications of what we call character or temperament. In order to discern the mechanical motion of living movement in which purposeful control of the mechanical happening is at work, it is useful to give a name to the inner function originating the movement. The word used here for this purpose is *'effort'*. Every human movement is indissolubly linked with an effort, which is, indeed, its origin and inner aspect.[11] Starting with an action in which fighting against certain motion factors prevails, it can be said that a *presser*, a *slasher*, or a *dabber* fight against two motion factors, and indulge in one.[12]

The Mastery of Movement on the Stage is divided into five sections. After an introductory Prologue (much of which is excerpted below), there is a long chapter, 'Movement and the Body', which includes over three hundred movement exercises that are notated, but not using his dance notation (perhaps because Laban thought that this notation would be too complex for actors?). Although at first sight the exercises seem pointlessly simple, they can form the basis of an effective form of physical training. The next two sections are called

'The Significance of Movement' where he makes a fascinating study of the effort-characteristics of animals and 'The Roots of Mime' (from which further excerpts are taken). The final, much shorter, section is called 'The Study of Movement Expression' and is followed by three 'Mime Plays' (which like the plays reviewed above are in the genre of fairy-tales).

The opening excerpt from the Prologue to the book offers a detailed analysis of a representation of Eve's plucking the forbidden apple in the Garden of Eden. Laban is not simply interested in the outer aspect of the movement, but Eve's inner motivation. This leads on to a broader discussion of movement on the stage, and a distinction between the virtuoso mover only interested in displays of technique, and the mover who is capable of effort-thinking, that is, about the meaning of the movement. The argument then broadens even further as he discusses the importance of movement-thinking in society – a theme we have seen him pursue from his first writings. The excerpts from Chapter 2 focus on effort-thinking, more particularly how the actor can analyse a character in terms of their effort profile, and this of course means, in terms of their ethical orientation in the world. Just as Laban's dancer was given a great deal of artistic licence and responsibility in the creation of the stage production, so his actor is given a very creative role through this focus on effort-thinking.

PROLOGUE[13]

Man moves in order to satisfy a need. He aims by his movement at something of value to him. It is easy to perceive the aim of a person's movement if it is directed to some tangible object. Yet there also exist intangible values that inspire movement.

Eve, our first mother, in plucking the apple from the tree of knowledge made a movement dictated both by a tangible and an intangible aim. She desired to possess the apple in order to eat it, but not solely to satisfy her appetite for food. The Tempter told her that by eating the apple she would gain supreme knowledge: that knowledge was the ultimate value she desired.

Can an actress represent Eve plucking an apple from a tree in such a way that a spectator who knows nothing of the biblical story is made aware of both her aims, the tangible and the intangible? Perhaps not convincingly, but the artist playing the role of Eve can pluck the apple in more than one way, with movements of varying expression. She can pluck the apple greedily and rapidly or languidly and sensuously. She could, too, pluck it with a detached expression in the outstretched arm and grasping hand, and in her face and body. Many other forms of action are possible, and each of these would be characterised by a different kind of movement.

In defining the kind of movement as greedy, as sensuous, or detached, one does not define merely what one has actually seen. What the spectator has seen is only a peculiar, quick jerk or a slow gliding of the arm. The impression of greed or sensuousness is the spectator's personal interpretation of Eve's state of mind in a definite situation. If he should observe Eve grasping quickly into the air – that is to say, if he sees the same movement performed without the objective aim – he would probably not be induced to think either of the object or of the motive. He would perceive the quick, grasping movement without understanding its dramatic significance.

It may, of course, occur to the spectator to ask whether this movement, apparently without an objective aim, was made in order to reveal certain traits of Eve's then mood, or of her character. It is unlikely that one movement could convey to him more than a passing impression, since it could never give a definite picture of her character. On the other hand, several concurrent movements, as for example those including Eve's carriage and walking before the snatching gesture, would offer additional and clearer indications of her personality. But even then Eve's behaviour in the act of plucking the apple would be less characteristic of her personality than of her momentary eagerness in the particular situation. On other occasions she might develop quite different rhythms and shapes of movement which, comprising several actions, would show her general character in an altogether different light.

So movement evidently reveals many different things. It is the result of the striving after an object deemed valuable, or of a state of mind. In its shape and rhythm it shows a special attitude to meet the situation in which the action takes place. It can characterise the momentary mood, or the personality of the moving person. Movement can also be adapted to the surroundings of the mover. The milieu of a scene or action will heighten the movements of the actress. They will be different in the role of Eve in paradise, or of a society woman in an eighteenth-century salon, or of a girl in the bar of a public-house in the slums. All three women might be similar personalities exhibiting almost the same general movement-characteristics, but they would adapt their behaviour to the atmosphere of an epoch, or a locality.

A character, an atmosphere, a state of mind, or a situation cannot be effectively shown on the stage without movement, and its inherent expressiveness. Movements of the body, including the movements of the voice-producing organs, are indispensable to presentation on the stage.

There is yet another aspect of movement which is of paramount importance in acting. When two or more players are to meet on the stage, they have to make their entrance, approach one another (either touching, or keeping a due distance), and later they have to separate and make their exit.

The grouping of the actors on the stage occurs in movement, which is expressive in another sense than individual movement. The members of a group move in order to show their desire to get in touch with one another. The ostensible object of meeting might be to fight or to embrace, or to dance, or just to converse. But there exist intangible objectives, such as the attraction between sympathetic individuals or the repulsion felt by persons or groups antipathetic to each other.

Group movements can be brisk and pregnant with the threat of aggression, or soft and sinuous, like the movement of water in a placid lake. People can group themselves as hard, detached rocks on a mountain or as on a leisurely flowing stream in a plain. Clouds frequently form most interesting groupings which produce a strangely dramatic effect. Group movements on the stage resemble in a way the shifting clouds from which either thunder rolls, or sunshine breaks.

The individual actor will sometimes use his movements as if his limbs were the members of a group, and this is probably the solution of the riddle of the expressiveness of gesture. When Eve plucks the apple in a greedy or a languid manner, she will express her attitude by the movement of parts of her body. In greed, the limbs, the whole body, shoots out suddenly, avidly, all together in one and the same direction towards the coveted object. The languid approach is characterised by a nonchalant, slow lifting of the arm, while the rest of the body is lazily curved away from the object. It is almost a dance-like movement, in which the outward action is subordinated to the inner feeling. No words are needed to convey this feeling to the spectator. . . .

The art of movement on the stage embraces the whole range of bodily expression from the actors' speaking and acting, through dance-mime, to pure dance and its musical accompaniment. . . .

The whole complexity of human expressiveness, as comprised in the art of movement, is represented in the following diagram [Figure 18.1].

We never know whether man regards himself as taking part in a tragedy or a comedy with himself as the protagonist in the drama of existence and Nature forming the chorus. Yet it is an undeniable fact that man's extraordinary power of thought and action has placed him in a peculiar situation so far as his relationship to his surroundings is concerned. . . .

The actor who tries to do more than represent life in a skilful manner uses the movements of his body and his voice-producing organs with his interest focused on that which he intends to convey to his audience and less on the external shapes and rhythms of his actions. This kind of actor concentrates on the inner efforts preceding his movements, and pays small attention to the skill with which his efforts are presented. A different quality of contact with the public thus results if, instead of skill, the inner participation is stressed.

It is obvious that the virtuoso will easily be tempted to restrict the number of his movements to those which best suit

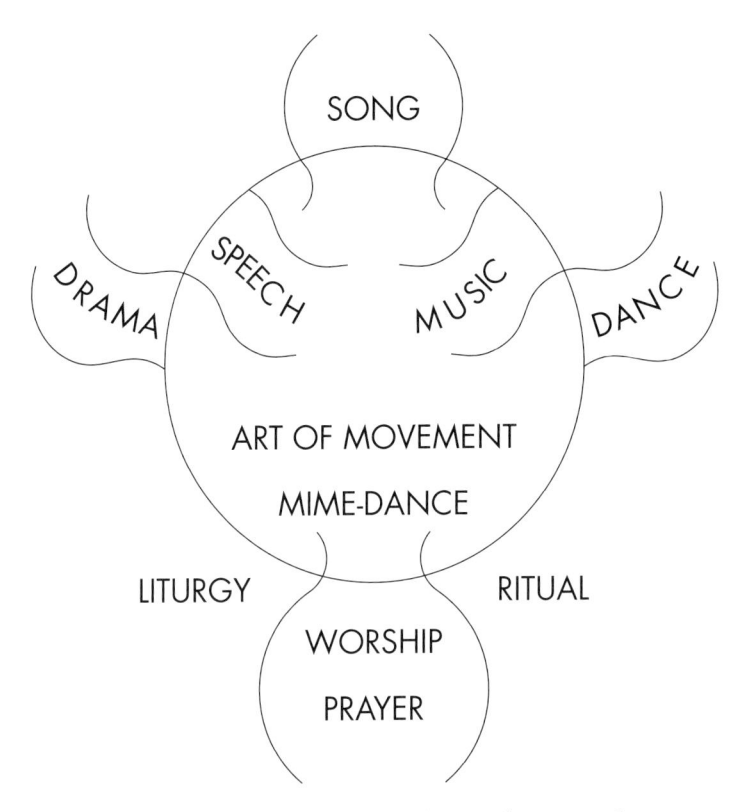

```
                    SONG
       SPEECH            MUSIC
  DRAMA                        DANCE

         ART OF MOVEMENT
           MIME-DANCE

   LITURGY                RITUAL
              WORSHIP
              PRAYER
```

Figure 18.1 [Human expressiveness in the art of movement]

his skill. The other type of actor will be inclined to reject all selection, and almost any exercise of single movement-forms which to him are mere acrobatics. In his endeavour to get his spontaneous movements to flow freely, he will often be more erratic and impulsive than the virtuoso.

On the whole, it can be said that these two contrasting viewpoints apply movement to two differing aims: on the one hand, to the representation of the more external features of life, and on the other, to the mirroring of the hidden processes of the inner being.

The actor, striving for the second of these two aims, has a deeper inclination, and a greater chance, to penetrate into the remoter recesses of what we have called the workshop of thought and action. In putting this kind of actor – provided he is perfect in his own type – on a higher rung on the ladder of theatrical values, preference is given to the less primitive, and therefore more complex, form of human mentality and taste. This preference could to a certain extent be justified today, because it seems that modern man needs a deeper penetration into the inner recesses of life, and the inner content of human existence, which, if brought to the surface, might help him to recover some lost but essential qualities. . . .

Mime based on mobile effort-thinking is the basic theatrical art. The conflict of effort in the struggle for value is most truly revealed in mime. Too many words and too much music are both apt to overshadow the truth revealed by bodily action and effort-display. Pure mime is now almost unknown, and its loss is of deep concern. The art of mime flourished in the early periods of human civilisation, in humanity's adolescence. There are values, such as youth, ingenuousness and innocence, which can be lost by individuals and races and can never be recovered. It is the same with certain forms of happiness, gaiety, harmlessness and, to some extent, with beauty, charm and gracefulness – all natural gifts of youth and innocence. The struggle for such values, which one cannot attempt to gain or regain, is ridiculous in everyday life.

The miracle of recovering these values, which have been forever lost in ordinary everyday life, is possible on the stage. Why? Because the actor or mime can represent a great deal of character and circumstance if he knows enough about their inherent effort-characteristics. This seems a paradox, but not so on the stage, where values and the efforts by which they are reached have not to be possessed, but to be pictured and presented. Who does this picturing is irrelevant, so long as it is effectively done. One sees middle-aged actresses playing exquisitely the parts of young girls, and able to convey to us the truth about youth and its fate in the most touching manner. Youthfulness and innocence, and certain forms of inner beauty, gaiety, and charm, can be represented effectively in mime. Inner youthfulness coincides frequently with what is called virtue; vice is incompatible with innocence; nevertheless the effort-elements of a virtuous and a vicious person have the same elements of movement. It is useful for the actor-dancer to consider and to compare the typical movement-rhythms of various living beings, animals as well as men, in order to gain insight into the selection of efforts, or inner impulses, appropriate to character qualities, conditions, and circumstances used in primitive mime. . . .

Man expresses on the stage by carefully chosen efforts this inner attitude of mind, and he performs a kind of corporate ritual in the presentation of conflicts arising from the differences in these inner attitudes. In domesticating animals, man has learned how to deal with efforts, and how to change the basic effort-habits of living beings. In applying the principles of domestication to himself, he has broadened the scope of effort-training into the creation of works of dynamic art. The way in which man has achieved this kind of effort-education is very remarkable. It has a parallel in the evolution of animal efforts. . . .

It is perhaps not too bold to introduce here the idea of thinking in terms of movement as contrasted with thinking in words. Movement-thinking could be considered as a gathering of impressions of the happenings in one's own mind, for which nomenclature is lacking. This thinking does not, as thinking in words does, serve orientation in the external world, but rather it perfects man's orientation in the inner world of efforts, which surge within his mind and find an outlet in the decision to move and to act. Man's desire to become orientated to the inner maze of the continuous now of his intentions to move and to act results in definite effort-rhythms, as practised in dancing and mime. . . .

The old ways of effort-awareness and effort-training will certainly play a part in the investigation of the actor's movement. It is to be expected that mime as expressive of effort, and a fundamental activity of man, will, after its long period of neglect, become once more an important factor of civilised progress, when its real sense and meaning have been re-acquired.

The value of characterisation through dance-like mime movements lies in the avoidance of the simple imitation of external movement-peculiarities. Such imitation does not penetrate to the hidden recesses of man's inner effort. To effect contact with the audience we need an authentic symbol of the inner vision, and this contact can be achieved only if we have learned to think in terms of movement, and to use this thinking for the purposes of the real mastery of movement on the stage is the central problem of the theatre.

THE ROOTS OF MIME[14]

An actor when depicting a character has not only to mirror the general effort-make-up of the character, but he must also be able to convey the development of that character's inner attitudes during the happenings of the play. Some characters might remain unchanged, presaging their tragic or comic fate. Others will develop either in a positive or negative direction, and their adaptation to these new situations might be the essential feature of the play. In this respect the change of habitual effort-make-up expressed in body-carriages and movement will be one of the essential means by which the actor builds up his characterisation.

Characterisation is an art, and, apart from psychological truth, there exist many factors which determine the artist's choice of a definite movement plus effort. The actor might even be unconscious of the cause of his choice, or of the exact kind of effort plus movement, by which he tries to characterise a person. Yet when he becomes conscious of it, say by remembering it exactly, or by working it up into definite shape, the study and description of movement on the lines indicated above will prove helpful.

In addition to portraying a single person's character, it must be remembered that the clash or harmony between characters is in reality the clash or harmony between different effort-components.

Dramatic situations are created by an effort-chemistry which often results – as in chemistry proper – in destructive explosion, or in the creation of new elements.

The correlation of the efforts of different persons vis-à-vis one another is a special aspect of the study of mime which employs a kind of effort-dialogue, similar to the spoken dialogue in drama. The behaviour of a gentle person in an effort-dialogue with a brute reveals details of the effort-characters of both, especially in their attitudes towards certain values. . . .

The change from an indulging attitude to a fighting one involves either quickening, or proceeding more direct, or waxing stronger, little by little. The change from a fighting to an indulging attitude involves either an increase in sustainment, or of flexibility, or of lightness, little by little. Considering the time factor, there is much more probability of the brute suddenly changing his occasional softness into hardness, than of the gentle man changing his seeming hardness slowly into softness. The sudden anger of an habitually jovial and gentle person will dissolve slowly; the slowly developing softness of an habitually brutal person will show suddenly his true character, and be of some permanence. Such probabilities are not rules, because the conflict of efforts is so very complex. The fact is that man is able to disguise his effort-nature as well as his effort-designs to a certain extent. Such a disguise will deceive only an unobservant person, though leaving him with a vague feeling that something is wrong. This feeling results from subconscious observation, or rather from observation not brought to full consciousness.

Any effort of another which is perceived by our senses – mainly by eye or ear – causes an effort-reaction that can, but need not always, result in an easily perceptible visible or audible movement. The reaction can be twofold: it can produce a counter-effort which is either similar or dissimilar to the effort causing the reaction. A brute could meet inner hardness in a gentle person whom he harshly attacks, but this hardness in the gentle man might slowly dissolve into inner and external softness as he begins to pity the benighted mind of his attacker. The gentle person's softness might find a vague sympathetic response in a brute, but this is quickly transformed into an inner and external harshness. . . .

All effort-action or reaction is an approach towards values; the primary value being the maintenance or achievement of the balance needed for the individual survival. The maintenance of this balance demands the reciprocal functioning of body and mind according to a person's effort-capacities or character. Balance requires adaptation to situations, and a more or less clear recognition of the values towards which the individual habitually or only occasionally strives.

To discriminate between material values and mental values is not always easy. . . .

We see in other people's movements what they feel, and even what they think, and can sympathetically identify ourselves with them. If we can suffer with the suffering, or feel anger with the rightfully indignant, we are nearer to real charity than if we only want to help or to give for the sake of the personal pleasure that helping and giving excites. In this sense the actor can be a great giver of his own self, and become a mediator between the solitary self of the spectator and the world of values.

The mediating activity of the actor demands veracity in a high degree. The real value of speaking the truth is that it puts others in possession of the facts. The love of truth, regarding it as of independent value in itself, might lead to a ruthless sort of veracity. Its counterpart, the beneficial hiding of truth, if charity or compassion demands it, is not untruthful. The pleasure or advantage derived from the falsification of fact is the real lie. In the same way charity or generosity is of no value in itself. A person who needs help should be given help, and one who should know a fact must be told the truth.

The competent actor, mime, or dancer strikingly reveals the possibility of expressing the values of veracity and all their complications through bodily action. It is a great error to regard the theatre and acting as make-believe, and as dealing with false actions and ideals. Mime and the theatre introduce the spectator to the realities of the inner life and the unseen world of values. The attempts to understand the world through naturalism and materialistic realism are doomed to failure. The realities of the inner life can only be depicted by art in which reason and emotion are compounded, and not by intellect or feeling in isolation. To give the right answer to the innermost expectations of the spectator, the actor must master the chemistry of human effort, and realise the intimate relationship between that chemistry and the struggle for values of which life consists. Although a spectator might not have any other reason for visiting the theatre than the wish to be entertained, he is nevertheless dissatisfied if he does not glimpse the realities of the world of values, and that world can be effectively depicted only through external and inner mobility.

It has been stated that the change from indulging to fighting involves either the quickening of the actions performed, or giving them increased directness or strength. And it has also been stated that the reverse change from fighting to indulging involves either an increase of sustainment, or of flexibility, or of lightness in the actions. This can be tried out by imagining or performing scenes in which such hardening or softening occurs. . . .

The scheme is brought nearer to life if one understands that:

1. No individual persists always in the same effort, but changes continuously.
2. During the changes some effort-elements are

>   kept intact, while
>   some become over-stressed, thus altering the quality of the effort more or less visibly, while others are almost entirely lost. . . .

Anybody can start with any of the basic moods, no matter whether it is habitual to him or not. He can then with greater or less effort-mobility run through whatever scale of moods he likes, or outer circumstances compel him to assume.

Each set of such changes is an effort-phrase which speaks a clear language conveying rises and falls, hesitations and precipitations; and these, if frequently repeated, bring out habitual characteristics.

This chemistry of effort follows certain rules, because the transitions from one effort to another are either easy or difficult. In ordinary circumstances, no sane person will ever change to an absolutely contrasting effort because of the great mental and nervous strain involved in so radical a change. . . .

Sometimes, the acting person reverts to incomplete efforts, in which only one or two elements are charged with inner participation, while the rest of the effort-manifestation remains mechanical, and is not supported by any inner attitude. A person showing this undecided form of effort expression could be called presser-glider and be considered a rather vague character. Such a gesture might indicate anything, but its essence is the renouncing of strong action.

The curious thing is, however, that characters are met with, who, either habitually or in a special mood, constantly use incomplete efforts, consisting of two elements only or restricted to barely one element. Such moods of inactivity arising occasionally point to a depressed disposition of mind which can be caused either by external events, or by states of mind that inhibit the rise of full action-efforts. If these moods are constant, a character will be doomed to lifeless inactivity.

One can easily imagine the enormous range of effort-combinations placed at the artist's disposal. The possibilities of changing and varying movement expression are innumerable. It does not simplify matters that all these numberless effort-combinations can appear in movements of the limbs or of the whole body. But the basic idea is nevertheless simple enough. If one is able to observe people's efforts, it will be noticed that it is always one exactly describable movement containing one well-definable effort-content that happens at one time. It is, of course, a different thing to choose one of the many possibilities of movement plus effort-content in order to characterise a person's behaviour in a specific situation on the stage.

The actor in observing people might recognise certain effort-habit types, such as the dabber-glider, or, as a contrast to him, the slasher-wringer-floater, which might offer a good basis to build up a picture of an imaginary person's movement-behaviour. But how will the person behave in a particular situation?

It is probable that a cautious and self-centred person in whose efforts no special drive and forcefulness have been observed will, if confronted by a sudden violent attack, be inclined to retire rather than to stand his ground. The attacker might then modify his *punching* mood in order to reassure the cautious person.

Punching is relatively quick. If one modifies (that mean relents) the speed of the thrust, it becomes *pressure*. When the strength of *thrusting* is diminished, the thrust becomes a gentle *dabbing*. Thrusting occurs always on a straight line; gradually curving the path of thrusting is brought finally to a *slashing* movement. All this can happen in an appropriate situation.

Each one of the basic actions can, through change in its speed, or its degree of strength, or the curvature of its path, be modified more and more until it is finally transformed into one of the other basic actions. This transformation can be compared with the grading one into another of the colours in a rainbow. As the many shades of colour can be understood as transitions or mixtures of the basic colours of the spectrum, so also can the great variety of actions observed in our movements be considered and explained as transitions or mixtures of basic actions.

One must not assume that effort-changes are always created by situations. The contrary is also true. New situations are often created by individual effort-changes.

The chain of happenings which is the very stuff of dramatic action, and therefore also of mime, has its roots in the chemistry of human effort. The nourishing soil of the tree of mime is the world of values.

Notes

1 In JHA, Box 23, Folder 13, Item 1.
2 *MM* (1950: 103).
3 Ibid., pp. v–vi.
4 *MM* (1960: 20).
5 Ibid., p. 101.
6 Ibid., p. 98.
7 Ibid., p. 98.
8 *MM* (1950: 10).
9 Ibid., p. v.

10 *MM* (1960: 20).
11 *MM* (1950: 22–23).
12 MM (1960: 117).
13 All excerpts are from the 1950 edition.
14 Chapter II, Part II, starting at p. 120.

Chapter nineteen

Effort and Recovery (early 1950s)

Introduction

Dick McCaw

Effort and Recovery (*ER*) is Laban's last book. Letters in the archives give the lie to the rumour that because it was left in too incomplete a state the book could not be published. The first is from John MacDonald to Laban on 29 January, 1953:

> Can you give me any news of 'Effort and Recovery'? I had the impression quite a time ago that the typescript was nearing completion. I shall be glad to see it as soon as possible.[1]

Laban responds on 28 April:

> Finally I am able to send you the completed MS of 'Effort and Recovery'. Like my former writings published by you, it will surely need the kind of efficient care which you have applied to my English style. I am looking forward with great interest to this final improvement and thank you already now in advance, very much indeed. You have

heard that the last delay in the completion of my work was caused by a very serious illness which detained me for several months in an isolation hospital.[2]

Clearly it was prepared and intended for publication and the mystery is why it has not been published to date.

Effort and Recovery is subtitled 'Seventeen Studies of People in Motion', and is similar to *A Life for Dance* in its sometimes autobiographical content and its conversational tone. Laban put a pencil to great effect being able to create vivid portraits either in drawings or writing, and this book contains some fantastic word pictures of people's movement behaviour. Each of the chapters of the book begins with a word-sketch of how a person or group of people move, which is followed by an analysis in terms of how they expend and then recover their energy. I have chosen the first two chapters because they balance each other so well. In them, he describes two workers, the first a baker, the second a manual labourer, each of whom have very contrasting patterns of effort and recovery. The baker is returning home after a night-shift and bumps into his female cousin, his mother and Laban himself: his journey begins with him shattered and ends with him already somewhat restored. The same cannot be said of Vulcan, a labourer who faints as a result of his over-exertion and on coming round fights against what he perceives as this weakness – he contends against recovery, only giving value to effort. Once again, we encounter Laban's core concerns – rhythm, balance and harmony in work. The baker has found a way of balancing his Effort and Recovery whereas Vulcan is a 'dramatic' example of lopsidedness.

In this work, to the familiar Effort terms – the Motion Factors of Weight, Space, Time and Flow and the eight Effort Actions – he adds four new terms borrowed from Carl Jung: the Mental Factors of Thinking, Intuiting, Sensing and Feeling (he offers his definitions of these terms in his Glossary of terms as used in Movement Psychology, given on p. 351). This is not entirely new territory since we should recall that in *The World of the Dancer* he had written about the trinity of Feeling, Thinking and Willing, which though not the same are related.

In a telling reflective passage in an early draft of the Vulcan chapter, he explains how his interest in theatre has broadened to a more practical and ethical engagement with people working in factories. He explains succinctly how in this context a study of effort has also to be a study of recovery.

> My interest in the theatre has never entirely faded, but my movement observation became more acute during all these years and also gained a broader significance. I had the opportunity to help people with corrective movement exercises and training, especially in industry where so much unhappiness is caused by an absolute lack of understanding of the movement functions used in work. With the study of work effort, the study of recovery from the strain of effort has to go hand in hand.

A few pages later he explains his lifelong fascination with movement of all types – his world, from the very outset, was always one of 'more or less continuous motion':

> One has to search, to hunt, to notate, to compile and to compare movement impressions in order to get more clarity. The hunting ground of the movement observer is world-wide because everything, and so also people, is in a more or less continuous motion, or at least affected by the results of preceding movements.

This so elegantly sums up a life devoted to the study of movement.

The text has been lightly edited, and spellings and punctuation occasionally changed in order make the sense clearer.

THE TIRED BAKER[3]

One early morning when I was waiting at a bus station I recognised my neighbour in the queue, a young man in his twenties, as a baker at a factory where I had been observing work on the night-shift. I remembered him very well, how vigorous in his work, how decided in all his actions, and also how in the early hours of the morning he started to slow down when he became tired. Then the decisiveness of his gestures diminished, his normally round and cheerful face became drawn, and he lost his precision of action; and finally his attention, which had formerly been very conscientiously on his work, began to wander as his fatigue got more and more hold of him.

Now, advancing slowly in the queue, he climbed heavily into the bus, and there he was suddenly most elated to find two women who were obviously known to him, one elderly and the other a young girl. He took a seat between them, and it appeared from the talk that they were some sort of relatives, perhaps an aunt or a cousin. As the young man chatted gaily some of his former apathy disappeared, although this tiredness still showed in his expression and his general heaviness. In fact, with traces of flour still smeared across his face he looked rather like a sad pierrot, or a ghost among the living. There was some family resemblance in the movement expression of his companions and himself, in spite of the marked difference in his dreamy demeanour. Apart from the young baker and myself, all the people in the bus were now on the way to work after a good night's rest, and they were much more lively than we were.

It was curious that this young man, who had previously struck me as a definitely masculine character, now showed an almost feminine softness and slowness as he fumbled to unbutton his coat and get out the money to pay his fare. And he displayed a jerky kind of nervousness which did not at all correspond to his obvious equanimity and also to the pleasure with which he had greeted his companions. His voice, too, seemed different. I had heard him shouting across the factory with the same decisiveness that he had shown in his work, but now he was so wanting in the power of expression that the conductor had to ask him twice where he wanted to go. This abstraction and lack of attention were also shown in the wavering of his eyes to the right and left, although in a friendly way and not with any suggestion of nervosity [sic]. He seemed rather to be astonished at seeing so many lively people around him. His head, usually held high, was sunk in his shoulders, giving him a kind of double chin that contrasted oddly with his youthful face, his legs sagged apart, and his whole body was slumped down in the seat.

The young girl, who was obviously very pleased by his presence, showed a light coquetry, to which he tried to respond as best he could. But he could not rival the lively intensity of the girl's face and the quick play of her eyes. The elderly woman on his other side had also a robust vitality, although she yawned once or twice, but perhaps this was because my baker was so much more interested in his other neighbour.

After a short time the young man got up and, recognising me sitting in the bus, he nodded to me with a sudden flash of sympathy in his eyes as he remembered having seen me about the factory the whole of the previous night. His own fatigue from the bodily and mental strain of the night-shift showed again in his heavy steps as he walked down the bus. Nevertheless, something like a new lease of life was beginning to dawn, which became more obvious when, stepping on to the platform, he took a deep breath of the early morning air. Then his spine straightened again, his head went up, the double chin disappeared, and I saw him at last jump down quite vigorously from the still running bus.

In comparing the movements of the baker in the factory with those which he made in the bus-scene, one very obvious contrast is first of all observable. His matter-of-fact actions during his working effort were carried out by a clear awareness of his surroundings. He was fully awake and dealt with each one of his acts in an intensive concentration on the matter in hand. The actions were rhythmically precise and his whole demeanour showed a person of settled stableness.

In the bus-scene, at the start of his recovery, a reversion of his drive to action became visible. A vague state of feeling seemed to invade him. He was decidedly no more fully awake and little aware of the nearby persons and things, until he met his friends. But also in this encounter a rather remote detachment became visible, which strongly contrasted with his former intensive concentration on nearby things and persons. The conductor had to ask him twice for his destination, and how he was fumbling in his pockets for money, dropping thereby a coin on the floor, revealed an inner stir absent from reality. Instead of looking fully awake into the light of day, his [eyes] were as if looking dreamily into the dark. His settled and stable personality was changed into one being an easy prey to emotive inner stirs.

In his work his firmly decided movements performed a lot of well-determinable actions. Now in the bus one could not detect any precision of action. All that he did seemed to swim within an overflowing stream of feeling. One could assume that the meeting with his relations should have awakened a certain warmth. But this was not the case. He remained fairly remote even from the smiling coquetries of the young girl, though obviously elated by her presence. There was not much clear thinking in anything he said or did at the beginning of his recovery period. Here was an individual who in a particular situation exerted himself in clear-cut actions and who found his recovery in retiring into the remoteness of his freely flowing feeling.

The observation of the baker's change-over from work to recovery was one of the many other experiences of a similar kind. Before quoting further examples, I should like to explain a few of the terms used in my descriptions. A person getting lost in the flow as did the baker in his recovery shows prevailingly movements of a soft and well-rounded curve, interrupted by rests in which the energy of the person seems to sink inwards.

It is one of the powers of man that he can sink into himself and re-emerge into the reality of his surroundings. This is continually the case with every heartbeat. This power is here called the cyclic power of man. The contrast to the cyclic sinking which has a floating character is an energetic thrusting outwards and away from the body centre, a gesture of dynamic self-assertion. In certain circumstances the capacity for producing such energetic self-asserting movements gets impaired so that the observer feels justified to speak of the balance between the dynamic and the cyclic power. The capacity of immersion or indulgence in the ever recurring waves of feeling will of course also recede into the background, but this is considered a quite normal disposition with people engaged in lively action. The cyclic floating of movement characterising a prevailing inner attitude of feeling was noticeable with the baker during his recovery. In contrast to the simple character of his recovery gestures, he had in his work much more complicated movements which carried the suggestions of complex inner moods.

His work could not be done with energetic thrusts only. He had to use a good amount of fine touch, appearing in a clear rhythm of alternating sustainment and urgency, revealing changes between caution and daring, or otherwise expressed, he had to make use in his work of more than his dynamic power. We suggest that he showed a definite gift in the use of rhythm in his work which got lost, together with his dynamism, in his recovery state. We can therefore say that besides the dynamic power he asserted, his rhythmic power in his work, he lost both in his recovery when he solely indulged in his cyclic power.

A further fact which was observable when the baker grew tired was that he lost his dexterity; he got clumsier than he was before. There is the capacity in man to build up movement patterns, and with this capacity goes together the dexterity shown in the handling and shaping of objects. This exact pattern-building capacity is based on what we call here the kinetic power of a person. When the baker began to lose his kinetic power, he started to drop tools and to shape his material clumsily, as well as losing time with the weakening of his rhythmic power and the squandering energy with the loss of his dynamic power.

The various powers, differently named for technical convenience, are in reality several aspects only of the one general motion power. But as it arises, that one or more of these aspects of movement are used in a too weak or on the other hand in a too exaggerated manner, one has to distinguish them and to give each of them an appropriate name. The four main aspects of motion power, the dynamic, rhythmic, kinetic and cyclic aspects stand in an intimate connection with the four main motions factors, Weight, Time, Space and Flow, which I have elsewhere discussed in detail.

It is also useful to consider that four aspects of the inner faculties of man, the Sense power, the Intuitive power, the Thinking power, and the Feeling power, find manifestation in movements which can be, with certain restrictions, allocated to definite motion factors. The flowing character of feeling is probably quite understandable to everybody. That this flow shows a cyclic recurrence of inside and outside orientation may be perhaps a new notion, but I do not think that it needs here further explanation. The weightiness of sense power, the rhythmical sensitivity of the power of intuition, and the pattern-building orientation in space of the thinking power have perhaps not yet occurred to everybody. The relationship between all these factors makes it possible to talk about a meaning of, and an order in movement, which both certainly exist. The choice of the technical means by which these almost ineffable relationships can be nearest described is based on the assumption that man, living in the space and time of his physical environment, has to use certain inner powers, in order to switch on and to regulate his movements dealing with the objects of the outside world. That in the same process messages from an inside world which is not immediately visible, can be carried to the surface makes movement function and its observation extremely interesting but also a puzzling subject.

Returning from this diversion into theory to our baker, we have to show how the changes in the use of his strength, rhythm, pattern and flow are observable. Towards the end of his working time the baker showed a tiredness which was expressed in the gradual decrease of the constancy and efficiency of his actions. It became clearly visible how the regularity of the combinations of strong gripping and fine touch which his work demanded dwindled away. Visible was also the fact that the former continuity of his rhythm dissolved into periods of slowing down alternating with periods of an almost hasty speed. The pattern of his working movement became distorted visibly and his drive could be seen to fade away in as much as his actions became always more frequently interrupted. Instead of the constantly renewed participation of his senses of sight and touch one could see him gaze more and more into a far-away distance, and a kind of insensitivity of hands and eyes became also observable. The thinking expression of his face took on a dreaming character which could be as clearly seen as the fact that his mobility became jerky or sloppy. In his highly automised skill he intuitively avoided mishaps such as the slipping away of tools, as long as he was in full possession of his powers. But later when getting tired his intuition left him and one could see him let things drop.

The conclusion drawn from these visual observations, that his thinking, his sensing, his intuition have left him at the same time as his rhythm, his strength, and his capacity to create precise patterns, seems to be fully justified. One saw also that the flow of his movement was least affected, but it took on an almost pathetic expression which is again certified by the visual impression on the observer. He appeared now to feel helpless, whereas before he had given the impression of a person possessing all the attributes of a great self-reliance.

In the beginning of his recovery, he was quite naturally under the spell of his tiredness. His face took on an almost visionary expression, while a passionate desire to escape from his drowsiness flickered up from time to time in his eyes. All this was, however, drowned in the general flow of a feeling mood expressed by corresponding movements, which strangely contrasted with the effects of active drive shown beforehand.

Recovery started to set in shortly before he left the bus. One saw that his body carriage became more erect and his face expression got more composed. One could notice how his kinetic power was reawakened as his gestures gained a clearer pattern. The rhythm and the dynamism of his movement [were] temporarily re-established to normal when he jumped from the bus. There was of course also a bit of showing off for the spectators, the girl and perhaps also myself. He obviously pulled himself together for the moment. Whether he relapsed later on into his relaxed mood when he got home, we could not say with security, because we have not seen him to do so.

I wish I could conjure up before your inner eye a vision of the movement of the baker and his companions. I decided to use these in themselves unimportant extracts from my diary in the hope that, as an illustration of my theme, this will make it easier to visualise what I understand by movement observation.

To look at things and happenings from the point of view of movement observation does not require any special gift. Everybody observes movement, although few people become conscious of it. Speculations about the character or life-history of a person one meets are apt to blur the most important impression of total patterns from which the information about other people's drives and lives are mainly gained. These important impressions made by other people's movements are the source of the capacity to sum up a personality. With some people the summing up of a personality happens so quickly that almost everybody thinks it is pure intuition. Nowadays it has become clear that this is not intuition, no guess or chance product, but an incredibly quick, subconscious mental process, by which we become aware of certain characteristics of a personality almost instantaneously. A great deal of hard work had to be done before it became clear how this sudden subconscious testing comes about. . . .

I would be able to tell you at once what this little adventure of the tired baker said to me in terms of movement. But as most people are not yet sufficiently acquainted with forms of movement, I have to proceed slowly. All I can tell now is that I saw a healthy young man displaying vigorous efforts in his work. Afterwards I saw him getting tired, losing his intensity of movement and reading for the necessary recovery of his lost energy. In the bus I was lucky enough to get a glimpse of how the recovery from his fatigue was growing, leading again to more vigorous efforts. This is not, of course, the whole story of the baker, because he probably got home and, as I hope, had a good breakfast and some well-earned rest in sleep. But as I had not opportunity to observe this I have to discard my speculations and stick to the observed movement facts. But what I have really seen is enough to give me a further confirmation of my experience that movements used in working differ tremendously from those used in the state of recovery. My conviction about this fact could not be based on a single experience only, and I had also to discover in what difference between the two types of movement really consists.

VULCAN THE FANATIC[4]

For this example I have to go back to an experience of my early youth, when still almost a boy. I watched a railway bridge being built across the River Danube, at a point where the river is nearly a mile wide and very deep. In order to build up the supporting pillars of the bridge, relatively narrow steel cylinders had to be sunk into the river bed and the water pumped out of them. The workmen then descended into these cylinders to lay the foundations of the pillars of the bridge. I was anxious to go down one of these cylinders myself, and contrived to persuade one of my teachers to make a school party which should watch the building of the bridge. After long deliberations, it was decided that some of us should be allowed to descend into one of these narrow tubes. We went down in couples, because there was no room in them for any more.

My schoolmate and I climbed down the primitive ladder and found at the bottom two men hitting hard with their axes at a stone emerging from the muddy ground. In the dim light of a rather primitive lantern – because the art of engineering had at that time not progressed to electric projectors – the two workmen threw fantastic shadows on the walls of the tube. As I watched their shadows gliding in a weaving pattern over the background, I suddenly saw the shadow of one axe stand still high in the air and then glide down slowly and vertically. I looked at the workman who had handled the axe before in a ferocious way, reminding me of Vulcan, the ancient god of the smiths. Now, suddenly, he smiled weakly, almost like a knocked-out boxer, and slowly collapsed to the ground. In the confined space, bringing him to the surface was a difficult task, because there was not in those days anything approaching modern technical equipment. Finally, however, the people at the top managed to haul him up very awkwardly along the primitive ladder into the fresh air. Several of the rescuers were themselves not far short of collapse after their exertions, and nor were we two boys climbing up in the rearguard. We had several times to stop and take deep breaths before being able to go on with the climbing.

At the top of the tube, the casualty was put on a kind of

improvised stretcher and covered over with a sheet of tarpaulin, and a doctor was summoned from the nearby riverside town. But the man was already recovering, and seemingly ashamed of his weakness and annoyed at finding himself the centre of so much attention, he jumped up angrily from the stretcher and demanded in his former ferocious way to go down the tube again and resume his work. His workmate, however, more alarmed by the incident than he was, flatly refused to return and there was a heated altercation with the foreman. But the argument was finally settled by the order of the doctor that nobody should go down before further investigations had been made and precautions taken.

The sudden change in the movement expression of this workman from ferocious effort to the sickening sweetness of his fainting, and the later reawakening of his old ferocity, which was now, however, entirely uncontrolled, was amazing.

I have since observed many people getting exhausted, fainting and falling asleep, and I even saw people in various circumstances falling into their last and final sleep. Yet I never again saw such an extraordinary contrast between exaggerated effort and its sudden and total vanishing into a fantastic shape of expression, followed by a brisk recovery to the savage intensity similar to, but nevertheless different from, the earlier working efforts. After the recovery, there was no swinging of the axe, no action, only the intention and decision to act expressed in a fearful flinging about of the arms, and accompanied by a rolling of the eyes in the distorted face. There was a grotesque pattern in the movement lacking all the purposefulness of a real effort.

I told myself: the man is a fanatic – though I could not discover at what object or aim his fanaticism was directed. Perhaps it was an urge to hit, or male pride of independence, but here it was, the fanatical expression of almost all his movements. I tried to explain the gist of my exciting movement observations to my classmate and friend who was with me down the tube. He showed, however, no understanding and only asked me whether I had heard the physical and physiological explanation of the causes of the accident expounded by our teacher who was leading the expedition.

I had to answer negatively and tried to make up my mind about what had happened in my own way. Vulcan, as I have called the man working at the bridge for myself, laboured obviously under the spell of his natural fanaticism. There was a settled stableness of character and purpose in his working behaviour, but it was not humanly warm, it was remote and exulted. No definite rhythm appeared in the work, but rather a frightening pattern of the swinging of his axe. His mood was not bright, not governed by a mind clearly awake. His mood was dark and dreamlike. In his short recovery there was an inner stir, becoming visible in the sickening grin during his fainting. He seemed to be awake to another intuitively felt reality.

More than in his work, he showed in his recovery a heaviness which brought him nearer to the earth than his former exulted remoteness shown in his work.

His awakening from the faint seemed to be a continuation of his recovery. He stood now obviously under the spell of an inner stir, the intuitive impact of which shook his whole body. What he wanted was not so much to get back to his work, but to assert his will. It was an intuitive desire to get again under the dark spell of his working hits. He had not yet regained his initial stableness or rather the stubbornness of his purpose and the remoteness of the pattern of his movements was not entirely re-established.

The sudden stopping of the functional action of Vulcan to hit at the rock with his axe was a reversion of the flow of animation in his whole bodily system. The everted[5] flow of animation leading towards working effort as been changed into the inverted flow of animation receding towards recovery. It is surely wrong to say that the capacity to do an effort has suddenly been abolished. What happened was that the positive flow of animation which usually leads to functional actions had changed into the negative flow of animation which recedes into recovery. Recovery is found in many bodily and mental attitudes, such as rest, fainting, sleep. In all these attitudes, the capacity to exert an effort is present. It has however become latent, but it has not been extinguished altogether, otherwise the individual would be inanimate, dead. There is a latent flow of animation in resting, fainting or sleeping. On normal awakening from sleep the direction of the flow animation changes from the inverted, retiring away from working effort, to the everted striving after function.

If I now compare Vulcan's work with that of the baker, which latter consisted of clear-cut actions, I find that Vulcan seemed not to work but to exert a spell directed towards the rock, which he frantically wanted to destroy. He did not want to master the object of his exertion, he was filled with the wish to destroy it. So his recovery did not consist of a simple gliding off of a natural action into the flow of feeling. His recovery was sought by him in an intuitive awareness of a state of heightened will manifested in a general rhythmic vibration. Other people such as the baker are used to finding relief from this want in the familiarity and homeliness of normal working actions.

In summarising the general impressions gained by Vulcan's work, and juxtaposing them with the impressions gained by the baker's movement, one could say:

In Work

The Baker's Work	Vulcan's Work
Done with the purpose of performing clear-cut actions. Action accompanied by the warmth and earthy nearness of rhythm, performed with brightness of a clear wakestate.	Done under the command of an innate necessity, a spell. Spell standing under influence of an exultation, far remote from ordinary behaviour, becoming visible in shapes of movement and governed by a dark dreamy mood.
Summarised general bearing:	Summarised general bearing:
Action With Stability, Proximity, Brightness	Spell With Mobility, Remoteness, Darkness

In Recovery	
The Baker's Recovery	**Vulcan's Recovery**
An escape into the world of feeling, filled with the elated performance of flowing shapes, in dreamy mobility, caused by an inner stir.	An immersion into the world of intuition, after fainting soon going over into a wakestate, in which the inner mobility found outlet in the wild and earthy rhythms of his gesticulation
Summarised general bearing:	Summarised general bearing:
Feeling With Mobility, Remoteness, Darkness	Intuition With Mobility, Proximity, Brightness

Notes

1. In JHA, Box 26, Folder 23, Item 6.
2. In NRCD L/E/58/37.
3. In NRCD, edited from L/E/54/8 and L/E/55/10, entitled 'Chapter 1' in the typescript.
4. In NRCD, edited from L/E/54/9 and L/E/55/15.
5. Laban's use of this archaic word is quite logical: 'everted' is the opposite of 'inverted', i.e. directed outward rather than inward.

Chapter twenty

Excerpts from *Effort and Recovery* and notes taken from Withymead (early 1950s)

Introduction

Janet Kaylo

Rudolf Laban's work continues to provide a rich resource for the practice of Dance Movement Therapy, as well as for therapeutic dance which generally takes place outside of clinical settings. Within these realms, Laban's movement terms are used to describe an individual's movement repertoire – whether client or therapist – in order to generate palettes of creative movement exploration and development, as well as for specifically defining and measuring progress in treatment goals, and building plans of intervention.

Some of the early dance therapists in the UK included teachers and therapists inspired and mentored by Laban and the Art of Movement Studio, such as Audrey Wethered, Chloe Gardener and Veronica Sherborne; as well as Marion North who later helped establish the first MA training in Britain. Following in their footsteps and those of several other pioneers, Walli Meier states in e-*motion* (2008) that Wethered and Gardener 'ran regular courses on Laban fundamentals for intending dance movement therapists', where she was also invited to teach.[1]

Contemporary use of Laban-based work in Dance Movement Therapy/Psychotherapy generally includes theoretical and practical contributions of two of Laban's prominent students and exponents, Warren Lamb in the UK and Irmgard Bartenieff who was one of the early Dance Therapy pioneers in the USA. While not all Dance Movement Therapists/ Psychotherapists use Laban-based work as a primary means of describing and understanding movement content in therapy sessions, most professional and university programmes include Laban Movement Analysis (LMA) as a significant component of movement observation training. Many – though not all – early dance therapists in the USA also carried Laban's work into clinical settings to varying degrees: some using LMA as a 'tool' and others pointing to Laban's work 'as a psychotherapeutic philosophy and a dance therapy methodology in and of itself'.[2]

Do Laban's broader assertions of movement meaning contain inherent therapeutic philosophy, and foreshadow and underscore Dance Movement Therapy/Psychotherapy practice today?

Taken as a holistic or therapeutic resource, Laban's references to movement parallel contemporary dance therapy theories which are based on the premise that body and mind are inseparable and that movement not only reflects inner states of being, but can also effect changes in the psyche when used as a primary means in a therapeutic setting or relationship.[3] Recent publications by clinicians Frances LaBarre (2001), Suzi Tortora (2006) and Katya Bloom (2006) testify to the usefulness of LMA in therapeutic practice, each of them using it in expertly nuanced and individualised ways while still drawing on Laban's original premises.

In Laban's pairing of movement expression and health lies his belief that individuality is a living dynamic principle, existing in a cycle of movement rhythm. This cycle requires a balance of effort and recovery, which he contends is specifically experienced and expressed through childhood and adolescence, and often lost or squelched later through the inhibitions of traditional education, and the drudgery or boredom of repetitive work actions. In *Effort and Recovery*, Laban describes the movement rhythms of effort and recovery as a 'life-giving reality'.[4]

Laban states that '[t]he value of effort study and of its practical application lies on an entirely different ground' from simply advocating movement as a panacea for all ills. Movement provides 'specific experiences which [man] cannot get otherwise',[5] but most importantly, which are revealed spontaneously rather than through conscious reasoning.

In the broadest sense, Laban was convinced that '[t]he spontaneity behind any movement makes it a unique and fundamental source of all experience'.[6] As such, movement demonstrates the expression of various feelings, and descriptions of the movement which characterises those feelings are possible.[7] '[H]uman movement,' Laban explains, 'can give an insight into the functions of the mind, both in health and in disorder.'[8] Unlike purely psychological description, Laban's vocabulary and distinctions are rooted in the movement itself. As part of a treatment for 'disorders', he claimed: '[Therapists] have found that my movement observation and training can be of help in their professional activities', assisting with recovery 'from illness, and especially from mental disturbances'.[9] Still, he warns that movement corresponding to particular feelings cannot be dispensed 'like medicine'; while he does allow that pairings of movement and feeling can assist in recognising the vitalised and devitalised aspects of a person's inner life. The therapists Laban refers to as benefiting from his work probably included British occupational therapists (such as Chloe Gardener), who trained with him at the Art of Movement Studio, and brought his work into clinical settings; as well as Jungian-based therapists working at Withymead, where he acted as consultant in the dance and movement activities.

ADVENTURES WITH PLAYING CHILDREN[10]

The expressive variants of basic actions, which we call frantic, passionate, suggestive, visionary forms of basic actions show some attributive qualities which can be clearly discerned. These qualities are characterised by a change in their space, time or weight components of the action. Thus a passionate action of any kind will lose the precision and clarity of its space-component. It will no more be definitely direct or flexible but rather bound by some inner impediment or it will be exaggeratedly free flowing. One could say that in the passionate action the space-content is replaced by a flow-content so that to the thinking part of the action it is imparted as intense feeling quality.

Whether the first impression is doggedly fixed and does not leave the person obsessed by it, or whether this first impression causes in its overpowering intensity a continuous sparkling sequence of dispersional vibrations, the enlargement while still showing the binding or scattering characteristics of the inner states by which the shadow moves are caused, leads to the abolition of the spell under which the individual has been brought through the overwhelming experience.

I should like to refer in this connection to my remarks about the sensations of people on the threshold between life and death in serious illness. I have found people suffering from serious mental disturbances to have a very similar inner picture of existence. This might express itself in an endless number of variations, but the core of the disturbance is always, that these people somehow and somewhere get a glimpse of the vast ocean of nothingness – or shall we say of another side of reality – and now, in spite of being otherwise generally healthy, they cannot get rid of this experience. A person recovering from physical illness forgets bit by bit the extraordinary awareness of the turning point at which he has faced the other side of the medal. The mentally disturbed cannot turn back from his experience, which was perhaps although not so clearcut as that of the almost dying physical malade.[11] The mentally disturbed hangs on this experience and tries even to peer into the strange land behind the threshold, in finding there laws and ordering principles according to which he feels compelled to live. It is obvious that this makes him unfit to function in normal everted life and in our language which we have learned to use in this book we see that the mentally ill person uses specific combinations of efforts and movement shapes reminding one of the demeanour of the almost dying physical malade. It is most curious that some of these efforts are also shown in the plays of children as well as in genuine discharge of the attempts at ritualistic excitement. Uneasiness and fear caused by extraordinary experience result in ritualistic movement play.

The normal and healthy person changes back easily from an occasional 'floating-fainting' into the struggling and 'punching' of everyday reality. One could also say that the changing over from dream or extasis[12] into awake activity is no problem for a mentally sane person. This changing over happens almost automatically. To get from the visionary aspect of reality back to normal life is much less easier for people whose mind is almost habitually reverted towards the landscape of the visionary aspect of existence. Without aiming to establish here an exhausting explanation of this turning away into visionary existence with its characteristic suffering and felicity so different from everyday experience, I should like to give a slight hint at least of the effort peculiarities which can be observed with people immersed in this beyond and in the natural remedy against abnormal states of mind which ritualistic epochs have found in movement play.

One will have to remember earlier passages of this book in which the action or passion character of certain effort combinations was illustrated. Some of these efforts have also been explained to serve visionary or spellbinding purposes. Mental states of cool remoteness in contrast to rhythmical warmth and nearness have been met, together with the opposition of the strong motility against the desire of stabilisation. The prevalence of either feeling, sensing or thinking and intuition as regulating factors of movements of different kinds have been discussed and demonstrated.

It has also been shown how certain basic effort, such as floating and gliding differ from others like punching and slashing, and how this basic difference – which is vital for the matter discussed now – can be expressed in terms of contrasting behaviour in space directness or flexibility, in time as sustained or urgent, and in strength as firmness or fine touch. It was also mentioned how incomplete efforts served the hiding of appetites and desires, but also how these incomplete efforts became the expression of the inner urge to play, and to dance, as with the factory girl Angela.[13]

Out of these few hints on effort as a function of our space, time and weight sensations it will be possible to shed a light on certain categories of movement more frequently used in states of recovery or also in the deep relaxation from physical illness or in the persevering invertedness of the flow of effort in mental disturbance. In all these states no real action occurs, that means no action which has a practical purpose in the sense of the alleviations of the normal everyday needs of man. Real action life is extinguished. This extinction has its shades, it can happen in different ways. Speaking in terms of effort, one must remember that ordinary basic action consists of a space-component, a time-component and a weight- or strength-component. The result of the compounding of these components are then pushing, pressing, gliding, floating movements which have a certain number of variations. The expressive variants of basic actions which we call frantic, passionate, suggestive, visionary forms of basic actions show some attributive qualities which can be clearly discerned. These qualities are characterised by a change in their space-, time- or weight-components of the action. Thus a passionate action of any kind will lose the precision and clarity of its space component. It will no more be definitely direct or flexible, but rather bound by inner impediment or it will be exaggeratedly free flowing. One could say that in the passionate action the space-content is replaced by a flow-content, so that to the thinking part of the action it is imparted as intense feeling quality.

In a similar way one can see, that if the clarity of the time rhythm of an action gets diminished or the time-content of the action gets neutralised and replaced by a more general flow feeling, the action gets definitely spellbound or spell exerting. Another possibility is the decrease of the strength-content of an action and the substitution of weight by intensity of free or bound flow, which makes the action visionary. Action and passion are much more part of everyday life, than spell and vision. It is thus that a ritualistic act, or the behaviour of a dying person and very similarly for if the behaviour of a mentally disturbed person and even of children in play is much more in the line of spell and vision than in that of straightforward action and even passion. As different combinations of effort elements are used in these various forms of movement it becomes possible to characterise the mental states connected with such movement forms in the terms of basic efforts. The observation of effort and especially the more elaborate assessment of effort combinations is therefore apt to reveal the kinds and degrees of the normality or abnormality of behaviour. In the same way it is also possible to discern appropriate recovery measures through movement play or exercise. It becomes understandable that the inner state of a person or of a group of persons whose recovery one would like to further through some kind of movement play can be first assessed and afterwards playfully remedied.

Notes taken from Withymead

The Withymead Centre was founded in the 1940s by Irene and Gilbert Champernowne, and continued into the late 1960s, with Laban and some of his students at times providing the dance and movement element in the arts therapies utilised there. The Champernownes had close ties to the Elmhirsts and Dartington Hall: prior to its sale to the Elmhirsts in 1925, Dartington Hall had been in the Champernowne family for centuries.

Laban's notes from these sessions at Withymead provide practical examples of how Laban might utilise movement as indicators of 'vitalised and devitalised' aspects of the personality: one of his primary claims for movement observation in *Effort and Recovery*. Though still highly interpretive in psychological as well as spiritual dimensions, Laban's observations and attendant 'indications for practice' present fascinating and complex associations between movement capacity and potential for overall balance and well-being through movement. Discovering just how to accomplish these recommended 'practices' within a therapeutic context, however, would challenge an experienced dance movement therapist even today.

It may be significant to note that the necessity for a movement-derived, therapeutic relationship between the movement 'artist' or facilitator and the patient/student, is not mentioned in these notes. Laban does demonstrate here, once again, his own facility for moving in and out of representational depictions of movements *as conditions of* the people who inhabit them. Perhaps in the context of Withymead's arts-based approach to therapy this worked well as an innovative attempt to make psychological parallels with body movement strengths and weaknesses. When seen against a backdrop of what Meekums refers to as 'contemporary imperatives to evidence the profession [of dance movement psychotherapy]',[14] the interpretive framework of his movement description can appear dubious. Laban himself attached far-reaching implications, both globally and locally, to his form of movement observation.

Laban's movement observations attempt to define a phenomenology of movement even though his interpretations lie well outside of the experience of the movement itself. It is vital to differentiate between these stages of observation and interpretation and thus avoid an essentialist approach to movement description. Does movement have unequivocal meaning and thus offer itself for universal, psychological interpretation? The confidence and assertion with which Laban employs his interpretive framework here would suggest that he believes it does. I would consider we read Laban's 'Notes from Withymead' as interpretations of movement within his individual and collective, historical and cultural times. Read this way, what can they tell us now?

VISIT TO WITHYMEAD, 19–26 SEPTEMBER, 1949[15]

Extracts from Notes concerning movement observation and movement practice

Notes have been made concerning:

1. Individual sessions with student-patients
2. Individual sessions with non-patients,
3. Other movement observations:

During clinic for children and adults in the art therapy workshop.
During everyday activities, meals, etc.
During leisure time, social gatherings, etc.

Extracts from Notes. Group A. Student-patients

(Names in the order of first sessions.)

1. RB
2. NG
3. MB
4. DH
5. JH
6. MR
7. SW

These seven student-patients (with the exception of 6 and 7) have each been observed in several sessions and seem to represent a reasonable cross section of personalities as well as of degrees and kinds of maladjustment. Therefore the assessments can give a survey of the various possibilities of how the Art of Movement could be applied for remedial purposes in similar cases.

1. RB

Observation of RB showed a noticeable inefficiency in the use of the left side of her body. This lack was neuro-muscular as well as expressive. Stiffness of back and shoulders was the witness of withheld energy which occasionally exploded in other parts of her body-mind.

Fighting against space, time and weight was characteristic of her movements. The fighting against space in brusque direct movements prevailed in self-invented movements.

She rarely indulged her weight in relaxed movements or in sustained slowness.

Movements in the form of exercise were inhibited through too much thinking about them.

Free movements (dance-like) were better coordinated and more flowing.

Her main gift seemed to be dramatic movement in which the fight of conflicting thoughts and feelings finds an outlet end produces compensatory movements which are otherwise lacking.

Dramatic movement (mime) was also the form in which pleasure was best experienced. It was not a pleasure of harmony, but of contrasting emotions of all kinds without much discrimination of physical mellowness and/or spiritual values.

Movement scenes of varying character, partly invented by herself seemed to relieve her one-sided crampedness, and exclusive fighting attitude.

Indication for practice

Occupation with human conflicts and situations in acting (mime) will help her to gain such security and all-roundness of movement expression out of which the intellectual search for spiritual values can be cautiously attempted. Otherwise the dramatisation of spirituality will distort her inner images.

(Note: Besides this individual practice, which in dramatic movement can be usefully supplemented by working with a living (not imagined) partner, general group work (in small groups) would also be indicated. This group work will introduce her into more abstract and impersonal movement habits. The character of desirable group work in general will be discussed later.)

2. NG

Observation of NG was interesting as a total contrast to 1. (RB).

The almost sloppy mobility of the whole body resulted in smooth movements which never exploded anywhere.

Indulging in space, time and weight was throughout characteristic. This character was less outspoken in time, where sometimes quickness (fighting against time) appeared in a form of small hasty but weak movements.

Reacted more to dreamlike formal movements than to dramatic incentives. A natural inclination for give and take series was evident in which a good coordination was achieved. Shrank from conflict and fight because of a great lack of physical force and endurance.

A good deal of her available energy is absorbed in her painting classes. It is therefore necessary for her to restrict herself to short energising morning exercises which will free her also from a certain crampedness of her abdominal muscles.

Indication for practice

Morning exercises. If later energy increases, it will be easy for her to invent formal movement sequences, consisting first mainly of her habitual dreamlike efforts with a slow and cautious addition of movements of a more fighting character. Occasional group work indicated.

3. MB

Observation of MB showed extreme contrast between fine movements of spiritual significance (reminiscent of ritual movements of medieval character) and rough movements of an almost brutal expression of childlike even baby-like vehemence and simplicity.

The fine movements showed an exaggerated indulgence in space, time and relaxation.

The rough movements showed an exaggerated fighting against space, time and weight.

There is nothing in between and no transitions. Long torpor-like rests and apathetic little tensions are followed by the unexpected outbreak of one of the two typical forms of her movement make-up. During these outbreaks an excellent movement coordination is shown, although the expression is always exaggerated except in the attempts to follow movement suggestions. During these attempts she shows hesitations which are the expression of doubt and suspicion. Once the hesitation has been overcome the movements flow freely to an exhausting climax of inner participation. Exhaustion of this kind and also of poor sustainment in physical energy makes the possible periods of coordinated activity relatively short and rare. The lengths of the intermittent rest or torpor periods vary in an irregular rhythm between durations of a few hours and whole – perhaps several – days.

Indication for practice

The goal of any re-education of personal effort capacity through movement is here obviously a complicated one:

a) The exaggeration of both fine movements (indulging in the movement factors of space, time and energy) and rough movements (fighting against space, time and weight) should be systemically reduced.
b) The transitions between fine and rough movements should be cultivated.
c) The rhythm of activity and rest should be brought to normal proportions.
d) The sustainment of physical energy (endurance) should be trained.
e) The hesitation in the acceptance of movement suggestions should be overcome.

Most of those aims are inter-related as far as the use of bodily actions is concerned. They are, however, also inter-related in their mental and spiritual significance which the patient intuitively understands and fundamentally loves and enjoys.

It seems that the two interferences a) by physical stimuli such as shocks and drugs and b) by verbal explanation even of the most poetic and spiritual kind are in the present state of the patient more apt to destroy self-regulating movement attempts than to help to advance the aims postulated above.

Cautious attempts in somehow propitious movements, but as far as possible at regular intervals to provoke movements which increase to and decrease from the two contrasting types of indulgence and fighting. The duration of such movement practice should be slowly increased and the intervals of their application slowly reduced.

As long as the patient is not able to work autonomically, a professional movement trainer would be needed who understands the technical meaning of the necessary prescriptions.

(Note: The prescription character of the initial movement treatment should of course include self-invented or improvisatory action. Care has however to be given that the trainer does not submit himself to all shades of the patient's mood which will be for a long time dictated by triplicate rhythm of extreme indulging – torpor – extreme fighting which has to be gradually reduced to a balanced interplay between moderate indulging and fighting efforts until a new centre is found within the balanced transitions.

Group work is indicated, whereby the patient can function sometimes as follower and sometimes as leader.)

4. DH

In the observation of DH, the shock-like reaction to movement was at first very pronounced. It can at least be partially explained as a sudden realisation of a personal all-round movement capacity and its long neglect, and further as a sudden understanding of the human and remedial value for himself and also for his professional ambitions.

The totality (all-roundness) of movement capacity leads to a confusion of symmetrical innervations. The discernment of left side and right side innervations is marked. Otherwise the coordination between indulging and fighting efforts is excellent as well as in all transitions. A relative preponderance of weak movement is due to the habitual lack of physical action. Weakness has however been overcome after a few sessions. A greater mastery of natural (childlike) clumsiness is to be expected through a self-regulating of movement habits. It was relatively easy to introduce the student to the typical forms of static and dynamic movement differentiation, mentally as well as bodily. He did functional exercises as readily and as well as emotionally expressive movement sequences. The mental-spiritual components are well understood, but some of them are more neglected than others. As an example the lack of self-assertive expressions could be mentioned.

Movement imagination and memory is of great latent capacity.

Indication for practice

Besides the training regulating the neuro-muscular inadequacies it will be possible for the student to find relief from self-induced moods and also of such moods which have been overtaken from other persons (as, for instance, from MB). The best form is a kind of personal or occasional ritual in which the noxious moods are first represented in bodily-mental movement and afterwards dissolved into compensatory evolutions of the body-mind.

A strengthening against hyper-sensitivity of mood-impressions might arise from the repeated performance of such 'personal rituals' but might later necessitate special exercises which cannot yet be determined and are not easy to describe in this short survey.

(Note: The participation in group movement is very strongly indicated. The increasing mastery of all movement factors might [predestine] DH to a leader of group movement. For the time being, however, he will greatly profit from the fitting into group evolution especially in order to overcome some of his shortcomings such as the confusion of symmetrical innervations or the clear discernment (in action) of personal and general space-time and energy.)

5. JH

The observation of JH showed that the general effort make-up is relatively all-round but is roughly handled. That means that the Inner attitudes (indulging and fighting) against the movement factors (space–time–energy) are careless and lack a certain cleanness of decision and precision. This indolence – if it may be termed thus – is not that of a child or young animal. It is rather that of an adult who contemptuously or desperately neglects relationships to objects and persons.

Coordination and interest increase however if rhythmically repetitive elements are stressed. In the first session she got more exact and gained in inner participation in clapping and stepping definite rhythms. The attempts to induce voice rhythms ended however in failure. The capacity for large movement is better developed than that for small movement (voice organ movements are small). The development of harmoniously large movements leads to dance and abstract movements, not to mime for which no special gift has been shown. So in fact in the second session JH found the figure 8 space rhythm helpful for the awakening of emotional participation. This has led further to other formal space rhythms out of which grew a remarkable differentiation of decision and precision and pleasureful participation. The combination of symbolically meaningful shapes found an excellent response. Inventiveness and memory reached surprising heights.

The movements have been performed without music, but it is probable that music will occasionally heighten the remedying effect.

Indication for practice

Dance-like evolution of well-harmonised large movements mainly shapes. The performance of mime-actions including face expression and of working efforts is for the time being less recommendable in individual exercise. Can be attempted in group movement.

(Note: The highly abstract tendency seems to correspond to a need to eliminate the intellectual approach to her problems. The patient seems to be a typical example of a person to whom dynamic art therapy could bring relief and perhaps also sanity. Group movement might help to extend the range of her inner participation and capacity of an intensified human relationship.)

6. MR

The observation of MR showed the outspoken artistic gift of this student to be impeded by a great lack of physical force and also of a decisive enthusiasm. Her movements are narrow and weak but fine touch is well-developed, the capacity to make strong movements is imprisoned in crampedness (exaggerated and misplaced strength). A well-reasoned desire of normal life conditions might help her to find balance in an artistic activity.

In the one session with her, stress was given to her future adjustment to the studies in which she wishes to embark. No special indications shall therefore be given here.

(Note: As a type she needs evidently group movement which will relieve her solitariness. Certain elements of mime-action might develop her capacity to experience and to appreciate the great manifold human relationships of which she seems to be totally unconscious. She is particularly unable to create a centre of action from which she can irradiate. She lives in personal space-time and energy without having any living notion of general space-time and energy. She accommodates herself to the exigencies of general surroundings in a solely passive and submissive way which her well-developed reasoning faculty recommends to her.)

7. SW

The observation of SW showed good neuro-muscular mobility connected with a very stiff and immobile neck. Her movements are all very realistically adapted to everyday actions. Emotional movements are sentimental in the bad sense, which means that clichés are used instead of genuine expression. Yet there is feeling in her which seems, however, to be buried in fixed opinions. Except in her left body side, strong movements (fighting against weight) prevail. The left side is weak, passive, almost lazy. Light and generally indulging movements, however, are not lacking altogether and the transitions are fluent although inexpressive (non-creative). There exists no real centre of creative irradiation. A remarkable feature of the one session with this patient was the miming of her life story without it having been asked for. This mime had a duration of approximately three minutes and she really brought into it all realistic features including emotional contents, which were conventionally, sentimentally presented. Some hints of spiritual significance, as her awe in face of her dead mother [and] the loneliness when she was abandoned by all her sisters and brothers, were also obvious and more genuine than her relational feelings. In showing how she brought up the family, she did some working action movements which were, however, muddled and externally imperfect. The physical joy of her childhood was represented by a gay jumping of a gymnastic character (almost pure bodily function). It will be noticed that this mime comprehended the four movement types several times alluded to:

bodily function,
emotional expression,
working actions,
praying attitudes.

This fullness of movement experience, no matter how inadequately centred, resulted in a great relief after which her movements in other exercises seemed to be more centred as if she had found the crossing point of the various inner and outer experiences.

The attempt to keep her on the level of a more integrated expression stressing rhythm and using her own humming singing as an accompaniment was partially successful.

Indication for practice

Symbolic mimes and dances awakening her imagination might result from a fostering of more realistic representations. Improvement of localised movement defects (stiff neck, left side's apathy) might be sought in special functional exercises.

She might be able to become a general trainer of fundamentals. It is improbable that she will reach the level of mental-spiritual guidance.

(Note: Group movement is an essential condition of her development. It is, however, necessary to assort [sic] her carefully to partners with whom coordination will be possible. There are not many who would appreciate her realistic simplicity. She should rather work in groups with healthy people or children – even backward children. Here she could even be a leader.)

Notes

1. For more on British pioneers in DMT, see Meekums (2008).
2. Reed, in Levy (1992: 163).
3. *ER*, p. 29 (all references are to the draft of *Effort and Recovery*).
4. Ibid., p. 272.
5. Ibid., p. 265.
6. Ibid., p. 265.
7. Ibid., p. 256.
8. Ibid., p. 1c.
9. Ibid., p. 1.
10. In NRCD, edited from L/E/54/36 and L/E/55/29.
11. Laban uses this French expression to denote a 'sick person'.
12. Laban uses the Greek *extasis* (literally 'out of its place') to convey this dimension of ecstasy.
13. He tells her story in Chapter V, where he observes her doing an extremely repetitive job and suggests she might like a change to a 'sorting job, in which various things had to be taken out of a basket, measured, counted, separated into different heaps, and then carried away and new material fetched for sorting'. She hated it because it prevented her from daydreaming. 'I thought about a letter I'd received, or about the shopping, or what I would do at the weekend.' He realised that for some people their waking life only begins after work ends. He noted that the rhythms of her movements in between those working the machine followed her daydream moods.
14. Meekums (2008: 99–106).
15. In JHA, Folder 12, Item 14.

Chapter twenty-one

The Harmony of Movement (early 1950s)[1]

Introduction

Carol-Lynne Moore

Throughout his peripatetic career as a visual artist, dancer, choreographer, writer, teacher, consultant and theorist, Laban never stopped wondering about human movement. When his observations and ruminations reached a temporary conclusion, he published. Then his relentless curiosity drove him on, to new examinations and formulations. As Bartenieff describes, 'It was an unending process of defining the inner and outer manifestations of movement phenomena in increasingly subtle shades and complex interrelationships.'[2]

Many of Laban's final theoretical explorations remain unpublished, but fortunately these works have been preserved in the Rudolf Laban Archive, a vast collection of writings, drawings and other materials now housed at the National Resource Centre for Dance, University of Surrey, England. The following article, drawn from this collection, addresses a theme to which Laban returns again and again – the harmonic structure of human movement.

Laban is well aware that this dance/music analogy is not immediately obvious, and he takes great pains to provide examples and develop his argument. Nevertheless, like Henri Bergson, another great philosopher of time and motion, Laban's discussion is not tightly structured. Instead, various themes are sounded and new notes are introduced as Laban sketches his vision through freely flowing iterations. This vision can be grasped more readily by revisiting the research problems Laban faced and the imaginative structures he developed to grapple with these problems.

When Laban began his dance and movement research in the early twentieth century, technical tools for recording and analysing movement, such as film, were not readily available. Instead, Laban had to develop conceptual tools that would allow him to identify elements of human movement analytically, and then explain how these elements come together harmonically, resulting in the fluent sequences of action that characterise dance as well as skilled labour, both mental and physical.

Laban's system of movement analysis starts from a recognition that movement occurs in two different domains – space and time. Movement through space goes from place to place; movement through time shifts from mood to mood. Movement from place to place belongs to the outer world where actions can be seen. The shifting landscapes of mood belong to an inner world of changing needs, impulses and reactions. These motions cannot be seen directly but must be inferred from the dynamic rhythms or 'efforts' employed in visible actions. Thus Laban conceives movement as a psychophysical phenomenon involving the whole person – body, mind and emotion.

In both outer and inner domains, Laban views movement as an oscillatory phenomenon, a vibratory shift between opposites. Laban refers to many opposites in his discussion: grace and clumsiness, authenticity and artifice, theoretical understanding and practical ability. As the discussion of harmony becomes more movement-specific, he introduces additional pairs of opposites: contrasting spatial directions, stable attitude poses and mobile arabesque extensions, and fighting and indulging effort qualities.

This conception of movement as vibration provides a foundation for the many musical analogies that Laban points out in the article and leads to his formulation of movement harmony. Key elements such as order, balance and kinship are stressed. For while harmony rests upon a richly varied range of motion, contrasting effort qualities and opposite directions in space require orderly intermediary steps to be balanced and brought into an agreeable relationship.

The most difficult harmonic correlation for the reader to grasp may be Laban's description of the space around the dancer's body as an 'invisible keyboard'. Here it is necessary to understand that Laban appropriated various Platonic solids, using their corners, edges and internal rays to map movement paths through space. The twelve corners of the icosahedron provide a particularly useful grid, not only for their commonsensical correspondence with corners of the cardinal planes but also for the more abstract association with the twelve semitones of Western music.

This association allows Laban to extend his harmonic analogies. Just as a composer draws upon tones to create melodic contours, so the dancer draws upon points in space to generate movement sequences, tracing geometric shapes and letters with various parts of the body. Spatial form (the movement from place to place) becomes analogous with melody, while Laban relates effort (the movement from mood to mood) to rhythm. The simultaneous movements of two or more dancers can result in consonant and dissonant harmonies, capable of expressing a range of tensions and emotions, from the soothing to the terrifying.

Laban admits that consonance and dissonance are less obvious in physical behaviour than in music, perhaps because it is easier avert one's eyes than to stop one's ears. Yet as the bombardment of moving images increases, there is a growing need to wonder about movement and its effects on the observer. Thus the question of what constitutes harmony and disharmony retains its pertinence and mystery.

THE HARMONY OF MOVEMENT[3]

The desire of man to live harmoniously is very much bound up with the way in which he performs his movements, because his movements are not only the basis of his actions but also the basis of the visible and audible expression of his inner state of mind. When someone behaves clumsily and knocks things about, it will be easy to see that his movements are not well harmonised. However, it will be less easy to see if someone is expressing through his movements the harmony of his inner attitude. The key to any observation of whether or not these expressions are a part of the harmoniously ordered inner life of a person is the regularity or irregularity in the flow of his movement. Regularity in the flow of a person's movement is a fairly evident witness of a certain coordination between the inner state of mind and practical movement action. The important thing is, however, the quality of this coordination.

If you look at human nature from a very large angle, you will notice that certain utterances and actions will refer to specific domains of human life. For instance, one could say about a person that all his moral and ethical utterances and actions seem to be well harmonised, but it does not follow that he is also harmonious in practical actions of everyday life. This is proved in the case of a scientist who may show a harmonious development of his thoughts and thinking faculties, but in his practical life he may utter and do things which are rather grotesque and disharmonious. He may forget things and put them in the wrong place and seek for them in a rather helpless manner, just because his thoughts are concentrated on some profound problem of deeper significance. On the other hand, you may see a person who superficially looks very harmonious in his or her movements, which are perfect, well-curved, and have an excellent flow and rhythm. But behind this glamorous appearance there may be hidden a hollowness, a lack of morals and intelligence, combined with muddled feeling. We can therefore say that a person will be most harmonious who shows in all fields of intellectual, emotional and active behaviour, an ordered state of mind, which is clearly expressed in the flow of his movements; it may be noticed that one has to consider the train of thoughts as a movement, which, in its more or less well-associated currents within the nervous system, it actually is.

One may surmise that such an all-round personality, who shows everywhere a certain ordered and well-flowing expression, may not be able to reach the same depths in all fields of human activity. This may be true. An athlete, who is perfect in the mastery of his body and superb in the overwhelming of obstacles of a physical kind, will hardly have the time to penetrate philosophical ideas with the same thoroughness as another person who specialises in this subject. The athlete is in form in his physical actions while the professor is astonishingly all-round in the field of thinking. But both the athlete and the professor can be harmonious personalities who are not particularly clumsy and helpless in the domains which are not their speciality. The athlete need not be stupid, and the professor is not bound to be a practical imbecile.

We may add the artist to this list of specially developed people. A good artist needs without doubt a very rich and all-round development of sensitivity and emotional understanding. This is true for all artists in any field of art whether he is a painter, musician, dancer, or poet, or engaged in anything else which is called artistic activity. Now in some cases the artist may lack the perfection of bodily form and movement which the athlete possesses. He may also be less complex in his methodical thinking which is admired in the professor or scientist.

The arts cover a very wide range and are enormously different. From the simple decorative and entertaining qualities of a work of art one can discern a ladder of many degrees leading up to the expression of deepest religious feeling. One may suppose that an artist fond of entertaining people in a pleasant way will sometimes have the disadvantages of the aforementioned superficial people who are very nice to look at but are lacking in depth. Other artists who are deeply religious in their work, showing here signs of great sincerity in an ethically valuable manner, will not always be able to present their work in an easy and fluent-looking style. One may even expect that the sincerity of the deeply religious artist will lead him to a certain crudeness which looks almost clumsy and is quite the opposite to any superficial charm of external harmony. The real clue to the idea of harmony is that some vestiges of inner harmony must still be present in external charm, very much as some trace of external beauty must be present in a strongly developed inner harmony. If one of these two features is entirely missing, one cannot speak any more of real harmony.

As movement is a feature in which all qualities of the mind, the heart, and the willpower are strongly represented, one can say that to study the harmony of movement is perhaps one of the best ways to deal with the nature of harmony itself. The most natural way to do so is of course to speak about harmony in terms of movement, but these terms need specification. It will not be enough to describe movements in the ordinary mechanical way. One can say that a person has a wonderful gait, and then go into detail and speak about the poise of the movement, the erect carriage of the spine and head and of other attributes connected with a pleasant and free form of walking; one can speak about the rhythm of the steps and of many other things but none of these remarks will penetrate the core of the idea of harmony in movement.

There is more behind it, and here we must introduce the idea of balance in order to get a bit nearer to the essential point of the description of the harmony of movement. Put in the simplest way, balance is the equalising of two opposites. If one puts an object in one side of a pair of scales, one has to put another object of equal weight in the other side, so that the scales will keep still on an equal level or at least so that neither side of the scales goes down too low or up too high. It is the same with all human attitudes, states of mind, and actions: one can exaggerate one of the possible opposites which all these features of human behaviour show and then the other side will seem unduly neglected. It is this which makes the professor's everyday actions clumsy and disharmonious, that he does not balance or secure his flow of movement by using well-measured steps and gestures, but instead he stumbles and fumbles, going in all kinds of unnecessary roundabout ways to his goal. The same thing applies to an athlete who balances all physical things perfectly, but if he has to express his thoughts, he may be helpless and splutter out incoherent words and clumsy combinations of ideas, which show the lack of balance in the movements within his brain. So also the artist who indulges in perfect sentiments and is able to express them in colourful tunes, may in ordinary life be cold and unresponsive to the sufferings of his fellowmen. There is no balance in these people and this lack of balance will be observable somewhere in their movements.

One can be touched by the clumsiness of a person, whether it is mental or bodily clumsiness, but being touched is not a recognition of harmony. One is inclined to pity a person who has little harmony, but if one wants to observe harmony, one must not be deterred by pity or contempt or any other feelings which may blur the judgment of the investigator.

When meeting a person who in his whole behaviour and actions has the capacity to balance the opposites, we may be inclined to say that he is really harmonious. How will this be shown in his movement, not only as a whole but also in details? First one should be clear as to what the opposites are for which we have to look. The deeper aspect of opposites consists in that any human fundamental tendency, as, for instance, his inner drives or higher psychic operations, has two possibilities to function. One could be called 'the activation' and the other one 'the restraint'. These two characteristics are very well known to the student of movement as 'free flow' and 'bound flow'. The terms introduced into effort study, in which a person either indulges in one of the movement factors or fights against it, are in reality, the same thing. If one indulges in something, one gives way to this thing whatever it may be in a free-flowing inner attitude. The free flow can also appear in the shape and rhythm of the outer action. The other way is not to indulge in, but to fight against something. This involves the total or partial restriction of the intended action, thought, or feeling – a proceeding cautiously with bound flow, whereby every step is exactly and deliberately mastered.

In the formal sphere of movement, one comes to two fundamental body actions which the dancer traditionally discerns; these are the arabesques on the one hand and the attitudes on the other hand. If you look at an arabesque, you will see that it is more direct and outward pointed, intruding into the outer space, while the attitude attempts to enclose a portion of space in a sphere-like form up to a definite, almost static, final position. It is difficult to continue an attitude because it is, so to speak, the end of a movement; and it is almost impossible to stop in an arabesque because its whole tendency is to go on.

We come here to the significance of the parts of a movement, whereby the rest or the poise of the position is to be included as an essential part of the realm of movement. It is not only the change from one position to another which is essential in movement, but also the positions themselves. Man is able to fill the space around him with his movement and positions, or he can restrict himself to straight lines in space, neglecting or not using any but one of the many extensions of space. Man can be heavy when he goes down to earth and light when he strives up towards heaven, but this is not harmony itself. It is a simple adaptation to the physical law of gravity. The adaptation to gravity and the economy of effort connected with it does not spring from the feeling or desire of balancing opposites within the moving individual's personality. One will easily understand that a person who always accentuates gravity with heavy steps is not necessarily harmonious in his movements. He may avoid unnecessary elevations and his behaviour, adapted to the gravity of his body, may be most appropriate in a practical sense. But he is lopsided in neglecting one of the opposites present in every person's psychical make-up.

It is a curious thing that we never see such behaviour, or only very rarely, with a dancer, who strives to give to movement its own significance. A dancer is apt to reverse the natural tendency towards gravity and to attempt the impression of an almost supernatural lightness. The way he does this is dictated by his desire to balance and reconcile the heaviness of his body with his desire to express the lightness and independence of his inner feeling. In which way this reverse function of directions can be applied to expressive movement is a most fascinating subject of study. The conciliation of movement patterns and of that which the dancer has to say with these patterns, along with the physical necessities of bodily structure and function, are the most important features of the real harmony of movement.

If the content or meaning of movement can be as easily described as in everyday actions, or even in mime, there is no great difficulty in explaining harmony. The difficulty arises only in those pure dances, which do not contain any story or comprehensive action.

The comparison of movement harmony with musical harmony is perhaps the best way to approach this intricate phenomenon. Before such comparison is made, the differences between music and dance must be briefly mentioned.

The art of dancing presupposes a mentality which is able to see a miracle in the structure and the movement activities of the human individual comprising his body as a whole. Music is an art in which some partial qualities and activities of man are specially stressed. The body and its harmonious appearance in space do not play any role in music. Both arts are, however, something like a cult of nature and life, the rituals and ceremonies of which are in their more profound meaning as ineffable in dance as in music.

The enhancement of spiritual willpower represented by the dancer finds a response in the spectator. Dance and its effect on the spectator are thus an entity transcending verbal interpretations although the bodily and mental functions used in it are perfectly describable in terms of space-pattern and rhythm, while music is described in terms of sound-pattern and rhythm.

Harmony exists between things which have a certain relation or kinship to one another. Things which are not at all akin to one another are opposites which can only become harmonised by intermediary steps leading from one of the opposites to the other.

In the presentational art of dancing, the feel of harmony is created in the audience through the interplay of certain elementary units, such as sounds, colours, shapes, thoughts, moving between opposites. Thus we see a musician using the keyboard of a piano to fix melodies and harmonies which he has in his mind. We see him choosing from certain notes those which fit his purpose. The notes are arranged on the keyboard to make a scale, a simple progression of elementary units. In creating melody or harmony the musician is seen to leap to and fro, up and down, and crossways on the keyboard, trying to find the connections that will sound more or less harmonious to the human ear. The inner vision of the composing musician uses the letters of the language of music by forming with them something like words and sentences. The notes of the piano – in fact all the sounds used in musical composition – offer a choice between those which are closely akin to one another and others which, becoming less and less akin to the first tone, lead finally to its opposite. The single steps can be taken as the basis of such a progression and to each one belongs its own progression of [kindred] sounds entirely different for the feel of the harmony from all the other progressions. The feel of the harmony of sounds is based on a natural phenomenon. If we produce a sound, or even if a sound is heard in a natural happening, say, in the singing of the wind or in the ringing of a waterfall, not only this one sound is heard but there is also a rush of subsequent pitches of sounds following in a definite sequence. Each basic pitch has its own characteristic sequence of follower-sounds scientifically called overtones. In spite of the progressive fading out of their intensity this line or row of sounds leading from a basic one to its opposite can be clearly discerned by the human ear. Each pitch consists physically of a definite number of vibrations. The overtones have a regularly increased number of vibrations.

What has been said of the composing musician can also be said of the dancer when building up a dance. The dancer has a kind of invisible keyboard around his body. It is a complication of the ordinary space directions which everybody knows: up and down, right and left, backwards and forwards. And the curious thing is that these six directions are all doubled according to the structure of the body, which has a left and right side, an upper and lower half, and a front and a back. The combinations of these elements give twelve directions – exactly the same number as the twelve tones in a chromatic scale on the piano within an octave. In choosing this or that point and connecting it with another point or a third one, the dancer has the feeling that one or the other of these connections will fit what he wants to express but at the same time it will not offend or disturb the eye of the spectator. There is a kinship between the several directions of space which form together a space pattern. In this connection the dancer distinguishes a great many well-known shapes comparable to geometrical forms, such as triangles, quadrangles, circles, etc., or comparable also to the more complicated patterns of writing such as the forms of ciphers or letters of the alphabet. Obviously the dancer's aim is not to write a text or a mathematical equation into the air, and the similarity with such writings is only an accidental one if ever it occurs. But as in geometry the forms can always become more complicated, leading from a surface with three edges to one of four, five, six, seven, and so on; so for the dancer a progressive difference is felt between the borderline of movement shapes, the angles of which become always more and more obtuse. There is a certain relationship between directions which makes them more easy to be performed or led into one another by increasing the obtuseness of the angle between them.

Special importance is attached to patterns having seven border lines, which are called seven rings. They correspond in many respects to the diatonic scales on the piano, consisting of seven sounds within an octave. It is a curious fact that one could translate a harmonious musical composition into movement-pattern by putting for each sound one direction in space. This of course would not be a satisfactory artistic procedure, because music and dance have to say things which are very different, in spite of the fact that dance is usually accompanied by music. It can at any rate be stated that the fundamental combinations of space directions and patterns unfold following a natural regularity which is similar to the unfolding of the combinations of sounds in music.

The twelve directions mentioned above form around the body a kind of scaffolding, in the middle and centre of which the dancer stands. It is possible to make a scaffolding of sticks meeting at twelve corners, and to step into it so that the directions become clearly visible to the student of movement harmony. In practice of course and especially on the stage the dancer has to imagine this scaffolding which he carries invisibly around with him when he moves to and fro on the stage.

The exact knowledge of harmony is a matter of study but many people have by nature a certain gift of composing their movements in patterns harmoniously akin. It is a quite different thing to study the theory of the harmony of movement than to experience harmonious movement in dance exercises. One will understand this much better if here again one compares dance with music. One meets many people who sing and play music without having the slightest idea of the fact that a theory of musical harmony exists. Such people are often not able to read music notation. Others can read notes but they are unable to write down even the simplest tune. One meets excellent musicians who have just a nodding acquaintance with the deeper issues of musical harmony and its scientific theory. With dancers there is no difference, except perhaps that a much greater percentage of dancers are illiterate in their art than musicians. This is not so surprising because dance notation, though existing for several hundred years, was never so well developed and widespread as music notation. The notation of words is several thousands of years older and there still exists a lot of analphabets or illiterate people. We have stated that many people have the gift of composing their movements in harmonious patterns, which is not so astonishing because the harmony of these patterns is based on natural laws. Such people are mostly gifted dancers. Other people have no feeling for these relationships and they are less suited to dance harmoniously. It is the same in the case of the unmusical person who will not be able to distinguish the sounds of a tune as easily as the musical person can.

Another feature of the harmony of movement appears when two or more people are dancing together. It is the same thing as when people are singing in a choir and the melodies of the tenors, sopranos and altos are coordinated according to the rules of harmony. What they produce together is a harmony of a new kind where several tones are produced simultaneously by the singers, and these sounds must fit one another, which means they must be in a definite relationship of kinship to one another, in order to avoid dissonance. Dancers can adapt their movements to those of their partners, and if they do so they use movements of such directions which are reciprocally harmonious with one another. One may also dance in contrasts which results in movement forms comparable to the highly dissonant music as heard in modern compositions.

Artistic dissonance or disharmony will, however, never be a haphazard one, resulting from the clumsiness or insensitivity of the producers of the voices or movements, but they are purposely arranged in a manner which shocks the ear or the eye and perhaps expresses emotions or tensions of a terrifying or disturbing character. Here is the key to that which the harmony of movement can express. It can evolve into the smoothest and sweetest combinations of space-patterns such as we see sometimes in traditional dancing, in which gracefulness and harmony of movement are extremely stressed. The expression can become more vigorous and less harmonious as seen sometimes in energetic folk and national dances and can be finally most bizarre and even repulsive in performances in which the forces of inner or outer struggle causing terrible suffering and despair are represented.

Harmony does not mean therefore only the selection of sweet and smoothly running space patterns, but harmony means that even the most disturbing and distorting combinations of movement elements are chosen purposely and characteristically in a way which is based on the feeling and the knowledge of their kinship. In everyday life also a person can show the sweet and graceful movements, but we have noted above that this sweetness is sometimes very deceptive because there is no deeper feeling behind it. The cause is probably that this sweetness is a mask, and the person who is always sweet hides something behind this smooth surface of charming movement. What it hides is often too ugly and disgusting to be openly shown. Thus a person using crude combinations of movement like those of a peasant or a hard labourer may be harmonious, because he expresses that which is real in himself with well coordinated movements. And if these movements do not collide with one another and are not too muddled, we may find the movement expression of such a person much more harmonious and more pleasant than the affectations of insincere coquetry.

One point must not be forgotten. A melody or sequence of sounds, which has a definite harmonious kinship with another, is performed in a definite form of rhythm. The musician invents the harmonious lines of sounds and the rhythm at the same time. Both the melody and its rhythm form together the essential expression of a musical idea. In dance the harmoniously arranged shapes are performed with different efforts, which are in a certain sense, equivalent to rhythm. But in dance another means is paramount, and this is the body. The same harmonious pattern connected with a definite effort can be performed one time with an arm and the other time with a leg or another part of the body. Shapes of dances are in this way much more differentiated in expression than the shapes of music. But if the parts of the body are considered as different instruments, a new similarity between dance and music can be established.

One question may occur to the attentive observer: why is it that musical harmony and disharmony are more conspicuous than the harmony or disharmony of movement? The answer is a very simple one. We can easily look away or shut our eyes to movements, while we are not able to avert our ears so easily to the impact of sounds. It is true one can cover the ears with the hands when hearing unsympathetic noises, but this is by no means so effective as the shutting of our eyes or the turning away from a disagreeable visual impression. Nevertheless it seems to be most important for many practical and ideal reasons to pay more attention to the harmony and disharmony of movement. Not only the artist but also the educator or the observer of industrial working actions will derive great benefit from a thorough knowledge of the rules of the harmony of movement.

The curative value of the harmonious flow of movement, not only for the body but especially for the mind, is becoming more and more recognised in musical science.

In conclusion, it may be said that the technical means by which harmonised movement behaviour can be controlled is the invisible icosahedron which man carries around himself. Very similarly to the expression which the musician elicits from the keyboard of a piano, man plays on his icosahedron when he dances. It must also be noted that the icosahedron is not an invention of man. The lawfulness of movement is given to man together with his innate bodily structure. The limbs of the body are best able to reach the points represented by the corners of the icosahedron. If someone neglects the consideration of the ease and regularity of movement represented in this crystal shape, he will be compelled to make contortions which are not only ugly to see but also strenuous and even painful for the performing body.

We revert to the beginning of our article where we said that the desire of man to live harmoniously is very much bound up with the way in which he performs his movements, because his movements are not only the basis of his actions but also the basis of the visible and audible expression of his inner state of mind.

Notes

1   In NRCD, L/E/38/4.
2   Irmgard Bartenieff, 'Space, Effort, and the Brain', *Main Currents in Modern Thought*, vol. 31, no. 1 (September–October 1974), p. 37.
3   This text is lodged in the Rudolf Laban Archive, NRCD, L/E/38/4.

Chapter twenty-two

Themes and contradictions in Laban's work and thinking

Dick McCaw

Although it might appear that one could characterise Laban's career as falling into two distinct halves, the first in Germany, the second in England, the first focusing on dance, the second on much broader applications of movement, we have seen several important areas of overlap between the two periods – his concerns with industry, education, mime, and even, as we shall see, therapy. As Albrecht Knust noted when celebrating Laban's 75th birthday, movement was the central preoccupation throughout his life. 'Typical of him, I think, is this very versatility and secondly the fact that all his activities and all his endeavours are focusing on one centre only. This centre is the problem of movement.'[1]

Laban was not interested in the externally observed movement, but rather the meaning – ethical, aesthetic, pedagogical – of that movement in relation to the person who is moving. Just as the Introduction to this book traced themes back to *The World of the Dancer*, so this conclusion will draw on further passages from this same book to illustrate the continuity and development of strands of Laban's thinking.

From his first writings, he was concerned by the deadening effect that machine-work in factories was having on workers, and he was keen to bring together the worlds of artistic movement and industrial movement (witness his massive pageant of trades and crafts in Vienna in 1929). Passages already quoted from *The World of the Dancer* (1920) lament the inequity and humanity of industrial labour – the 'price' of many goods is not simply what you must pay now but what the worker has already paid in the 'hours of torture'[2] which went into its making. Whether writing about gymnastics with machinery or processes involving industrial plant, Laban demanded that the human body be allowed to move according to its own rhythms. Failure to understand this results in loss of production through sickness, absenteeism and staff turnover. He returned to this theme in *Effort* (1947), both books flatly contradicting the arguments of F.W. Taylor's hugely influential *Principles of Scientific Management* (1911) which focused purely on finding the 'one best way' of performing a task, 'best' often meaning 'quickest'. Laban and Lawrence argued that if a person is allowed to adapt a task to their own way of moving, they will work harmoniously and more happily. Happiness is a value for Laban – whether it be in education, recreation or work – this is not simply about celebration, it is also about the best use of human energy. This is to understand Laban's concerns about balance and harmony, and the emotional content of movement, in a different key.

Attention to the outer form and the inner intention of movement is constant throughout Laban's studies. Effort could be seen as a later variation of his earlier notion of Spannung which is both an outer and an inner tension – a directed intentional force linking the inner mental state with the outside world. A passage from *The World of the Dancer* explains this:

> In a word, our sensation is stimulated into a movement that aims away from or towards a point by forces operating in certain directions. The stimulatory forces have consequential correlations, degrees of relationship among themselves. The movements are longings for growth of our inner being which attract or reject each other on curved paths of the direction of the force. . . . The training

and shaping of our body through movement exercises hence is down to us. The tensing, the relaxation of muscles, breathing in and out, flying and falling take on a deeper meaning in this approach. Our will itself, our inner striving can open or close itself, can be one-sided, many-sided, bipolar, multi-polar, can lower and increase its tendencies. The will can be subjected to forces or it can vanquish them.[3]

This passage develops his notion that human movement is a vector that projects out from the self into the world. Turning to his later theory of Effort, we have seen how actions like Punching or Wringing are external and functional movements while incomplete Efforts (consisting of two or three movement factors) are expressive. Common to all of his thinking about human movement in the 1910s and 1920s and the 1940s and 1950s are the distinctions between outer and inner movements, between the functional and the expressive. Whether writing about the design of a Rococo chair, the stacking of wood or the significance of a hand gesture, he was always equally interested in the practical as in the expressive. His ability to make distinctions between types of movement, his constant search for precise descriptors (like weight, space, time and flow) indicate an extremely acute feeling for the detail of all types of movement.

It has been argued that Laban owed his unusual gift for observing movement to his first training as a painter, but in his first book he argues that to see and to understand movement we also need to feel it: our eye is informed by our own kinaesthetic experience. Again, perception is chordal rather than singular; not just the eye and the intellect, but the whole body.

> In order to be able to fully experience the spiritual form of an artwork the eye must be trained. This training is instinctively sought by modern man. It should be noted that the person who develops his own agility among others in sports, games and dance penetrates further into formal spirituality, through observation of his own movements and of others, than the mere spectator of artistic or

any other performances. The practising dancer shall not pass by any event, any image, with a feeling of indifference. He shall grasp the gestures and characters of individual people, as well as group tensions of an overall image, quickly and with understanding, and thus face life and art differently, with a deeper appreciation than the one to whom the eye serves only as a means of reading letters and numbers.[4]

In Chapter 9 of *Choreutics*, he looks at the question from the other side, seeing all space as movement, whose life is expressed in endless changes of form:

> Movement is the life of space. Dead space does not exist, for there is neither space without movement nor movement without space. All movement is an eternal change between binding and loosening, between the creation of knots with the concentrating and uniting power of binding, and the creation of twisted lines in the process of untying and untwisting. Stability and mobility alternate endlessly.[5]

This is the first seeming contradiction in Laban – between plastic form and the process of movement. Throughout the passages in this book we have seen Laban struggling to explain that a movement should not be considered purely in terms of its starting and end-points but the nature of the passage between them. To understand this process one has to break it up into sections, into 'snapshots', as he puts it in *Choreutics*, where he adds another metaphor:

> When we wish to describe a single unit of space-movement we can adopt a method similar to that of an architect when drafting a building. He cannot show all the inner and outer views in one draft only. He is obliged to make a ground-plan, and at least two elevations, thus conveying to the mind a plastic image of the three-dimensional whole.[6]

We can only grasp movement intellectually as snapshots which we then run in a sequence, like Muybridge's sequences of photographs that 'break up' the running of a horse or the performance of everyday movements. This is also a point made by Bergson (for a full discussion, see Moore 2009: 88). To understand is to 'articulate' which literally means to break up into bits or phases.

Another way of tackling this seeming contradiction between painting and movement is to look at the shift to abstraction in painting that Kandinsky and the *Blaue Reiter* group were making in Munich. Their canvasses gave form to inner movements of the mind rather than representing outer movements:

> In modern painting the subject-matter is abstracted from ordinary sense impressions received from the surrounding world. In like manner the modern or abstract dancer attempts to convey an insight into a strange spiritual world of his own. It is assumed that this world constitutes 'the primary heritage of embodied human spirit' as one of the modern dancers expresses it. Dance is for these artists a manifestation of those inner forces out of which the complications of human happenings grow.[7]

But while these painters privileged the inner meaning over the outer (which acquired the pejorative sense of being superficial), Laban was equally interested in both the everyday and the spiritual. He bridged contradictions effortlessly.

One step along the 'path to abstraction' was the move towards using the pure forms of geometry – circles, squares, and in particular, triangles. But compare Oskar Schlemmer's *Triadic Ballet* of 1927, where the human figure was obliterated beneath oversized geometric costumes which limited movement to small steps, and Laban's exploration of movement within geometric shapes. Laban was both geometric and human, rather than opting for one side of the opposition. From his earliest recorded experiments Laban was exploring the correlation between the inner structure, the tensile structure of Plato's regular solids and the nature of human movement. Indeed, as Knust makes clear in a letter from the late 1950s, Laban's movement scales, which were based on these inner tensions, were not something that he invented, but that already existed in nature:

> I too believe, as you say, that 'the typical Form schemes or shapes are a fact of nature and not a reflection of individual discoveries'. If you got the impression from what I said that I regard the scales taught by you as your invention, I hope to correct myself to say that I don't regard these things as your invention but as your discovery. In some cases, as for instance with the practical execution of the A- and B-scale, I am convinced from personal experience that you have discovered a sequence of fundamental harmonic stances and movements.[8]

At the heart of Laban's conception of the spiritual in art (to borrow Kandinsky's phrase) was a belief that the movement forms he was discovering were a fact of nature. This explains his frequent jibes at cheap mysticism and superstition – for him, the laws of natural harmony were part of the structure of matter.

In a turn of thought that is surprisingly contemporary, Laban demands the simultaneous exercise of practice and theory, body and mind. Throughout *The World of the Dancer* Laban insists that the world of movement cannot be understood through one strand of intellection alone – i.e. through physical sensation, intellect or emotion; body, mind or soul – but through their simultaneous action, acting as a chord.

All of Laban's approaches to movement – industrial, artistic, recreational and educational – demanded harmony and balance and deplored 'lopsided' movement:

> Dance education never achieves its impact through one-sided, intellectual teaching, emotional excitement or through compulsion. In nature, in humanity and in the truest expression of its overall experience, in art, a living force is at work which does not need to cause divisions in the mind, heart and senses of man in order to cultivate and inspire a healthy will to live. This force expresses itself in the drive for creative activity.[9]

This chordal or unified approach is opposed to specialisation where processes are reduced to singular ways of doing or seeing. Taylor saw only one side of movement in industry and when it came to education people saw movement in the category of either Dance or Gymnastics, but not a third thing containing elements of both, something closer to this 'healthy will to live', to a joyful celebration of life through movement.

Throughout his career, Laban was passionate about integrating movement into a person's education. From his experiments with *Tanz Ton Wort* in the 1910s in Zurich to *Gymnastics and Dance for Children* in 1926 to *Modern Educational Dance* in 1948 he pioneered and championed a vision of education that addressed the imagination of the student through creative movement. Knust describes Laban's approach:

> The educational means was likewise suited to the individual students and situations. At one time he allows the abilities of the students to grow quietly, another time he draws them out, stimulates and intensifies them passionately. The one he supports in his actions, the other he causes to complete exactly the opposite of that which the student intended or desired. At a given time he excites the imagination in order once again to train the memory of movement. He teaches through analysis recognition of movements in their various forms and to grasp the relation of these forms to each other. He teaches likewise intelligent joining of one movement to another and how to vary them.[10]

There is a lability and adaptability even in his approach to education! In his two books on Gymnastics and Dance he pleads for a 'free' dance, a 'free' gymnastics. Laban's idealistic visions ran counter to the vested interests of institutions. Gymnastics (like Taylor's approach to industrial movement) tends to be objective and scientific, often using machines – it deals with measurable inputs and outputs, with tangible and reproducible results. Its appeal lies precisely in its predictability which is then taken to mean reliability rather than suggesting uncreative and unresponsive. In the England of the 1950s as in Germany of the 1920s, he fell foul of traditional (Laban would say 'mechanical) Gymnastics. In an interview with the renowned British educationalist Peter Slade, towards the end of his life, he admitted that 'the PE world has ruined my work'. Then he turned to Lisa Ullmann and noted miserably that his 'great mistake' was to have chosen education rather than theatre. 'But [Peter] in a very wise sense calls it "drama". I do, I struggle. I call it drama action. That's what we should have stuck to Lisa.'[11] Apart from this being a heartbreaking estimation of his educational work, it is evidence of his struggle to balance his artistic interests and his need to make a living in England.

Laban's choice of the words 'drama action' rather than 'drama' is indicative of his approach to works for the stage – he always created pieces of 'dance theatre'. His second wife Maja (later Maria) commented on this:

> He was not a romantic dancer, he was more of an actor. ... At first he was like an actor, but later he became a better dancer. He became more skilled, he had a kind of 'hovering' quality which was very beautiful and he stepped in a very distinctive way.[12]

The common term that links both periods is 'mime', which we have seen used from the 1910s up to the 1949 review of the performance of his Bradford students. A review of a performance entitled 'Dance and Pantomime' in November 1917 at his school in Zurich connects mime and cinema:

> He [Laban] began to produce film pantomimes; on the one hand as a practice of dance, and on the other, as an artistic production in cinema. With the most simple contrasts and counterpoints he is able to portray the strongest and most intimate spiritual convulsions and anguish. One watches amazed as one experiences a body, a hand, a face, as an immeasurably clear and perceptible means of expression. Pantomime underlines what is meaningful, or, to put it better, it draws what is meaningful out of a pile of unimportant trivia – at least that is what it seems.[13]

Once again, it is too easy to try and define Laban in terms of an either/or, dance or drama. He created Dance Theatre and this still remains a valid artistic form today – particularly in the work of Pina Bausch (a pupil of Kurt Jooss, himself one of Laban's students).

While the above might demonstrate a continuity in the content of Laban's work, it cannot be denied that the form of his activities did change – Effort became the unifying conceptual tool for his activities in the 1940s and 1950s and Laban's focus shifted away from the organisation, creation and promotion of modern dance. When he arrived in England he was 59, in ill health and without the infrastructure that he had been building in Germany over 30 years. It was perhaps inevitable that the second phase of his career would be a more modest enterprise.

The one 'new' addition to Laban's list of movement-related activities in England appears to be therapy, but even this dates back to the 1910s, as Mary Wigman recalls how Laban helped a lady in Ascona who was crippled with a kidney complaint:

> He put her on the chair with the gentleness of a mother. Then, 'Let's start to work.' I was standing behind the chair and was trembling because I was afraid something might happen. I knew all the exercises by heart. I had studied them all through – they were very hard to do. You could never do them with a sick person. He started, let her move her head down and up, down and up. She moved her head, first it didn't work, after a while it started, then her face changed. He let her move her head to one side and then over to the other side. At first it didn't work but then it gave her back her courage: it was very clever. Anyhow, he got her to move her head without difficulty, then he let her bend and lift her shoulders. She was sitting comfortably on the chair, a cushion to her back. She was enjoying it. I had never, never in all my life seen the change in a face. . . . Happy she was able to move from the body. There was not a word said. The damn kidneys were not thought of.[14]

It is Laban's non-verbal, movement-based therapy which helps this poor woman to enjoy life once again.

Possibly one could adapt Knust's statement about Laban's career and state that it focused upon the celebration of life through movement. His ethics and education are based upon a belief that if you allow a person to express themselves freely, then their movement will spontaneously express their natural, inborn joy of life. This is why laws in ethics, drilling in education, and treating humans as machines in the workplace, are all denials of the expression, the flow of this life-force. There is surely a connection with Bergson's *élan vital* (vital impulse) and his belief that morality is discovered through feeling rather than the intellect. For Laban, movement was a way of celebrating this life-force:

> Festival producers are bringers of insight. The awakening of the will to work and pleasure at work is the task of those who organise the active part of the rest period. In a nutshell one can call this active part of the rest period festivity, celebration.[15]

Seen from this perspective, recreational dance, or celebrative events, are not something that can or should be separated from Laban's other activities.

This culture of celebration (*Festkultur*) was not Laban's personal preoccupation – it was espoused by theatre-makers and cultural commentators across Europe. With an accent on active, participative culture, the audience was no longer considered a passive recipient of artistic productions. Thus the proscenium arch theatre which separated actor and audience was rejected in favour of the Greek open-air amphitheatres. We have seen Laban's plans for theatres where every member of the audience has an equally good view of the stage; he also dreamt of a massive open-air stage for movement choirs. To mention but two other examples: in the *Festspielhaus* at Hellerau, opened in 1913 (where Dalcroze briefly had his school), there was no division between stage and auditorium, and in Georg Fuchs' Munich Art Theatre, opened in 1907, he dreamt of a 'theatrical experience which could be closer to ritual and able to involve a mystical union of spectators and performers'.[16] *The World of the Dancer* is Laban's vision of a new age in which all people will dance. Karl Bergeest, one his students from the 1920s, understood this vision:

> Those familiar with his *World of the Dancer* (and every serious dancer should read it, in spite of all its difficulties) know how Laban looks upon the dancer as the creator of a new festival culture, as an agent of the highest value. From this knowledge he has always cultivated festive dancing during the whole of his development, everywhere where he had influence on festive organisation, among his students, at festivals.[17]

It was probably with this vision that Laban wrote the following words in the programme for his *Vom Tauwind und der Neuen Freude*, the pageant created for the 1936 Berlin Olympics (mentioned in the Introduction):

> Everyone at some time or other has opened his arms to a strong inward emotion, and has felt some kind of tension touch his body.
> Perhaps one has wanted to shout with joy because of a beloved person, or because of a beautiful natural scene: 'Oh! It is wonderful', but one has remained silent. The inner voice has said that words are never the right expression for this experience. Instead the arms were raised and this gesture showed clearly what words could never express. It is this type of experience that underlies all dance.[18]

Typically, Laban has chosen to stress the superiority of physical gesture over that of the spoken word. Typically, the accent is on the joyful individual who is dancing with other individuals.

Photographs of hundreds of people dancing together no longer conjure up such visions of inner and communal harmony but have rather become associated with the heartless regimentation of the Nazis. Joseph Goebbels, Minister for

Propaganda in Nazi Germany, wrote in a journal for dance and movement choirs in 1935 that 'there is a limit to the survival of the individuality itself. For it may clash with the interests of the public. For no-one has the right to experience themselves simply as an individual.'[19] Superficially, Laban's movement choirs and a massed parade might look the same. But when Goebbels saw *Vom Tauwind*, he immediately saw the world of difference between a vision where all conform to one set of strictly drilled movements (remember how Laban detested drilling) and one in which everyone freely joins together to enact a spirit of celebration in dance; the difference is between dancing in unison and dancing in harmony with each other (Figures 22.1–22.3). In his notes on *Titan*, Laban had written:

> In the third scene the formative wish is awakened which leads to the suffering of conformity. Then there is an intermezzo in which the group possessed of restless movement becomes relaxed and cheerful. The fourth scene passes over the peak of rigidity to the cry for personal liberation.

Goebbels had grasped the propaganda value of the form of *Festkultur* and used its form to promote an entirely different content: National Socialism as opposed to a personal expression of joy at the wonder of life. Indeed, one could use the same words with which Goebbels had denounced Laban: 'it is dressed up in our clothes and has nothing whatever to do with us'.[20]

To many, such an argument will still be unconvincing and the question will remain: Why did Laban remain in Germany, and accept Goebbels' patronage? There seem to be no public statements or writings by Laban himself that explain his decision. A close friend, Felicia Sachs with whom he corresponded for much of his life, offers an explanation in an interview with John Hodgson in 1977:

> Laban was a weak character, no doubt about it. And he was partially infantile. I mean, it was all extremely charming – but there was a certain infantilism there; he did not

Figure 22.1 Dietrich Eckhart Stadium, venue for the 1936 Berlin Olympics
Source: John Hodgson Archive, Brotherton Library, University of Leeds.

face reality. Reality hit him constantly over the head, and he suffered tremendously, but his character – and I don't blame him for it – he was in a terrible position, many, many times in his life: sheer survival, not a cent in his pocket.[21]

Some weeks after this interview, she wrote Hodgson a letter expressing how difficult it was to balance her love for Laban with her profound disapproval of his actions (she and her husband were Jewish):

> Why is it, I asked myself, that both my husband and I during these crucially dangerous times, before Laban fled, felt overwhelming pity for him, and he became more and

Figures 22.2, 22.3 Dress rehearsal of *Vom Tauwind und der neuen Freude* at Dietrich Eckhart Stadium, from the brochure commemorating the opening of the Dietrich Eckhart Stadium, venue for the 1936 Berlin Olympics

Source: John Hodgson Archive, Brotherton Library, University of Leeds.

more for us the victim to be loved and protected? The victim to whom our door had to be open day and night for talks, telephone calls, who must always know that he has a place to go, an emotional haven – whereas the cold reality was this: We were the victims. He was going in and out of the Chancellery as the Führer's guest and had handed himself over to the Nazi movement. . . . And at the same time that all this happened – as people do when they experience the utmost depth of human bestiality together, he and we at opposite ends of the pole – we reached a profundity in our relationship, where the best was brought out in us. And thus it happened, that Laban spoke to me words of wisdom and spirituality which still live with me to this day. I can never forget his words, when he taught me that there exists not time and space in moments like these. That, should we never see each other again, never be able to write to each other, or should one of us die, what he has taught me, if I survive, will live on, we will always be in contact of soul and mind, and he knows that he will survive in my work, no matter what form it will take. He gave at that time the finest, the best, to both of us, as a friend, to me as a teacher – he was dear to our hearts, we trembled for him and he for us – and it did not matter that fundamentally he was a traitor to himself and what he stood for.[22]

Hopefully this long extract will provide readers with reason to pause before they leap to condemn Laban for his collaboration. If anyone had just cause to criticise it was Sachs, and yet she realised that despite his flaws he was a man worthy of her love, respect and gratitude.

And the future of Laban's ideas? A glance at the work of the contributors to this Sourcebook or at the bibliography gives an idea of the extent to which his ideas have spread. Valerie Preston-Dunlop has written books that explain and thus bring his very difficult ideas about Choreutics to a wider audience. Laban's Effort-work still has currency among theatre practitioners. His Effort-analysis can be a subtle means of describing the finest nuances of movement (and therefore character) or it can be reduced to a banal typology with such stereotypes as the 'dabber' or the 'wringer'. Laban and Lawrence were alert to the temptation and danger of such static categorisation: 'one must never forget that these absolutely fundamental types do not exist in reality,'[23] adding that 'Such a search would rather restrict rather than help the extension of effort investigation.'[24] The difference is that between a dynamic and a static use of his thinking. In his Preface to *Effort*, Warren Lamb takes the argument further when he states that Effort and Shape (Eukinetics and Choreutics) should not be studied separately since all movements have both shape and dynamic characteristics. His ideas influenced Irmgard Bartenieff who set up the Laban Institute of Movement Studies (LIMS) in New York, and the work of psychoanalyst Judith Kestenburg. Lamb uses Movement Pattern Analysis to correlate a person's movement profile with their style of decision-making. In her Preface to 'Shadow Moves', Marion North mentions her own research into Personality Assessment. More generally, the time may be ripe for a re-examination of Laban's ideas. Modern techniques of brain imaging have allowed researchers to begin to describe the intricacy and complexity of how body and brain function together. Books like Denis Noble's *The Music of Life* demonstrate how the whole bodily system works as one and can only be understood as a single organism.

It is impossible to sum up Laban's intellectual achievement. This conclusion has pursued several seeming contradictions in his thinking, but maybe Laban would join with the ebullient Whitman and respond:

> Do I contradict myself?
> Very well then I contradict myself,
> (I am large, I contain multitudes.)[25]

Laban's thinking was multitudinous and multiform – rather than either/or he would put 'and'. Bartenieff understands this:

> So he was a terrific comprehensivist. And also the core of everything he did was that everything changes. . . . He got you into all of these things that are based on variation and

motivation – that's why it is a true movement theory. He speaks about a person going from a state of greater stability to a state of greater mobility – but it is a flux thing.[26]

He shared the turn-of-the-century fascination with symbolism and esoteric thinking which led to abstraction, and yet he remained very much connected to the living world around him. His thinking is sophisticated but not scientific: to describe the planes of movement he uses homely terms like Wheel, Door and Table rather than the more technical terms Sagittal, Vertical and Horizontal. His concept of Flow is easily grasped because it appeals to a sense of movement we all possess, and yet it defies scientific definition. It is a phenomenological rather than an objective category, something felt but which cannot be measured. But maybe the most intractable and productive contradiction is that between flux and form, change and stasis. As Laban knew all too well, the problem lies in the very enterprise of writing about movement: the unfolding of language is unilinear, whereas the experience of movement is multilinear. On the one hand, one is trying to 'pin it down' intellectually, while, on the other, trying to retain its sense of it being a process of change. No surprise then that Laban the painter spent so much time giving plastic form to the shapes and changes of movement in space.

Notes

1 In JHA, Box 23, Folder 21, Item 1.
2 *WD*, p. 71.
3 Ibid., pp. 127, 230.
4 Ibid., pp. 118, 215.
5 *Cho*, p. 94.
6 Ibid., p. 5.
7 *MM*, p. 156.
8 Letter to Laban, 8 December 1957 (in JHA, Box 23, Folder 21, Item 3).
9 *WD*, pp. 63, 118.

10 A. Knust, article on Laban (in JHA, Box 29, Folder 39, Item 2g).
11 Undated interview with Peter Slade (in JHA, Folder 45, Item 4).
12 Interview with Maria and Etalka Laban, Munich 1973 (in JHA, Folder 41, Item 10c).
13 *Der Bund*, Zurich, 17 November 1917 (in JHA, Box 11, Folder 12, Item 11).
14 Mary Wigman's reminiscences, translated by Lisa Ullmann (in JHA, Folder 45, Item 21).
15 WD, pp. 71, 132.
16 *The Oxford Encyclopaedia of Theatre and Performance*, ed. Dennis Kennedy (Oxford: Oxford University Press, 2003), p. 488.
17 Karl Bergeest, 'With Laban in Hamburg 1923–25' (in JHA, Box 30, Folder 39, Item 3).
18 Festival Brochure, pp. 34–35 (in JHA, Box 18, Folder 10, File 2).
19 *Singchor und Tanz* (The Specialist Press for Vocal and Dance Choirs), 7 August 1935 (translated by Richard Ellis, JHA, Tape 4).
20 Preston-Dunlop (1998: 196).
21 Interview with Felicia Sachs (in JHA, Folder 45, Item 3c).
22 In JHA, Box 30, Folder 42, Item 6.
23 E 60.
24 E 57.
25 *Song of Myself*, Stanza 51.
26 Bartenieff in Johnson (1995: 234–235).

Glossary of terms as used in Movement Psychology[1]

Action: A bodily movement expressed through the Motion Factors of Weight, Space and Time; performed for a functional purpose with a measure of conscious volition.

Adapting: The extroverted adjustment of one's Self with the outer world, and the introverted relating of one's Conscious Self with the Subconscious. Revealed in the Motion Factor of Flow and the Mental Factor of Feeling.

Adream: The Inner Attitude of unawareness – sombre or irradiant – overpowering or diffused; compounded of the Motion Factors of Weight and Flow and of the Mental Factors of Sensing and Feeling: forming part of the Externalised Drives of Passion and Influencing.

Adrift: The negatively neutral quality of Space in which the interplay between Flexibility and Directness is cancelled by a disorientation which negates the Reflective and Attending aspects of Thinking.

Agogic: A term referring to the explanation of human expression or modification of the rate of motion.

Asymmetric: The patterns traced in Space by two parts of the body which are not similarly related to the centre of the body.

Attending: Turning the mind tentatively to motivate an Inner Attitude or Externalised Drive or to activate an Action. Revealed in the Motion Factor of Space and the Mental Factor of Thought.

Bound Flow: The contending Element of the Motion Factor Flow. A feeling of movement of sticky viscid fluidity, arrestable at any stage of development with a continuous readiness to stop.

Chordic: Movements of separate parts of the body in different directions and tensions which are in a common relation to the centre of the body.

Contending Elements: The masculine Elements of Strong, Direct, Quick and Bound which fight against the Motion Factors of Weight, Space, Time and Flow.

Deciding: The intuitive relating of the past and future with the present. Revealed in the Motion Factor of Time and the Mental Factor of Intuiting.

Direct: The contending Element of the Motion Factor – Space. An intentive movement traversing either a straight line or a flat curve in a single plane of Space.

Doing: The Externalised Drive of exerting and reacting, compounded of the Motion Factors of Weight, Space and Time and of the Mental Factors of Sensing, Thinking, and Intuiting. Flowless, Feelingless and Unrelated. A fusion of the Inner Attitudes of Stable, Near and Awake.

Effort: The sequence of Inner Attitudes and Externalised Drives which activate an Action.

Externalised Drives: The four Drives of Doing, Passionate, Influencing, and Visionary. The mental states which are motivated by the subconscious Inner Attitudes and which activate us into the conscious Actions. Each Drive is revealed as a compound of three Elements of movement.

Feeling: One of the four Mental Factors. The emotion of liking or disliking, interest or disinterest, etc. Revealed in Movement as Flow – Free or Bound.

Feminine Elements: The four Elements which yield with the Motion Factors, namely Light, Flexible, Sustained and Free.

Fighting: Synonymous with 'Contending' q.v.

Flexible: The yielding Element of the Motion Factor – Space. A reflective movement which is roundabout, being both concave and convex, in two or more planes of Space.

Flow: The cyclic Motion Factor which expresses the Mental Factor of Feeling and the inner participation of Adapting and Relating. The feeling of the viscosity of Movement. Subdivided into the Elements of Free and Bound.

Free Flow: The yielding Element of the Motion Factor – Flow. A feeling of streaming, unarrestable, fluidity of Movement.

Gathering: A Shape movement toward one's own body with an emotional content of closing-in. Frequently associated with Bound Flow and sometimes observed as a defensive withdrawal into oneself.

Harmonious: Movements of separate parts of the body in a balanced relation to a common point.

Heavy: The negatively neutral and impotent quality of Weight in which the interplay of Lightness and Strength is cancelled by an inertia which negates the receiving and transmitting intentions of Sensing.

Incomplete: Efforts Movements compounded of less than three Elements, observed particularly in Shadow Moves expressing Inner Attitudes but seen also in Actions.

Indecisive: The negatively neutral and dream quality of Time in which the interplay of Sustainment and Quickness is cancelled by a timelessness which negates the relating of the past, present and future in the Decisions of Intuiting.

Indulging: Synonymous with 'Yielding' q.v.

Influencing: The Externalised Drive of dominating or surrendering; compounded of the Motion Factors of Weight, Space and Flow and the Mental Factors of Sensing, Thinking and Feeling. Timeless, Intuitionless and Decisionless. A fusion of the Inner Attitudes of Stable, Remote and Adream.

Inner Attitudes: The six subconscious states of Stable, Mobile, Near, Remote, Awake and Adream which can be activated by bodily movements. Each attitude is revealed in our movements as a compound of two Elements.

Intending: Stimulating the mind purposefully to motivate an Inner Action of Externalised Drive, or to activate an Action. Revealed in the Motion Factor of Weight and in the Mental Factor of Sensing.

Intuition/Intuiting: One of the four Mental Factors. Insight by the mind without reasoning. Revealed in our movements as Time – Sustained or Quick. Now (and not 'here').

Irrelated: The negatively neutral and frozen quality of Flow in which the interplay of Free and Bound is cancelled by an emotional fixity which negates the extraverted and introverted aspects of the Adapting and Relating of Feeling.

Kinaesthetic: The sensation of movement in any part of the body.

Light: The yielding Element of the Motion Factor – Weight. A light sensory muscular exertion which does not involve noticeable change of normal muscle forms.

Masculine Elements: The four Elements which contend against the Motion Factors, namely Weight, Space, Time and Flow respectively.

Mobile: The Inner Attitude of Adaptiveness – revealed or concealed – acknowledged or unacknowledged; compounded of the Motion Factors of Time and Flow and of the Mental Factors of Intuiting and Feeling; forming part of the Externalised drives of Passion and Vision.

Motion Factors: The four Factors of Weight, Space, Time and Flow into which all movements can be analysed and which express the four Mental Factors of Sensing, Thinking, Intuiting and Feeling. Each Motion factor is subdivided into two Elements which yield with or contend against the Factors.

Motoric Awareness: The intuitive perception and knowledge of one's own bodily movements.

Near: The Inner Attitude or relationship – human or materialistic – warm or cool; compounded of the Motion Factors of Weight and Time and of the Mental Factors of Sensing and Intuiting; forming part of the Externalised Drives of Doing and Passion.

Passion: The Externalised Drive of constructing and destroying; compounded of the Motion Factors of Weight, Time and Flow and of the Mental Factors of Sensing, Intuiting and Feeling. Spaceless, Thoughtless and Attentionless. A fusion of the inner attitudes of Mobile, Near and Adream.

Quick: The contending Element of the Motion Factor of Time. An intuitive urge into the future.

Relating: See 'Adapting', q.v.

Remote: The Inner Attitude of solitude – sociable or unsociable – altruistic or egocentric; compounded of the Motion Factors of Thinking and Feeling forming part of the Externalised drives of Influencing and Vision.

Scattering: A Shape movement away from one's own body with an emotional content of opening out. Frequently associated with Free Flow and sometimes observed as a casting away or giving of one's Self.

Sensing or Sense Perception: One of the four Mental Factors. Sensory perception through the five senses. Revealed in our movements as Weight – Light or Strong.

Shadow Moves: Movements by any part of the body performed without conscious volition expressing Inner Attitudes and External Drives.

Shape: An emotional expression of Flow and Feeling with patterns traced in Space by Flexible and Direct Movements; and frequently observed in a recovery from an Effort. The five principal Shapes are: (1) Angular – two linear movements enclosing an angle. (2) Circular – curved about a centre in one plane. (3) Linear – a succession of straight lines through a series of points. (4) Plastic movement in a succession of planes. (5) Twisted – curving in a roundabout pattern in two or more planes.

Space: The kinetic Motion Factor which expresses the Mental Factor of Thinking and the Inner Participation of Attending. The reflection of thoughtful movements is in one or more planes of space. Subdivided into the Elements of Flexible and Direct.

Stable: The Inner Attitude of unadaptive – receptive or commanding – self-contained or practical; compounded of the Motion Factors of Weight and Space and of the Mental Factor of Sensing and Thinking; forming part of the Externalised Drives of Doing and Influencing.

Strong: The contending Element of the Motion Factor – Weight. A sensory muscular firmness in any part of the body and involving a considerable exertion of muscles.

Sustained: The yielding Element of the Motion Factor – Time. An intuitive clinging to the past.

Symmetric: The pattern traced in Space by two parts of the body moving simultaneously in a similar relation to the centre of the body.

Thinking: One of the four Mental Factors. Formation of ideas through intellectual reflective reasoning. Revealed in our movements as Space – Flexible or Direct.

Time: The rhythmic Motion Factor which expresses the Mental Factor of intuiting and the inner participation of Deciding. The intuitive perception of the relation between the past and the future. Subdivided into the Elements of Sustained and Quick.

Viscosity: The quality of movement observed in Flow, varying in feeling from an absence of viscosity in Free Flow to an emotional viscidity in Bound Flow.

Vision: The Externalised Drive of ideas and problems; compounded of the Motion Factors of Space, Time and Flow;

and of the Mental Factors of Thinking, Intuiting and Feeling. Weightless, Sensingless, and Intentionless. A fusion of the Inner Attitudes of Mobile, Remote and Awake.

Weight: The dynamic Motion Factor which expresses the Mental Factor of Sensing and the inner participation of Intending. The impact of receiving or transmitting sensory stimuli. Subdivided into the Elements of Light and Strong.

Working Actions: Punching, Pressing, Slashing, Wringing, Dabbing, Gliding, Flicking and Floating. The eight basic Actions in which all consciously performed functional activities can be analysed. Compounded of the Motion Factors of Weight, Space and Time.

Yielding Elements: The feminine Elements of Light, Flexible, Sustained and Free which yield with the Motion Factors of Weight, Space, Time and Flow.

Note

1 Photocopy of typescript by Rudolf Laban, dated 'Feb. 1954' (in JHA, folder 45, item 2).

Glossary of German Terms

Stefanie Sachsenmaier and Dick McCaw

Celebration [Fest]

For Laban, this notion has a key function and is closely connected to the 'round dance' [Reigen]. It is translated here as 'celebration', with the emphasis on it constituting a sociable event where dancing could take place. With its root in the Latin 'festus', which translates both as 'festive' as well as 'joyful', terms such as 'festivity' and 'festival' are related, yet their connotations to religious or music events are misleading in this context. Laban referred to 'Fest' as a communal gathering in which the individual would be able to express and further their body, mind and spirit through dancing.

Compression [Ballung]

Laban uses this term mainly in relation to **Spannung**. 'Ballung' has been translated previously as 'agglomeration' and 'nucleation'. Both terms, however, do not quite give a sense of a state of 'energy' that seems to be vital in Laban's concept. 'Ballung' in the context of movement describes a process of compression and densification, a compacting of energy that creates a concentrated, packed form. The German notion of 'geballte Kraft' is a widely used expression for a concentrated force, and the term is likewise used to describe a 'clenched fist' ('geballte Faust'). It should be noted that Laban used the term 'bound' in relation to flow later on when writing in English, which resonates strongly with 'Ballung' or 'geballt'. Yet to avoid confusion and a mixing of concepts, in the present translation of 'Ballung' in *The World of the Dancer*, the notion of '*compression*' has been chosen, describing a concentrated state that has the potential to be released again.

Round dance [Reigen]

The term has mainly been translated as 'round'. Since Laban wrote extensively about geometrical shapes, in the present translation of *The World of the Dancer* the term 'round dance' has been chosen for 'Reigen' in order to clarify its description of a specific dance practice and not the 'round' as a geometrical shape. The *round dance* describes a folk dance practice which is dance in a round or circle, formed by multiple participants.

Space [Raum]

The term is usually translated as 'space', as in the present translation of *The World of the Dancer*. However, 'Raum' has further facets that translate as 'room' and 'area'.

Swinging [Schwung, Schwingen]

Both terms translate readily to 'swing' or 'swinging'. 'Schwung', however, entails further nuances that are of importance with regard to movement. Implicit in the term are the notions of 'impetus' and 'momentum', and a common German expression ('in Schwung kommen'), literally translated as 'to get into swing' would be translated as 'to gain or gather momentum', 'to get going'. Further it can be suggested that somebody has 'Schwung', meaning that the person is full of energy or spirits.

Tension [Spannung]

The term is mainly used by Laban in relation to **Ballung**. 'Spannung' has previously been translated as 'tension' as well as 'tensility', and the former is the term that is being preferred in the present translation of *The World of the Dancer*. Yet it should be noted that 'Spannung' in the German language has further aspects to its meaning that are not implicit in the term 'tension'. 'Spannung' can suggest 'excitement' or 'suspense' in the context of 'anticipation', as well as 'electric voltage'. The term is also used in the sense of 'energising' something ('etwas unter Spannung setzen'), and is by way of example used to describe the drawing of a bow. In terms of (muscular) movement, we find 'Spannung' both as '*An*spannung' as well as '*Ent*spannung', the former being a process of 'contraction', whereas the latter means 'relaxation', again with 'tension' at stake in both processes.

Bibliography

Books by Rudolf Laban

Die Welt des Tanzers [*The World of the Dancer*], 1920, Stuttgart: Verlag von Walter Seifert.
Gymnastik und Tanz [*Gymnastics and Dance*], 1926, Oldenberg: Gerhard Stalling Verlag.
Kindes Gymnastik und Tanz [*Gymnastics and Dance for Children*], 1926, Oldenberg: Gerhard Stalling Verlag.
Choreographie [*Choreography*], 1926, Jena: Eugen Diederichs.
Effort with F.C. Lawrence, 1947, London: Macdonald and Evans, 2nd edn 1973.
Modern Educational Dance, 1948, London: Macdonald and Evans.
The Mastery of Movement on the Stage, 1950, London: Macdonald and Evans, 2nd edn 1960.
Principles of Dance and Movement Notation, 1956, London: Macdonald and Evans, 2nd edn 1975.
Choreutics, edited and annotated by Lisa Ullmann, 1966, London: Macdonald and Evans.
A Life for Dance, translated and annotated by Lisa Ullmann, 1975, London: Macdonald and Evans.
A Vision of Dynamic Space, ed. Lisa Ullmann, 1984, Laban Archives and London: Falmer.

BIBLIOGRAPHY

Books about Laban

Bartenieff, Irmgard and Davis, Martha A. (1965) *Effort-Shape Analysis of Movement: The Unity of Expression*, New York: Albert Einstein College of Medicine, Yeshiva University.

Bartenieff, Irmgard with Dori Lewis (1980) *Body Movement: Coping with the Environment*, New York: Gordon and Breach Science Publishers.

Bonham-Carter, V. (1958) *Dartington Hall: The History of an Experiment*, London: Phoenix House.

Bradley, Karen (2009) *Rudolf Laban*, New York: Routledge.

Davies, Eden (2001) *Beyond Dance: Laban's Legacy of Movement Analysis*, London: Brechin Books.

Dörr, Evelyn (2004) *Rudolf Laban: Das choreographische Theater*, Hamburg: Norderstedt.

Dörr, Evelyn (2008) *Rudolf Laban: The Dancer of the Crystal*, Plymouth: Scarecrow Press.

Foster, John (1977) *The Influences of Rudolf Laban*, London: Lepus Books.

Green, Martin (1986) *Mountain of Truth: The Counter-Culture Begins, Ascona, 1900–1920*, Hanover, CT: University Press of New England.

Johnson, Don Hanlon (1995) *Bone, Breath, and Gesture*, Berkeley, CA: North Atlantic Books.

Jordan, Diana (1938) *Dance in Education*, London: OUP.

Hodgson, John and Preston-Dunlop, V. (2001) *Mastering Movement*, London: Methuen.

Kandinsky, Wassily (1977) *Concerning the Spiritual in Art*, London: Dover Publications.

Karina, Lilian and Kant, Marion (2003) *Hitler's Dancers: German Modern Dance and the Third Reich*, trans. Jonathan Steinberg, New York: Berghahn Books.

Lahusen, S. (1998) *An Extraordinary Life*, London: Dance Books.

Lamb, Warren (1965) *Posture and Gesture*, London: Duckworth.

Lamb, Warren and Watson, E. (1979) *Body Code: The Meaning in Movement*, London: Routledge & Kegan Paul.

Lange, Roderyk (1975) *The Nature of Dance*, London: Macdonald and Evans.

Maletic, Vera (1987) *Space, Body, Expression*, Berlin: Mouton de Gruyter.

Moore, Carol-Lynne (2009) *The Harmonic Structure of Movement,*

Music, and Dance According to Rudolf Laban, Lewiston: Edwin Mellen Press.
Newlove, Jean (1993) *Laban for Actors and Dancers*, London: Nick Hern Books.
Newlove, Jean and Dalby, John (2004) *Laban for All*, London: Nick Hern Books.
Nicholls, Larraine (2007) *Dancing in Utopia: Dartington Hall and its Dancers*, Alton: Dance Books.
Noble, Denis (2006) *The Music of Life*, Oxford: Oxford University Press.
North, Marion (1972) *Personality Assessment through Movement*, London: Macdonald and Evans.
Preston-Dunlop, V. (1963) *Dance in Education*, London: Macdonald and Evans, 2nd edn 1980.
Preston-Dunlp, V. (1998) *Rudolph Laban – An Extraordinary Life*, London: Dance Books.
Preston-Dunlop, V. and Lahusen, S. (1990) *Schrifttanz: A View of German Dance in the Weimar Republic*, London: Dance Books.
Russell, Joan (1975) *Creative Dance in the Primary School*, 2nd edn, London: Macdonald and Evans.
Sherborne, Veronica (1990) *Developmental Movement for Children*, Cambridge: Cambridge University Press.
Stevens, Anthony (1986) *Withymead: A Jungian Community for the Healing Arts*, London: Coventure.
Thornton, Sam (1971) *A Movement Perspective of Rudolf Laban*, London: Macdonald and Evans.
Wigman, Mary (1966) *The Language of Dance*, ed. Walter Sorrell, Middletown, CT: Wesleyan University Press.
Wigman, Mary (1973) *The Mary Wigman Book: Her Writings*, ed. and trans. Walter Sorrell, Middletown, CT: Wesleyan University Press.
Willson, F.M.G. (1997) *In Just Order Move*, London: Athlone Press.
Winnearls, Jane (1958) *The Jooss-Leeder Method*, London: Adam and Charles Black.

Works Cited in the Introductions

Adshead, J. (1981) *The Study of Dance*, London: Dance Books.
Bartenieff, Irmgard (1974) 'Space, Effort, and the Brain', *Main Currents in Modern Thought*, vol. 31, no. 1, September– October.

BIBLIOGRAPHY

Baudoin, P. and Gilpin, H. (1989) Progamme for William Forsythe/ Reggio Emilia Festival Danza, Book 2.

Bergson, Henri (2007) *The Creative Mind: An Introduction to Metaphysics*, trans. L. Mabelle, Mineola, NY: Andison Dover Publications.

Bloom, Katya (2006) *The Embodied Self: Movement and Psychoanalysis*, London: H. Karnac Books.

Curl, G.F. (1967) 'Philosophical Foundations', PF II, *Laban Art of Movement Guild Magazine LAMGM*, 38: 7–17.

Curl, G.F. (1968) 'Philosophical Foundations', PF IV, *LAMGM*, 40: 27–38.

Curl, G.F. (1969) 'Philosophical Foundations', PF VI, *LAMGM*, 43: 37–44.

Curl, G.F. (2001) 'Laban's Philosophical Foundations Revisited', in *Order or Chaos: Laban's Artistic and Philosophic Foundations . . . and Beyond*, Laban Notation Institute, University of Surrey,

Flavell, John H. (1985) *Cognitive Development*, London: Prentice-Hall.

Gleisner, Martin (1928) *Tanz für Alle*, Leipzig: Hesse und Becker Verlag.

Haynes aka Carlisle, A. (1987) 'The Dynamic Image: Changing Perspectives in Dance Education', in P. Abbs (ed.) *Living Powers: The Arts in Education*, London: The Falmer Press.

Hutchinson, Ann (1954) *Labanotation*, London: Phoenix House.

Jordan, D. (1938) *The Dance as Education*, Oxford: Oxford University Press.

Knust, Albrecht (1956) *Abriss der Kinetographie Laban*, Hamburg: Das Tanzarchiv, English version 1958.

Knust, Albrecht (1979) *A Dictionary of Kinetography Laban Labanotation*, Plymouth: Macdonald and Evans, 2nd edn, *Institut Choreologii*, Poznan, 1997.

La Barre, Frances (2001) *On Moving and Being Moved: Nonverbal Behavior in Clinical Practice*, Hillsdale, NJ: The Analytic Press.

Levy, Fran (1992) *DMT: A Healing Art*, rev. edn, Reston, VA: The American Alliance for Health, Physical Recreation and Dance.

Meekums, Bonnie (2008) 'Pioneering Dance Movement Therapy in Britain: Results of Narrative Research', *The Arts in Psychotherapy*, 35: 99–106.

Redfern, H.B. (1973) *Concepts in Modern Educational Dance*, London: Henry Kimpton.

Steiner, R. (1926) 'A Lecture on Eurythmy 1923' (trans.), London: Anthroposophical Publishing.

Tortora, Suzi (2006) *The Dancing Dialogue: Using the Communicative Power of Movement with Young Children*, Baltimore, MD: Paul H. Brookes Publishing.

Warner, Mary Jane and Warner, Frederick E. (1984, 1988, 1995) *Laban Notation Scores: An International Bibliography*, 3 vols, New York: ICKL.

Index

acrobatics 46, 171, 273
adream (also A-dream, one of the Inner Attitudes) 204, 351, 354, 355
Also Sprach Zarathustra (*see* Nietzsche) 18
amateur 52, 117, 243
anatomy, anatomical structure 59, 83, 242
arabesque 132, 318, 323, 324
art of movement 27, 30, 32, 50, 80, 83, 84, 87, 92, 123, 126, 127, 139, 158, 173, 185, 207, **208-215**, 244, 245, 246, 249, 250, 253, 272, 273, 307
Art of Movement Studio xiii, xiv, xviii, 8, 217, 265, 299, 301
artistic wisdom 57
Ascona vii, 5, **20-23**, 31, 34, 35, 38, 341, 364
Atkinson, Madge 238
attitude, bodily 151; of limbs, 98, 103; towards a Motion Factor, 103, 151, 203, 204, 209, 210, 213, 214, 225, 226, 227, 229, 248, 250, 251, 257, 258, 268, 271, 272, 277, 295, 308, 315, 318, 322, 324 (*see* Inner Attitude)

Awake (one of the Inner Attitudes) 190, 203, 204, 295, 303, 352, 354, 357

baby, baby movements 258, 259, 309
balance (in the physical sense) 11, 12, 45, 59, 60, 85, 92, 101, 103, 104, 109, 111, 132, 182, 183, 190, 193, 218, 277, 322, 323, 324
Ballet, 6, 7, 47, 51, 98, 99, 103, 114, 119, 131, 161, 163, 170, 176, 178, 180, 217, 246, 247, 248, 250, 266, 337
Ballet d'Action (*see* Jean-Georges, Noverre) 246
Bartenieff, Irmgard xiv, 6, 20 100, 112, 203, 204, 206, 300, 317, 331, 348, 364, 365
basic tensions 61
Bausch, Pina 341
Bayreuth 161
Beauchamp, Pierre 157, 181
Bereska, Dussia 127, 133, 160, 162, 173
Bergeest, Karl 343, 350
Bergson, Henri 10, 43, 67, 177, 318, 337, 342, 365

369

INDEX

Berlin xi, 6, 122, 128, 136, 139, 145, 161, 162
Berlin Olympics (1936) xii, 7, 343, 344, 345
Berlin State Opera 114, 168
Blake, William 69, 70
Blaue Reiter Group 5, 337
Bodmer, Sylvia xvii, xviii, 265
body/mind/spirit (*Korper/Geist/Seele*) 9, 10, 14,
body tensions 61
Bound (Flow) **199–200**, 212, 218, 220, 227, 229, 302, 304, 323, 352,353, 354, 356, 360
Brandenburg, Hans 5, 8, 9, 14, 23, 25, 27
Bratislava 3, 140

Carpenter, William (*see* Movement Psychology) 8
celebration [*Fest*] 16, 17, 24, 30, 44, 46, **51–57**, 66, 79, 83, 85, 117, 129, 140, 141, 147, 170, 171, 334, 339, 342, 344, 359
Central European (Modern) Dance 237, 238, 244, 254
Champernowne, Gilbert and Irene (see also Withymeade) 305,
Chekhov, Michael 7
Choreographic Institute viii, **121–130**, 132, 138
Choreography viii, xi, 6, 11, 12, 14, 19, 71, 84, **97–112** (Chapter five), 122, 131, 158, 195, 363
choreography 92, 98, 120, 125, 127, 130, **131–132**, 161, 168, 180, 181, 242
choreosophy 16, 130, **131–132**, 177, 180, 195,
Choreutics viii 7, 16, 99, 101, **175–196** (Chapter eleven) 336
choreutics 14, 84, 99, 126, 127, 158, **175–196**, 218, 239, 345, 348
Church, Esmé 8, 265
cinema, cinematography 6, 167, 340
Clegg, Sir Alec 239
combat 61, 66, 79
communal dance 51, 161, 253
community 5, 17, 21, 31, 51, 52, 66, 117, 118, 152, 179, 205, 262, 365
compression [*Ballung*] 15, 57, 58, 359
conservatoire 63
Congress, Dancers' Congresses 1, 6, 24, 31, 32, 34, 35, 121, 125, 127, 128, **131–135**
consonance 319
crampedness 308, 309, 314
crystal, crystallography 57, 58, 62
cube (*see* diagonals) 10, 11, 12, 14, 100, 101, 176, 185,

Dabbing (one of the Effort Actions) 200, 202, 210, 223, 281, 357
Dalcroze, *see* Jaques-Dalcroze
dance and life 46, 169
dance composition 42, 124, 126, 127, 133, 134, 161, 180, 241, 250, 252, 326, 327, 329
dance conscience 50, 55, 61, 78, 79
dance knowledge 49, 53, 55, 61, 98
Dance Movement Therapy 8, 205, 299, 300, 342, 266
Dance Notation 6, 8, 71, 109, 113, 114, 117, 124, 126, 127, 132, **155–164** (Chapter nine), 168, 180, 259, 268
Dance Notation Bureau (*see* Ann Hutchinson-Guest) 162, 164
Dance of the Setting Sun 33
dance sense 44, 48–49
dance script 97, 98, 113, 118, 119, 120, 138, 160, 170, 174
dance technique 46, 124, 126, 158, 250, 251–253
Dance Music Word (*Tanz Ton Wort*) 9, 23, 339
Dancers' Congress (*see* Magdeburg 1927, Essen 1928, Munich 1930) 1, 6, 24, 31, 32, 34, 121, **131–135**
Dartington xviii, 7, 164, 195, 305, 364, 365
Demons of the Night 32, 33, 34
Dervish dance 3, 17
diagonals (see cube) 12, 14, 94, 100, 101, 107, 108, 111, 185, 187, 190, **193–195**

INDEX

Dietrich Eckhart Stadium xii, 7, 344, 345
Dimensional Scale, 85, 95, 100, 101, 107, 108, 111
disharmony xviii, 87, 319, 330
dissonance 319, 329
Doing (one of the Drives) 204, 352, 355, 356
Drachentöterei [*The Killing of Dragons*] 167, 173
Drive (Doing, Passionate, Influencing, Visionary) xii, **203–204**, 291, 292, 323, **351–356**
Duncan, Isadora 240, **247–248**
dynamosphere 177, 178, 193

economics, life and dance 65, 66, 67, **145–147**, 221
Effort viii, xviii, 8, 84, 84, 99, 158, 195, **217–230**, 260, 334
Effort (*see* Dabbing, Flicking, Floating, Gliding, Pressing, Punching, Slashing, Wringing) xii, xiv, xix, 14, 63, 84, **99–100**, 101, **197–206, 208–215, 217–230, 231–235**, 240, 249, 250, 255, 257, 259, 262, **267–269**, 272, **274–282, 283–297, 299–305, 309–316**, 318, 319, 323, 324, 330, 334, 335, 341, 347, 348, **352–355**
Effort and Recovery ix, xix, 8, 20, 139, 207, 258, 260, 261, **283–297, 299–305**
Elmhirst, Dorothy and Leonard xxii, 7, 8, 195, 305
emotional understanding 49, 321
Essen (Second Dancers' Congress 1928; *see* Folkwang School) 6, 123, 127, 132
ethics 1, 4, 71, 74, 75, 76, 77, 84, 342
eukinetics 14, 84, 100, 126, 127, 197, 218, 239, 348
eurhythmics (*see* Emile Jaques-Dalcroze) 24, 35

festival, festivity 5, **16–17**, 21, 24, 25, **30–32**, 37, 38, 44, **51–57**, **66–67**, 83, 87, 127, 141, 143, **144–151**, 152, 153, 161, 249, **342–343**, 346, 359
Festzug Der Gewerbe [Pageant of the Trades] **139–153** (Chapter eight)
Feuillet, Raoul Auger xii, 97, 98, 157, 164, 181
Folkwang School, Essen, 6, 123
Forsythe, William 195
fleeting (German *flüchtigkeit*, a precursor of the Motion Factor 'Flow') 92, 93, 94, 108
Flicking (one of the Effort Actions) 201, 202, 210, 223, 357
Flight (a precursor of the Motion Factor 'Flow') 85, 92, 101, 104, 106 -108, 171, 197
Floating (one of the Effort Actions) 201, 202, 223, 288, 289, 303, 357
flux 177, 182, 241, 349
form, (spatial and movement forms) 9, **10–15**, 24, 29, 31, 55, 57, 59, 73, 65, 66, 74, 81, 86, 87, 88, 89, 94, 98, 99, 100, 102, 106, 109, 11, 130, 132, 151, 163, 170, 173, **175–178**, 179, 181, 185, 245, 247, 249, 251, 252, 273, 319, 327, 329, 337, 339, 349
study of forms [*Formlehre*] **103–105**
form tension 14, 15, 17, 42
form transformations 10, **102–103**
form image [*Formbild*] 104
Free Dance 26, 28, 29, 30, 67, 83, 99, 238, 241, 244, 339
free exercise 87
Free (Flow), 85, 101, 199, 200, 212, 227, 229, 246, 302, 304, 323, 353, 355, 356
Free Gymnastics 70, 75, 79, 83, 339
Freemasonry (*see* the Masonic Order of the *Ordo Templis Orientis*) 24, 32
Freud, Sigmund 177
Fricke, Martha 5
Fuchs, Georg 5, 342
functional (dance, exercise or movement), 86, 88, 89, 90. 99,

371

INDEX

101, 105, **109–110**, 112, 132, 133, 204, 258, 260, 262, 295, 312, 315, 335, 351

game 65, 66, 77, 79, 87, 88, 211, 250, 335
Gathering and Scattering 85, **94–95**, 110, 179, 253
Gaukelei xvii, 114, 119–120
gestural power 15, 46, 47, 50, 55, 61, 63, 65
gesture [*Gebärde*] 47, 48, 49, 50, 55, 58, 70, 62, 63, 86, 94, 102, 110, 111, 130, 132, 144, 171, 179, 183, 190, 193, 211, 246, 249, 261, 262, 270, 272, 280, 286, 289, 291, 322, 335, 336, 343
Gliding (one of the Effort Actions) 149, 201, 202, 223, 270, 293, 303, 304, 357
girdle 178, 187, 190, 193, 194
Göbbels, Dr Josef 7, 343, 344, 346
Goodrich, Joan 253, 254
Graf, Kurt 119
Graham, Martha 243
Green Table, the (*see* Kurt Jooss) 217
Gymnastics 15, 24, 26, 28, 46, 50, 65, 66, 70, 71, 73, 75, **77–78**, 79, 81, 83, 84, **85–90**, 91, 92, 102, 133, 238, 334, **339–340**
Gymnastics and Dance for Children 6, 15, 19, **69–82** (Chapter three), 83, 233, 208, 339
Gymnastics and Dance 6, 15, 19, **83–96** (Chapter four), 100, 122

Hamburg xi, 5, 113, 115, 116, 120, 154, 161, 162, 165, 265, 350, 366
harmony xviii, 10, 13, 16, 17, 25, 37, 38, 53, 56, 57, 58, 61, 71, 74, 84, 87, 88, 96, 99, 100, 118, 126, 168, 176, 178, 179, 180, 195, 213, 233, 234, 235, 239, 276, 284, 308, **318–331** (Chapter 24), 334, 338, 343, 344
health 1, 16, 17, 51, 61, 65, **66**, 69, 72, 73, 74, 76, 79, 87, 88, 90, 91, 133, 148, 151, 170, 211, 228, 292, 300, 301, 303, 316, 338, 339, 341, 366
Heathcote, Dorothy 265
Hellerau (*see* Emile Jaques-Dalcroze) 21, 342
Hepton, Bernard 265
hieroglyph 98
Hildenbrandt, Fred 134
Hitler, Adolf 6, 7, 364
Hodgson, John xxiii, 19, 346, 364
Hodgson, John Archive, xi, xii, xx, xxiii, 2, 19, 121, 135, 136, 137, 345
Husserl, Edmund 177
Hutchinson-Guest, Ann 164, 166, 366

icosahedron xii, 11, 12, 14, **100**, 169, **172**, 173, 176, 195, 319, 331
impulse 25, 50, 62, 93, 112, 118, 170, 173, 229, 275, 318, 342
impression (sense impressions, the relation between sensory impression and physical expression) 18, 24, 26, 48, **49**, 54, 63, 69, 71, 72, 74, 79, 117, 133, 147, 227, 270, 275, 285, 291, 292, 302, 312, 324, 330, 337
inclination (spatial inclination and its relation to attitudinal inclinations) 14, 58, **60**, 76, 99, 107, 179, 187, 193
industry xix, 1, 66, 141, 146, 205, 207, 208, **211–213**, 218, 231, 235, 238, 244, 247, 285, 333, 339
Industrial Rhythm 217, **231–235**
Influencing (one of the Drives), 204, 351, 352, 353, 355, 356
Inner Attitude, 203, 204, 214, 251, 257, 258, 268, 275, 276, 280, 289, 312, 320, 323, 351, 352, 253, 354, 355, 356, 357
intuition, 43, 67, 131, 222, 290, 291, 292, 297, 303, 354

INDEX

Jaques-Dalcroze, Émile 20, 24, 25, 28, 29, 238, 342
Jooss, Kurt 7, 41, 123, 162, 164, 217, 341, 365
Jordan, Diana 253, 254, 364, 366
Jung, Carl 18, 177, 205, 284, 301, 365

Kammertanzbühne Laban [Laban Chamber Dancetheatre], 127
Kandinsky, Wassily 5, 195, 337, 338, 366
Kestenburg, Judith 348
kinesphere 177, 178, **184–185**, 187, 193, 195
Kinetography Laban 127, 160, 162, 166, 174, 366
kinship 228, 319, 325, 327, 329, 330
Klingenbeck, Fritz 113, 153
Knust, Albrecht xi, xii, xv, 113, 161, **162**, 163, 166, 205, 333, 337, 342, 339, 350, 366
Krause, Lotte 153

Laban, Azra 5, 162
Laban, Etalka 350
Laban Guild 215
Laban, Maja (later Maria) 24, 340, 350
Laban Movement Analysis (*see* Kinetography Laban) 300
labile (or mobile, as opposed to stable) 12, 85, 104, 107, 108, 125
language (the 'language' of movement, as opposed to spoken or written language) 70, 111, 124, 125, 132, 134, 162, 163, 181, 257, 279
Lawrence, Frederick xviii, 8, 217, 219, 255, 334, 348, 363
Lay or Laic Dance (*see* Round Dance, Celebration, Recreational Dance) 85, 116, 117, 124, 128, 129, 154
Leeder, Sigurd 7, 163, 164, 365
Lichtwende [Dawning Light] 154
Life for Dance, A xxii, 3, 7, 133, **139–142, 144–153**, 284

Littlewood, Joan xviii, 265
London Contemporary Dance School, 243
Loeszer, Gertrud 127
logic (as in the logic of dance) 42, 43, 76, 131, 162, 181
Longstaff, Jeffrey-Scott 99, 101, 112, 195
lopsided 10, 16, 62, 208, 218, 222, 48, 284, 324, 338

Macdonald, John (of MacDonald and Evans, Laban's English publisher) xxiii, 166, 255, 283, 363–366
Magdeburg (First Dancers' Congress, 1927) 117, 121, 131, 161
Maré, Rolf De 163
Mastery of Movement on the Stage, The 8, 12, 205, 206, 208, **265–281**, 363
McColl, Ewan 265
Meier, Walli 299
melody, 25, 241, 319, 326, 330
Mental Factor 352, 356
Milloss, von Aurel 197
Mime, The Mime 15, 29, 65, 110, 111, 132, 170, 173, 214, 266, 267, 269, 272, 273, **274–275, 276–281**
mobile (or labile, as opposed to stable) 12, 107, 193; mobile Effort thinking 267, 274; mobile reading 12, 266
Mobile (one of the Inner Attitudes) 203, 204, 354, 355, 357
Möbius Strip 14
Modern Dance xviii, xix, 1, 5, 27, 99, 144, 170, 171, 238, 240, 244, 245, 246, 251, 252, 341
Modern Educational Dance 8, 195, 205, **237–253** (Chapter sixteen)
Monte Verità (near Ascona) 21, 23, 24, 25, 31, 34
Motion Factors (*see* Space, Weight, Time, Flow) 85, **93**, 101, 197, 199, 204, **219–222, 228–230**, 250, 257, 268, 284, 290, 351–357

373

movement choirs 5, 6, 16, 87, 118, 141, 143, **151–153**, 171, 342, 344
movement image 59
movement notation (*see* Dance Notation) 16, **127–128, 155–164** (Chapter nine), 186
Movement Psychology, 8, 20, 198, 206, 284, **351–357**
movement script 158, 162, 163
Movement Therapy (also Dance Movement Therapy), 59, 118, 205, 299, 300, 366
Muybridge, Eadweard 336
Munich (Third Dancers' Congress, 1930) 5, 8, 21, 27, 28, 35, 39, 140, 141, 170, 337, 342, 250
music xviii, 6, 9, 16, 23, 24, **25–29**, 30, 32, 36, 37, 46, 47, 48, 53, 62, 119, 125, 127, 131, 134, 135, 141–143, 149, 155, 172–174, 177, 178, 180, 209, 241, 244, 245, 272–274, 313, 317–319, 321, **325–330**, 348, 359, 364

nature (the natural environment) 30, 46, 73, 75, 89, 118, 169, 179, 183, 189, 190, 272, 325, 338
natural movement (see also Madge Atkinson) 10, 11, 70, 131, 238
National Socialist Party (Nazi) 139, 162, 343, 344, 347
Near (one of the Inner Attitudes) 203, 204, 296, 303, **352–355**
Newtown (Wales) 7, 237
Nietzsche, Friederich (*see Also Sprach Zarathustra*) 18, 70, 84
Northern Theatre School, Bradford (*see* Esmé Church) 8, 265
Noverre, Jean-Georges (*see Ballet D'action*) 240, **246**
numbers 57, 85, 336; numerical 57, 195

Obrist, Hans 5, 26
octahedron **11**, 14, **100**
opposites 87, 107, 318, 322, 323

Ordo Exempli Orientalis (*see* Freemasonry) 34

pantomime (*see* Mime) 32, 33, 35, 37, 116, 130, 167, 250, 266, 340
Paris 5, 6, 7, 24, 162
Passionate (one of the Drives) 204, 291, 301, 302, 304, 352
Pavlova, Anna 270
pedagogy 23, 25, 71, **130**, 133
Perrottet, Suzanne 4, 8, 20, 21, 23, 24, **25–26**, 36; André and Bibi (fathered by Laban) 205
Physical Education, 85, 171, **238**, 242, 254; Physical Education Association 238
planes (of movement: Wheel Plane, Table Plane, Door Plane) 12, 14, 104, 178, 319, 349, 353, 356
plasticity 10, 58, 65, 105; plastic tension 49
Plato (*see Timaeus*, regular solids) 11, 176, 179, 180, 319, 337
poetry xviii, 26, 27, 30, 62, 131, 163, 209, 244, 245
Practice-as-Research 42, 43
Prager, Wilhelm 67, 169, 173
Pressing (one of the Effort Actions) 200, 202, 223, 304, 357
Principles of Dance and Movement Notation 163, 363
psychology 42, 143, 177, 218, 224, 248, 267
Pythagoras 15, 176, 179, 180

Rambert Dance Company 255
reason (as in the faculty of reasoning) 48, 49, 67, 278, 301, 314, 354, 356
regeneration **65**, 77, 260
regular solids (*see* cube, icosahedron, octahedron, tetrahedron) 10–12, 14, 337
religion 4, 53
Remote (one of the Inner Attitudes) 203, 204, 287, 295, 296, 297, 303, 354, 355, 357
rhythm 10, **24–29**, **35–37**, 44, 47, **53–54**, 55, 58, 61, **63–64**, 65, 73, **76–78**, 86, 87, 103, 105, 112,

117–119, 125, 129, 130, **140–143**, 146, 148, 149, 151, 160, 168, **170–174**, 193, 205, 209, 211, 213, 217, 218, 221, 222, **231–235**, 241, 247, 258, 259, 260, **270–272**, 275, 284, 287, **289–291**, **295–297**, 300, 303, 304, 310, 311, 313, 315, 316, 318, 319, 320, 322, 323, 330, 334, 356; spatial rhythm 86, 160
ritual 9, 17, 32, 33, **54**, 116, 118, 250, 273, 275, 303, 304, 309, 312, 309, 325, 343
Robst, Hermann 127
Rosicrucian (Rosenkreutz) 5, 17, 20, 24
Round Dance [*Reigen*] 17, 41, 42, 43, 44, 47, 50, **51–53**, 54, 55, 144, 169, 170, 172, 359, **360**

Sachs, Felicia 346, 347, 350
scales 98, 100, 169, 172, 176, 177, **178**, 337, 378; A-scale and B-scale 100, 176, 178, 338; chromatic scale 327; diatonic Scale, 327; diagonal Scale 101; musical Scales 180, 326; standard scale **191–**193, 195; swinging scales **95**, **105–106**
Schlee, Alfred 160
Schlemmer, Oskar 337
Schrifttanz 98, 129, 138, 160, 165, 365
science (as a form of knowledge, movement and choreographic science) 43, 57, 87, 123–132, 177, 181, 248
sense impression 49, 337
Shadow Movements or Moves 204, 206, 213, **257–263** (Chapter seventeen), 302, 348, 353, **355**
Sherborne, Veronica 299, 365
skill 46, 52, 63, 116, 142, 208, 211, 215, **219–221**, 222, 228, 232, 233, 234, 250, 259, 272, 273, 291, 318, 340
Slashing (one of the Effort Actions) 200, 202, 210, 223, 281, 303, 357

Snell, Gertrud 127, 138, 161, 175
space [*Raum*] 3, 10, 12, 19, 29, 57, 58, 64, 85, 86, 91, 93, 99, 100, 101, 103, 104, 106, 107, 108, 109, 117, 126, 131, 151, 158, 160, **175–196**, 197, 199–204, 209, 212, **221**, 222, **226**, 227–229, 250, 255, 284, 289, 290, 293, 301–304, 307–310, 312–314, 318, 319, 325–327, 329, 331, 335, 336, 347, 349, 351–357, **360**; space harmony 71, 99, 100, 176, 178, 179, 195; spatial laws 58, 62; performance space 38, 117, 118, 133
sport 65, 66, 77 87, 128, 142, 335
stable (as opposed to labile or mobile) 12, 85, 104, 108, 193,
Stable (one of the Inner Attitudes) 203, 204, 287, 288, 295, 318, 352, 354, **356**
Steiner, Rudolph 17, 195, 366
Stephenson, Geraldine 268
swinging [*Schwung*] 53, 55, 58, 61, 64, 85, **95**, 96, 98, 104, 105, 107, 111, 151, 170, 173, 208, 212, 221, 294, 295, **360**
symbol 3, 4, 9, 14, 47, 49, 50, 52, 54, 57, 58, 59, 60, 94, 98, 127, 180, 186, 229, 230, 262, 276, 313, 315, 349

tableau vivant 140
Tannhäuser 161
Tanzbühne Laban [Laban Dancetheatre] xvii, 127
Taylor, Frederick Wilmslow 247, 334, 339
tension (inner and outer) 9, 10, **13–15**, 16, 17, 26, 42, 46, 47, 48, 49, **55**, 57, 58, **59**, **60**, **61**, 62, 88, 89, 92, 94, 98, 99, 100, 103, 104, 107, 108, 187, 192, 193, 209, 210, 260, **261**, 266, 309, 319, 329, 334, 336, 338, 343, 352, **361**
tetrahedron 11, 59
thought (as in inner mental activity, as distinct from feeling or will) 9,

INDEX

14, 42, 47, 48, 50, 56, 61, 62, 64, 76, 79, 111, 272, 273, 308, 320, 321, 323, 325; festive thought **56–57**; thought-movements 14; thought-rounds 42, 53; thought-tension 42
Timaeus, The (*see* Plato) 11, 176, 180
Titan xi, xii, **113–119**, 136, 137, 161, 344
tone 31, 110, 203, 263, 319, 326, 328

tool 53, 63, 65, 223, 232, 252, 289, 291
trace-form 23, 99, 177, 178, 182, 183, 190, 192–195
training xi, xviii, 8, 10, 24, 25, 34, 35, 37, 51, 65, 80, 86, 92, **94–96**, 122, 127, 129, 130, 138, 149, 153, 177, 208, 214, 215, 220, **222–223**, 233, 240, 242, 243, 249, 250, 252, 268, 285, 299, 301, 312, 334, 335; Effort-training 222, 224, 275; movement training xviii, 85, 126, 232, 233, **234**, 252
transversal 176, 178, **187**, 189, 194
turgor 13
Turnen [German for gymnastics with equipment] 84, 88, 91

Ullmann, Lisa 4, 7, 8, 19, 20, 39, 138, 153, 154, 163, 175, 178, 195, 217, 238, 265, 350, 363

Vienna 5, 98, 138, 139, **142–144**, 160, 208, 334
Vision of Dynamic Space, The xxiv, 19, 133, 363
Visionary (one of the Drives) 204, 291, 301, **303**, 304, 352
Vom Tauwind Und Der Neuen Freude (*see* 1936 Berlin Olympics) 7, 18, 343, 345

Wagner, Richard 127, 161
Wigman, Mary 3, 4, 17, 19, 23, 24, 25, 32, 35, 36, 37, 99, 134, 341, 350, 361
will (*see* thought, emotion, will) 17, 45, 48, 49, 52, 53, 61, 80, 96, 110, 131, 248, 275, 284, 295, 296, 322, 325, 335, 338, 339, 342
weight (one of the four Motion Factors, *see* Time, Space, Flow) 26, 85, 101, **199–201**, 203, 304, 218, 220, 221, 223, **225**, 226, **227**, 228, 229, 250, 284, 290, 301, **304**, 307, 308, 309, 314, 322, 335, 351–357
Withymead Centre 205, 299, **305–315**, 365
World of the Dancer, The vii, xxi, 3, 6, 9, 11, 15, 17, 19, 20, **41–68** (Chapter two), 70, 97, 99, 195, 208, 266, 284, 333, 334, 338, 343, 360, 363
work (Laban's work in Industry and with workers) 8, 16, 35, 44, 53, 54, **56**, 57, 61, **63–66**, 83, 86, **87**, 96, **141–146**, 148, 149, 170, 186, 190, 205, 207, **208–209**, **211–213**, 218, 221–224, 228–231, **233–235**, 238, 242, 244, **246–247**, 249, 251, **260**, 268, 284, 285, **286–290**, 292, 293–296, 300, 315–316, 330, 333–334, 342
Wringing (one of the eight Effort Actions) 200, 202, 223, 335, 357
Würzburg (*see* Choreographic Institute) 122, 123, 161

Youth Advisory Bureau 257

Zabekow, Rita xviii, 114, **119–120**
Zorn, Friedrich Albert xii, 159, 164
Zurich vii, 5, 6, 8, 20, 21, 23, 24, 25, 28, 35, 38, 167, 266, 339, 340, 350